Marketing Graffiti

Marketing Graffiti

The view from the street

Michael Saren

AMSTERDAM • BOSTON • HEIDELBERG • LONDON • NEW YORK • OXFORD
PARIS • SAN DIEGO • SAN FRANCISCO • SINGAPORE • SYDNEY • TOKYO
Butterworth-Heinemann is an imprint of Elsevier

Butterworth-Heinemann is an imprint of Elsevier
Linacre House, Jordan Hill, Oxford OX2 8DP
30 Corporate Drive, Suite 400, Burlington, MA 01803

First published 2006

British Library Cataloguing in Publication Data
A catalogue record for this book is available from the British Library

Library of Congress Cataloguing in Publication Data
A catalogue record for this book is available from the Library of Congress

ISBN–13: 978-0-7506-5697-9
ISBN–10: 0-7506-5697-2

For information on all Butterworth-Heinemann publications visit our web site at http://books.elsevier.com

Layout design by HL Studios, Long Hanborough, Oxford
Typeset by Charon Tec Ltd, Chennai, India
www.charontec.com
Printed and bound in Italy

05 06 07 08 09 10 10 9 8 7 6 5 4 3 2 1

CONTENTS

Marketing contexts page 1

Building relations page 39

Consuming experience page 93

Creating solutions page 139

Brand selection page 195

Moving space page 241

Rewrite this book!

The view from the street

As consumers in a marketing culture we are also part-time marketers. We all write on walls too, metaphorically at any rate.

So too with this book.

Like marketing, you as reader/consumer can access and activate it in any order you like. It is not a linear text.

The book is organized in six main sections. You can read them in any order.

Start anywhere and follow the links (i.e. 'see . . .') through the marketing topics that you are interested in discovering about.

This book is just the first access point to your knowledge of today's marketing values. You can begin at any section and write the book for yourself by following the key links between sections.

'ou design our own structure!

This book has a new content format with all information connected through keywords, pointers and cross-references. Essential further reading and links are indicated throughout.

consumers are marketers too!

About this book

Marketing affects everything – even nothing

Most marketing books discuss the subject as a business discipline, from a managerial point of view. How to 'do' marketing in companies and other organizations. But marketing is not just about being a marketing manager.

Marketing is all encompassing nowadays. Everything is marketed – the church, politics, science, history, celebrities, careers, sport, art, fiction, fact. Marketing involves promotion, selling and consumption. However, marketing is more than just an economic activity. It drives the consumer society, a culture of consumption. Marketing affects everybody; as consumers we cannot escape the market, even those who try to live simply.

Consumers are not passive recipients of what marketers do. We re-interpret marketing messages, display their logos; present ourselves through what we consume; make choices; complain; window shop; view celebrities as brands; compete with other consumers. This book explains marketing as consumers experience it, as active participants in it.

Marketing may appear to affect more and more of the world nowadays, but its powerful effects are not new. Over the centuries, trade, exchange, what we now call marketing, influenced how and why empires were built, technologies applied, property law, transport routes constructed, shopping architecture of cities, languages developed and spread. It was in order to calculate market exchange that Europeans imported from the Arabs the mathematical concept of 'nothing'[1].

The contents

Topics in this book reflect the view of marketing as a social and cultural phenomenon, not just a business function. Therefore, it does not adopt the managerial approach like most textbooks, rather it also seeks to explain how consumers, organizations, society can and do use marketing – for example, in areas of social marketing and the construction of consumer 'identity'.

The subject is covered from a relational approach. That is, how actors and organizations relate to each other in and through marketing.

It takes a critical perspective on the values of marketing, not only 'market value'. Beyond a critique of unethical marketing practices, it questions and analyses established, traditional marketing theories and the assumptions behind them.

The structure is not organized according to the core marketing functions used in companies – advertising, distribution, strategy, sales, product development, etc. It does, though, introduce how companies and managers think and go about marketing in their businesses, but not in the terms found in traditional textbooks. This book does not explain these using the old concepts and highly gendered, militarized language of traditional marketing – strategy and tactics, campaigns and offensives, intelligence and planning, control and implementation, targeting, market penetration, winning customers, beating competitors.

The contents cover how marketing creates solutions, how marketers build relations with customers, other companies, society, how they build brands, use media, how marketing moves space and time.

This book is not written from a single authorial perspective. It includes expert contributors on specific topics from experienced academics and practitioners, which cover a range of views about the subject. These are written in different styles and presented here in different ways, allowing for variety and reflecting the bricolage subject that is marketing.

[1] See Rotman, B. (1987) *Signifying Nothing: The Semiotics of Zero.* Macmillan: London.

The readers

This is not only an introductory textbook on marketing aimed at readers who are studying the subject. It is written also for advanced undergraduate and post-graduate students who want an alternative type of text taking a different approach. Many teachers of marketing have been clamouring for a new type of non-managerial text, beyond the '4Ps'. Hopefully the structure and contents here will enable and encourage marketing to be taught in many different ways.

This book will hopefully not put off the general reader. It is a short introductory book, which covers the latest ideas. We are all consumers affected by marketing. If you are curious to understand how, and perhaps keen to change some of it, this book provides a starting point for some answers.

How to use this book

If you are studying marketing for the first time, this book provides a short overview of the subject from a broad perspective. It provides a topical introduction to the range of activities and effects that marketing involves nowadays. It aims to be easy to read, allowing the reader to start with whichever topic interests you and follow through the cross-referenced links to related issues. Hopefully, whichever way your read it, you will get a flavour of the subject and can check out topics in greater depth using the suggestions for further reading.

Advanced students of the subject already familiar with marketing theories and concepts will find this book provides an alternative approach to the widely used texts which sets the subject in its wider contexts and covers the latest thinking, drawing on relevant ideas from associated literature, beyond conventional marketing.

Those readers who work in almost any organization, or for themselves, will hopefully find in these pages some useful ideas about marketing, from a more wide-ranging perspective. Some of you may want to put this relational, critical approach to the subject into practice. This requires a fundamental reappraisal of what constitutes marketing activity, which cannot be reduced and simplified into a set of point-by-point managerial prescriptions. For those readers interested in taking the implications for business and society further, the book provides a guide to the reading and rethinking required.

For teachers of marketing who are looking for new ways of introducing the subject to new students or developing new approaches for advanced classes, *Marketing Graffiti* can be used as an alternative and/or supplementary text. Your course can be built around the variable structure and links in the book, using your own further reading in addition to that suggested here.

List of contributors

Dr Mairead Brady
Trinity College, Dublin
Information technology sections

Dr Cláudia Simões
University of Minho, Portugal
Corporate branding

Professor Gerard Hastings
University of Stirling, UK
Building Social Relationships

Ruth Grima
Germany
Contributor to Brand selection

Alexea Grech
NMSglobal, UK
A virtual firm in a moving space

Professor Christopher Moore
Glasgow Caledonian University, UK
Fast fashion branding

Professor Christina Goulding
University of Wolverhampton, UK
Why consume?

Andy Barker
Research International Qualitif, UK
It's qualitative Jim, but not as we know it

Professor Jaqueline Pels
Universidad Torcuato Di Tella, Argentina
The role of institutions and networks

Dr Emmanuella Plakoyiannaki
Aristotle University of Thessaloniki, Greece
Organizational processes and capabilities

Michael Marck
University of Strathclyde, UK
Contributor to Moving materials

Dr Julie Tinson
University of Stirling, UK
The role of communications

Marketing contexts

Marketing does not take place in isolation. This section outlines the wide range of contexts which effect and are affected by marketing activities. Many of these are outside the organizations undertaking marketing such as the society, culture and the media, and others are inside the organization, where marketing fits, who does it. Another question is what are markets? They can be viewed in different ways and which perspective is chosen fundamentally affects how marketing operations are analysed and conducted. This section also reviews the values and history of marketing itself which lie behind the activities that today are undertaken in its name.

Views of markets

This book is about marketing and marketing is about markets, so it is important to be clear what a market actually is. And this is not as straightforward as it appears, because there are many views of what characterizes a market, differences between academic subjects such as economics and psychology, differences between management disciplines such as marketing and strategy, and even, as we shall see below, different views of markets within marketing. This is separate from different views people have as to whether markets are *good or bad things* (see Marketing values), it concerns the alternative perspectives or *ways of looking at markets* taken by authors in marketing.

In this chapter four views of markets are outlined:

- Markets as exchange
- Markets as competition
- Markets as networks
- Markets as information.

Exchange

Any market must have certain core elements, namely a buyer, a seller and *some form of exchange between the two*. What is exchanged can be a product, a service, knowledge, meaning, time-saved, an agreement or a promise. As in the case of a gift, or a free offer, there need even not be money exchanged in return – although many would argue something must be returned, if only satisfaction or obligation (see Consuming Experience).

There is also no need for the consumer to meet the buyer, even to know who they are. Internet markets are obvious examples, though more generally you do know who has exchanged or who makes the book you are reading. You have bought this book in a bookstore or perhaps on the Internet, but the author has no direct contact with you, nor necessarily does the publisher. Your purchasing it is the result of a series of exchanges, a long supply chain (see Moving Space), from woodcutter to paper manufacturer, to printer, to publisher, to bookseller, to you.

If there is an exchange between buyer and seller, both parties must expect to gain something. If there were no anticipation of mutual benefit, then there would be no incentive for each to conduct the exchange. The benefit may not actually occur – e.g. when the product fails to satisfy the customer (if you don't like this book) or the buyer fails to pay the buyer (if you stole this book) – but each must believe that they will benefit from the market exchange.

Things a market requires:

- *A buyer*
- *A seller*
- *An exchange*
- *Information and knowledge*
- *Something which is exchanged*
- *Potential for mutual benefit.*

Things a market does not require:

- *Money*
- *Direct contact.*

So, one way to view markets is as a transaction or exchange.

Exchange theory assumes that human beings are need-directed with a natural tendency to try and improve their material circumstances. It has its foundations in psychology and economics (Housten & Grassenheimer, 1987). At the consumer behavioural level then, in order to encourage consumer's readiness to spend their money with a particular firm, marketers must provide them with something beneficial in exchange. Exchange involves the transfer of tangible or intangible items between two or more social actors (Bagozzi, 1978). Many authors view it this way. In his influential text *Marketing: Theory and Practice*, Baker (1995) also takes a marketing-as-exchange position:

> . . . the recognition and acceptance of the need to improve our understanding of the manner in which the [marketing] system works which underlies the need to develop a workable theory of exchange.

Competition

Another way to view markets is in terms of competition. All markets must have a degree of competition involved. This view has several dimensions:

1 *Sellers competing with each other for markets, i.e. for sales or buyers.* This form of competition can be seen in most industries with the exception of

monopolies, where there is only one firm selling in the market. Even here, though, there is often a substitute from another industry which buyers can choose, e.g. customers can choose gas or electricity as power; or rail or bus transport. So even if there is only one supplier in each market, the availability of alternatives means that a monopoly firm in these cases still has to compete with other industries for buyers' choice.

2. *Buyers competing with each other for sellers' offerings on the market, i.e. for goods, services or other purchases.* You only have to attend an auction or watch buyers at the cut-price 'sales' to observe competition of buyers against each other. Unless there is great over-supply relative to the strength of demand from customers, they will always effectively be in competition with each other for availability, lower prices, and also sometimes buyers compete in the way they use and display their purchases (see Consuming Experience).
3. *Sellers competing with buyers, i.e. for best price or terms.* Even where there is only one seller and one buyer and one product and no alternative substitutes, there may be no competition in terms of types 1 or 2 above, but there still normally is an element of competition between the buyer and the seller. This occurs because each tries to maximize their benefits from the transaction, which in some markets takes the form of negotiation or bargaining, or 'haggling' over the price and quantity bought – so, for example, if lower price results the buyer benefits and where higher price the supplier gains.

Marketing writers have adapted theories of competitive advantage from economics and strategic management (Chamberlin, 1933; Alderson, 1957). The ability of a firm to create and maintain competitive advantage over rival firms is a central objective of its marketing strategy. The way in which this ability can be achieved depends on various factors, including: unique (hard to imitate) capabilities of the firm (e.g. skills of employees, higher quality products); the conditions of the business environment (e.g. government regulation, technological advances); the number and intensity of rival firms in the industry (e.g. barriers to new firms entering); and the conditions in the marketplace (e.g. customers loyalty, retailers power); as well as the overall competitive strategy followed by a firm (Porter, 1985).

So, according to this view, markets are *competitive arenas* where firms aim to achieve competitive advantage over their rivals. To some extent they are limited in their ability to achieve this because of the industry, technology and market conditions, but it is important to note the *proactive nature* of the firms' strategies, which can be achieved through strategic decision-making that is firmly based on knowledge superior to their rivals (Nonaka, 1994).

Collaboration and networks

Another view of markets highlights the fact that buyers and sellers not only compete, they also often collaborate. This emphasis has developed in the past 20 years largely due to the wider influence of the business thinking and culture of firms from the Far East and Asia. For example, Japanese business methods and ideas of collaboration, quality control, employee relations and procurement practices have all had an enormous impact on business methods and thinking in the West. Chinese culture and business also operates with the notion of *Guanxi* (see Marketing values).

So, also in marketing, several authors agree with Gummesson (1997b) that 'collaboration in a market economy needs to be treated with the same attention and respect as competition'. Rindova and Fombrun (1999) argued that a firm's competitive advantage depends on three key elements:

1 The efforts of the firm
2 The conditions of the environment
3 'The nature of the firm–constituent interactions.'

This last point refers to collaboration by the firm with other 'constituencies', i.e. suppliers, buyers, distributors, consumers, media, sponsors, etc. Rindova and Fombrun pointed out that competitive advantage can also be built on relationships and that 'relationships with constituents . . . are not just exchanges but sustained social interactions in which past impressions affect future behaviours', a view which is similar to the 'network theory' of competitive advantage (e.g. Håkansson & Snehota, 1995).

The types of collaboration in markets can be much broader than this, however. Three main types of collaborations can be identified, similar to those of competition:

1 Firms collaborate with other firms, even competitors – in alliances and joint ventures. For instance, airlines collaborate to provide global services (e.g. BA, Qantas, Swissair) and IT firms combine with suppliers and business partners to provide a 'platform' or whole offering for customers, e.g. Pentium, Intel, IBM.
2 Buyers collaborate with each other. This can be a formal cooperation – e.g. customer cooperatives, buying clubs, user groups (services, gym, health), enthusiast societies (e.g. cars, football supporters). Alternatively, this can be an informal or social arrangement – information sharing, instruction, friends.
3 Buyers and sellers collaborate. The very act of buying requires information sharing, dialogue, agreement and trust between the buying and selling parties. Especially in business-to-business (B2B) and service markets, the buyer is often involved with the seller in producing or making together some key aspect of the delivery or transaction or use.

The idea of market as collaboration links to the fields of relationship and network marketing (see Building Relations), which developed from studies of marketing in

B2B and services where collaboration and relationships have been found to be *central* to success. Although one review identified at least 36 separate definitions of the field (Harker, 1998), all these relational approaches emphasize long-term collaboration (as opposed to competition and exchange) between market and social actors.

It is actually possible for *all* marketing activities, problems, systems and behaviour to be conceptualized and conducted by focusing on the collaborations involved to identify best practices, analyse behaviour and provide solutions (see Creating Solutions). For example, network theory has been applied extensively to industrial marketing by the north European IMP group (see Mattsson, 1985; Ford, 1990). This has enabled them to explain the behaviour of marketing systems in terms of networks of relationships and collaboration using sophisticated sociometric methods, exchange theory and even chaos theory.

Payne (1995) pointed out that firms operate in several different types of markets (see Figure 1).

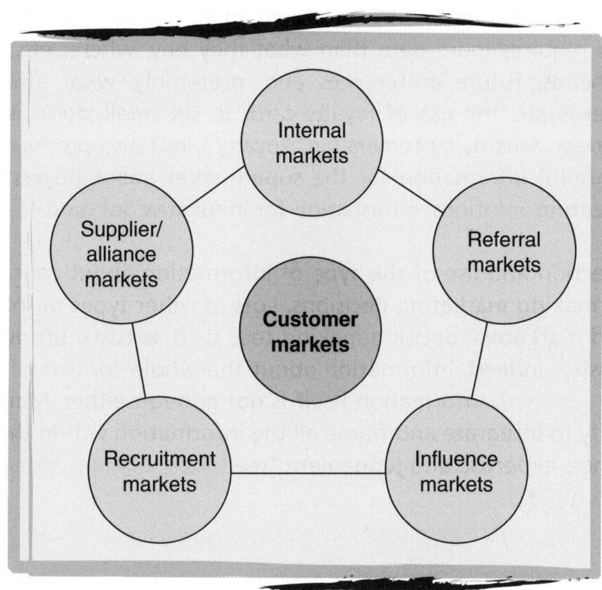

Figure 1 Six markets model. *Source*: Payne (1995)

Information

When a sale takes place, it is not only products, services and money that are exchanged – so too is information. Indeed, certain information must be known by both parties beforehand *in order for a sale to occur*. For example, by sellers, how

to reach buyers, how to communicate with them; for buyers, where and how to buy, price and how to use the product. So markets can be viewed as a process by which information and knowledge is produced, communicated and exchanged (see Moving Space: Moving information – the role of IT). Adverts, prices, availability, delivery, place of purchase and how to best use products are all types of *information that are useful for customers*.

Sellers too need information in order to engage in a market. Because satisfying consumers is the central focus of marketing (see Marketing values), marketers need information about consumers, their wants and needs, and what will satisfy them. Consumer information aids marketing decision-making – pricing decisions, promotion decisions, product decisions, distribution decisions and so on should all be aimed at satisfying the consumer, so this requires more data than what they buy, where, etc.; knowledge about their needs, future preferences and, preferably, what affects them is needed. For example, the use of loyalty cards in UK retail stores is not just to encourage repeat visits by customers (i.e. 'loyalty'), but also produces on a daily basis lots of useful information for the supermarket about buyers' purchasing habits (see Creating Solutions: Information for innovative solutions).

Even the collection and use of this type of information about consumers is not sufficient for making marketing decisions. Lots of other types of information is needed to aid marketers' decision-making too, such as costs, production, competitors, industry; indeed, information about the whole context of the market (see External contexts). Information itself is not enough either. Marketers must have the ability to integrate and frame all the information within the context of their experience, expertise and judgement (see Moving Space: Moving information – the role of IT).

So another way of viewing markets is as an information production, processing and communication system. Lots of information of various types mentioned above flows all the time between all the participants in the marketing process. Every purchase, every movement of goods, every advert, every shop display produces and communicates market information.

FURTHER READING

Markets as exchange

Bagozzi, R. P. (1978) Marketing as exchange: a theory of transactions in the marketplace. *American Behavioral Scientist*, **21** (March/April), 535–556.

Baker, M. (1995) *Marketing: Theory and Practice*. Macmillan Press: London.

Market competition

Day, G. S. & Nedungadi, P. (1994) Managerial representations of competitive advantage. *Journal of Marketing*, **58** (2), 31–44.

Porter, M. (1985) *Competitive Advantage: Creating and Sustaining Superior Performance*. Free Press: New York.

Rindova, V. P. & Fombrun, C. J. (1999) Constructing competitive advantage: the role of firm–constituent interactions. *Strategic Management Journal*, **20** (8), 691–710.

Market collaboration

Ford, I. D. (ed.) (1990) *Understanding Business Markets: Interaction, Relationships and Networks*. Academic Press: New York.

Gummesson, E. (1997) In search of marketing equilibrium: relationship marketing versus hypercompetition. *Journal of Marketing Management*, **13** (5), 421–430.

Market information

Glazer, R. (1991) Marketing in an information intensive environment: strategic implications of knowledge as an asset. *Journal of Marketing*, **55**, 1–19.

Menon, A. & Varadarajan, P. (1992) A model of marketing knowledge used in firms. *Journal of Marketing*, **56** (October), 53–71.

Perkins, W. & Rao, R. (1990). The role of experience in information use and decision making by marketing managers. *Journal of Marketing Research*, **27** (February), 1–10.

Internal and external contexts

Marketing takes place within the wider contexts of organizations, industries, cultures and countries. Also, our knowledge of markets and marketing has developed over many decades into theories and ideas from associated areas of knowledge such as economics, psychology and sociology. Another key context which affects marketing is its history – where it came from and how it has developed. These are the contexts of marketing.

The organizational or internal context

The most immediate context for marketing activities is the organization in which it takes place. Marketing is sometimes considered to be what the marketing department of a firm does. This is an inadequate definition for a number of reasons:

1 Although most organizations nowadays have a function or department labelled 'Marketing', sometimes still it is little more than a sales unit, which delivers advertising, personal selling and promotion activities. Such organizations have been labelled 'sales oriented'. As we explain in this book, marketing in today's world is concerned with creating and delivering 'solutions' for customers (see Creating Solutions), whoever they may be, not just selling something to them.

2 In order to aspire to be fully 'marketing oriented', *all the activities of the organization* must be centred on the customer. This means that so-called 'marketing' activities must be undertaken by *all functions* and personnel, not only those in the department called 'Marketing'. This is what Evert Gummesson (1997a) means when he says everybody in the organization is a 'part-time marketer'.

3 In order to provide something of value to their customers or users outside, the activities and departments involved *inside* the organization each must deliver their part of the process to the other units and functions. For instance, the research department must develop the new system for IT, who must integrate it into existing IT systems for manufacture, who must make the products to

order for sales and the service division must back up sales, etc. In this way, each internal activity can be viewed as having an output and thus a customer *inside* the organization. This is the notion of internal marketing (see Varey & Lewis, 1999) where all departments, not just that labelled 'Marketing', are users of others' output and have 'customers' in other functions.

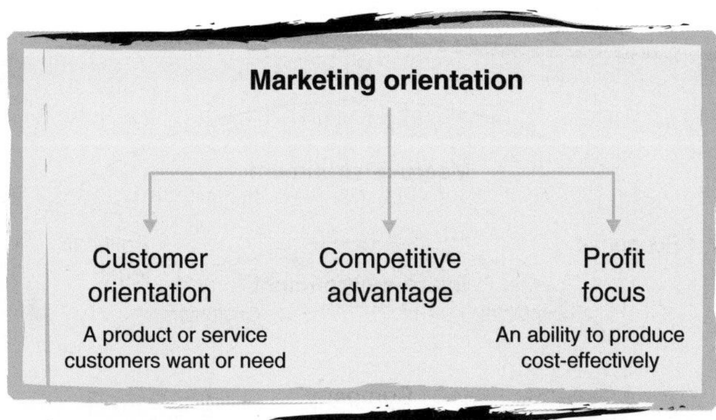

Figure 2 Marketing orientation

Many textbooks describe marketing as the business function that resides at and manages the 'interface' between the firm and its outside world; marketing integrates activities inside the firm in order to focus them outwards, especially to customers (e.g. Kotler, 1967 plus subsequent editions). One complication with any description of the marketing context nowadays is that the distinction between the organization and its environment is not so clear-cut as this 'internal' versus 'external' explanation suggests. In fact, many companies contract out to other firms and agencies large parts of their marketing and other business activities. For example, market research, advertising and technical research are contracted to outside agencies very often, even by large firms. This is done to save the cost of permanently employing lots of specialists and to allow more flexibility of costs and operation. Internally, they are more likely to retain control of overall marketing and key operations – that is, activities such as marketing strategy and planning, sales management, in-store promotions, costing and pricing. In practice, many marketing activities for firms usually span the internal/external divide, making the boundary itself between inside and outside the firm even more unclear (see Webster, 1992).

The environmental or external context

The idea behind the external marketing context is that at its basic level the marketing activities of a company take place between – and are crucially determined by – other organizations and people in the immediate *micro-environment* – suppliers, buyers, competitors, etc. The company has some influence over these immediate influences through its marketing activities – e.g. by lowering its price it may encourage buyers to purchase more, but also may encourage competitors to reduce their price. At a further distance other factors in the external *macro-environment* are also powerful influences, such as technology, cultural norms, economic conditions, etc. (see Figure 3).

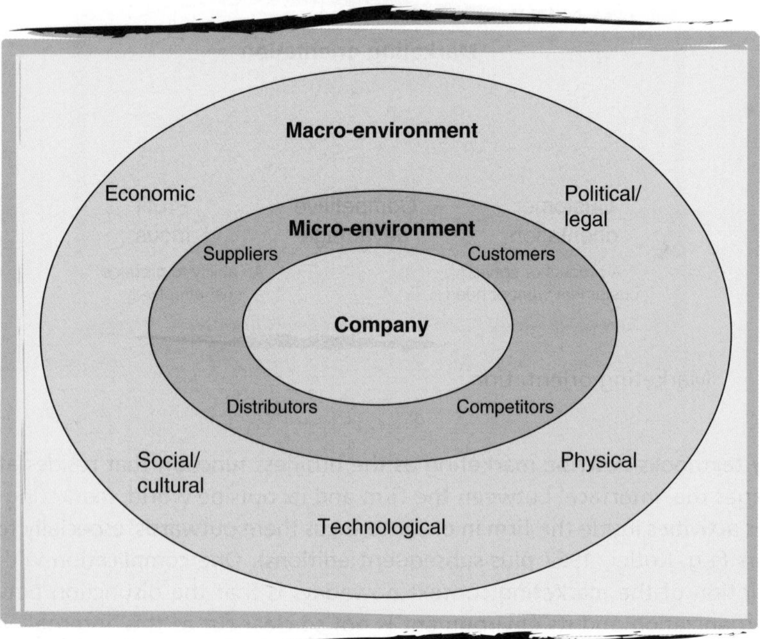

Figure 3 The marketing environment

Forces in the macro-environment affect marketing more indirectly by helping or hindering things such as the effect of advertising, the disposable income of customers, the opportunities for new products, etc. The company has much less influence over the macro-environment, determined much more by the state of the general economy, social forces, technological advances, government policies, etc.

A better way of viewing the marketing environment would be more appropriate, however, if it turned the 'onion' inside out, putting consumers at the centre and competing companies at the periphery. One criticism of the conventional view depicted in Figure 3 is that it is too 'marketer-centric', not customer-centric. The depiction of the marketing environment should be centred on the consumer, not the seller, according to the traditional marketing concept (see Marketing values). In Figure 4, therefore, the firm's environment shows the consumer at the centre, with sellers fighting for their trade from the outside, and also competing for distribution channels to customers, for retail space, advertising placements, etc.

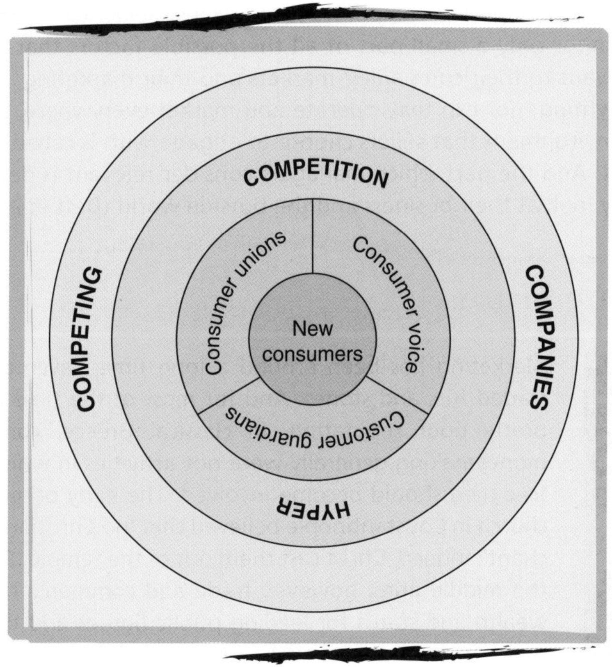

Figure 4 Consumers at the centre

External scanning and the enacted environment

The role of the external environment for marketing activities is not 'all encompassing', but selective and partial. Companies cannot possibly affect or even engage with all of the possible elements which it consists of. Indeed, most firms are not even aware of all the macro forces and trends in technology, society, economy and public policy that may affect them. There are many examples where managers complain that an important change came 'out of the blue'. Marketing managers will have a particular perspective on the outside forces that are important for their business and will also select a small subset of these to research and possibly exploit. This is what is called *environmental scanning*, which is systematic information gathering to monitor important trends in the environment.

For example, oil and gas companies undertake regular scanning of oil prices, availability, costs, etc., and forecast future possible scenarios. Also, they constantly monitor key long-term macro-environmental factors such as government stability and national policies in selected countries where they might have or seek exploration licences. Other factors are also assessed, such as new technologies, social dependence on cars, transport investments, road infrastructure capacity and regulation/taxation of automobile emissions.

In other words, managers in companies such as these *select* to investigate, forecast and monitor only a small part of all the possible factors that might be or become relevant to their companies' markets and their marketing. They cannot look at everything, nor can they operate and market everywhere. That part of the macro-environment that sellers choose to engage with is called the *enacted environment*. And the part which managers consider relevant is determined by the way they look at their business and the outside world (Daft *et al.*, 1988).

Marketing history

Marketing has been around a long time; cavemen no doubt traded furs and stones. And for most of the time it has had a pretty poor reputation. In classical Greece, commerce and moneymaking generally were not activities in which reputable free men should become involved. The early original Christian church in Constantinople believed that 'no Christian can be merchant'; indeed, Christ cast them out of the temple. By the end of the middle ages, however, trade and commerce had acquired wealth and status for leading public figures and the merchant guilds in particular played a major role in the rise of city-states such as Venice. A key element in the rise of the mercantilist class – and with it the early form of what we would now call marketing – was the legal establishment of free trade and property rights, which permitted citizens to confront one another on equal terms in the marketplace (Black, 1984).

Academic study and development of marketing as a separate discipline is essentially a twentieth century occurrence. It corresponds to the rise of US business schools and in them the first courses on marketing, which occurred at the end of the nineteenth century. The first of these was Wharton at the University of Pennsylvania in 1881 (Lazer & Shaw, 1988).

Early histories of marketing were written by Hotchkiss (1938; cited in Enright, 2002) and later by Bartels (1962). Hotchkiss took the long view, setting out three periods in the development of marketing, from the fifth to the twentieth centuries! Bartels, by contrast, sees it as an entirely twentieth century phenomenon. Both these seminal authors, however, regard the operation and channels of distribution as central to, if not the same as, marketing, particularly the increasing distance of the producer from the final consumers, over whom manufactures have thus lost control and influence, with distributors, agents and retailers filling the gap.

Figure 5 illustrates this shift in market structure and power over the period of the second half of the twentieth century. The rise of marketing was seen by both

There has recently been much more attention to studying marketing from a historical viewpoint, which is defined as the description analysis or explanation of events through time (see Savitt, 1980). These largely cover (i) the history of marketing thought and theories, (ii) the history of individuals and organizations critical to the development of marketing, e.g. scholars, companies, regulations, agencies, institutions, professional associations, and (iii) the history of core marketing activities and functions, advertising, retailing, merchandising, branding, product innovation.

See also: Kerin, R. (1996) In pursuit of an ideal: the editorial and literary history of the Journal of Marketing. *Journal of Marketing, **60** (1), 1–13.*

authors, in their different ways, as the solution to this problem for manufactures. In other words, marketing started to be used by producers in order to attempt to wrest knowledge, contact, control and influence over consumers, back from the various middlemen in the elongated distribution channels. And this was done by developing market research, public relations, consumer motivation research, advertising, direct sales methods – all of which first began to be employed by businesses in the USA in the 1930s and 1940s.

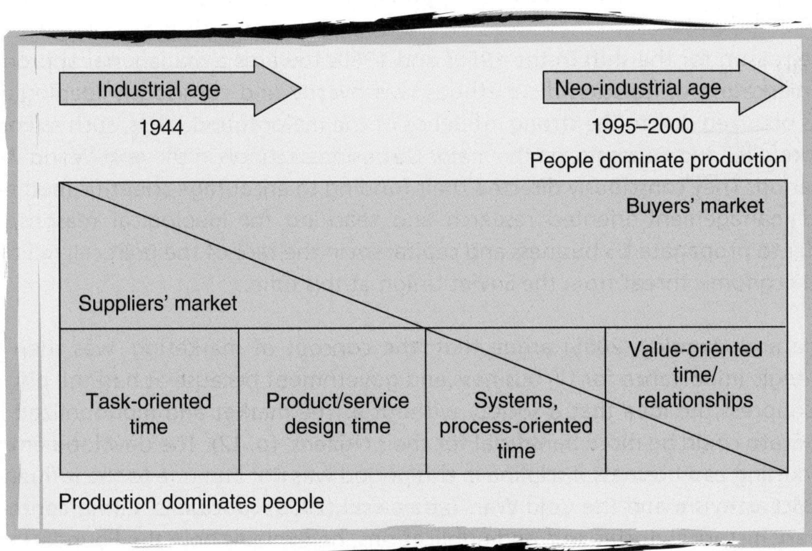

Figure 5 From suppliers' market to buyers' market

Later, in the 1950s and 1960s, a lot of marketing utilized the techniques, tools and language of psychology as it attempted to acquire the means to understand 'customer' behaviour, the customer being the espoused central focus of business. The buyer behaviourist view regarded the consumer as a conditioned organism, open to reconditioning and treated as a 'behaving machine', performing cognitive functions within a black box (Shankar & Horton, 1999).

The early editions of the main marketing publication, the *Journal of Marketing*, from 1936 contained papers that also used the term 'marketing' to mean primarily aspects of distribution as the flow of goods and services from the place of production to the point of consumption. The ways in which marketing ideas and theories developed have been plotted and categorized into various 'schools of thought' (Sheth & Gardener, 1988). Crosier (1975) lists 47 definitions, split into seven historical approaches. The key development in marketing thought, however, was from a functionalist, systems approach to analysing markets to one which focused on managerial and buyer behaviour (Lazer & Shaw, 1988).

Marketing and the Cold War

The choice of methodology, and with it theory, in marketing was affected by wider socio-political events, particularly World War II, the Cold War, the Space Race, the Nuclear Race and the Korean War. The Ford Foundation, and to a lesser extent the Carnegie Corporation, were hegemonic agents responsible for changing the direction of marketing education, research and theory.
Wooliscroft, 2004

The functionalist approach studies marketing behaviour as a system and tries to establish ways of making it work better, more efficiently. It is associated with the great marketing theory pioneer Wroe Alderson, writing in the 1950s and 1960s (Alderson, 1957). The managerial and buyer behaviour view of the 1960s and 1970s studied individual firms and consumers to discover how to control their market behaviour in order to maximize their profit (firms) and satisfaction (consumers). Managerial marketing is most closely associated with Philip Kotler (1967 onwards) and the buyer behaviour approach is typified by Engel *et al.* (1968).

One reason for the shift in the 1950s and 1960s towards a managerial approach to marketing using scientific methods was overtly and consciously ideological. This occurred due to the strong influence of the major foundations, such as Ford, Rockefeller and Carnegie, on the major US business schools in the post-World War II period. They consciously directed their funding to encourage scientific methods and management-oriented research and teaching for ideological reasons, in order to propagate US business and capitalism in the face of the political, military and economic threat from the Soviet Union at this time.

Faria and Wensley (2005) argue that 'the concept of marketing' was then of strategic importance for US business and government because 'it had the power to suppress the idea that a society without a free market and monopolized by the State could be more beneficial for their citizens' (p. 12). The development of marketing as a business discipline in this period was not immune to the influence of McCarthyism and the Cold War, Tadajewski (2006) concludes. Citing contemporary historical documents and publications, he explains how the Foundations' promotion of pro-American business values, methods, research and education can be seen as a response to the criticisms which had been levelled at the Foundations by the House of Representatives Un-American Committees. These included allegations of subversion for, amongst other things, funding social science projects based on ideologies opposed to the US free enterprise system.

During the 1970s and 1980s, this, by then dominant, ideological, managerial and mechanistic view of marketing extended its reach into just about every aspect of business, public, civil, charitable and even military and scientific activity in modern societies. It could, so its 'widening' adherents argue (see McKenna, 1991; Kotler, 1972), be applied to just about everything – actually it was not 'just about', but literally everything!

This book agrees that marketing today can be applied to everything. But not the marketing of the functionalists as an integrated system, nor just about the managerial aspects of marketing decisions and behaviour. Neither is it just about selling and advertising or distribution and retailing – and certainly not marketing as the *control of consumers*. On the contrary, marketing should be about liberating consumers, helping them consume better (which could mean less), creating their own value and using their market power for wider ends in society than simply consumption (see Marketing values).

FURTHER READING

Concept of internal marketing

Varey, R. J. & Lewis, B. R. (eds) (2000) *Internal Marketing: Directions for Management*. Routledge.

Internal vs external marketing boundaries

Webster, F. Jr (1992) The changing role of marketing in the corporation. *Journal of Marketing*, **564**, 1–17.

External environment and scanning

Daft, R. L., Sormunen, J. & Parks, D. (1988) Chief executive scanning, environmental characteristics and company performance: an empirical study. *Strategic Management Journal*, **9**, 123–139.

Review of marketing histories

Enright, M. (2002) Marketing and conflicting dates for its emergence. *Journal of Marketing Management*, **18** (5/6), 445–462.

More about marketing theories

Baker, M. J. (2000) *Marketing Theory: A Student Text*. Thomson Learning: London.

marketing values

Marketing has become the soul of the corporation.
Deleuze, 1992

Market value

The primary value in traditional marketing seems to be 'market value', i.e. creation of economic value to sellers and/or buyers. The very purpose of marketing according to some authorities is value creation (e.g. Doyle, 2000; Srivastava *et al.*, 1999). But the key questions remain – *what* is this value, *how* is it created and for *whom*?

As long as half a century ago, Wroe Alderson (1957) recognized that unless a firm creates and delivers value to customers, it has no real purpose, nor can it meet its business objectives. The creation and delivery of value to customers requires both an operational and a marketing component and, critically, the integration of the two. It is primarily from works on strategy, management, economics, consumer behaviour, engineering, operations research, accountancy and finance that the business concepts and measures of value have been developed.

Marketing mangers need to think in terms of different value propositions and how they can be created and delivered. According to Martinez (1999), these value propositions can then be analysed from three different perspectives – the customer perspective 'what customers get', the marketing perspective 'what marketing needs to do' and the operational perspective 'what the company needs to do'.

Creating value for customers is the key source of competitive advantage in the 21st century.
Woodruff, 1997

Before explaining the nature of value propositions, it is necessary to take one step back and see where this idea comes from.

The traditional 'engineering' view of value (i.e. value analysis, value engineering, etc.) looks at ways of maximizing functionality of a product or service process, whilst eliminating waste. This view is still seen today in engineering disciplines, with authors such as Womack & Jones (1994) encouraging companies to focus on the whole rather than the parts, thus allowing companies to distinguish value from waste. Similarly, Fawcett & Fawcett (1995) showed that a firm's ability to add value does not arise typically from any single functional expertise, but is attributed to the greater coordinated effort.

Many different definitions of value

One problem from a marketing perspective is that these definitions of value are mainly focused on the *producers' point of view* (organizational benefits), without

- *Porter (1985) – a firm is profitable if the value it commands exceeds the costs involved in creating the product.*
- *Merrifield (1991) defines value as the increase in value that occurs at each stage of the manufacturing process and value resides in the concentration of resources focused on selected business areas.*
- *Condra (1985) interprets value as a fair return in goods, services or money for some things exchanged that are worth, in comparison, with something similar (competitors' product).*
- *Treacy & Wiersema (1996) define value as resulting from the fulfilment of customers' expectations through which the organization achieves the economic benefit.*
- *Miles & Snow (1978) – value comes from choosing customers and narrowing the operation focus to best serve that market segment; customer satisfaction and loyalty doesn't, by itself, create unmatched value.*

giving much consideration to the customers' point of view. Marketing research shows that customers do not perceive product value in solely functional, product or any one-dimensional terms. For example, Wilson & Jantrania (1994) separated product-related aspects of value creation from vendor-related types and distinguished economic from non-economic components of value (see Figure 6).

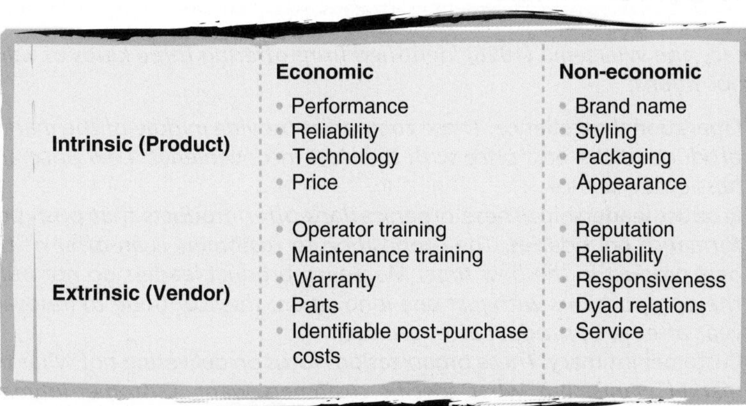

	Economic	Non-economic
Intrinsic (Product)	• Performance • Reliability • Technology • Price	• Brand name • Styling • Packaging • Appearance
Extrinsic (Vendor)	• Operator training • Maintenance training • Warranty • Parts • Identifiable post-purchase costs	• Reputation • Reliability • Responsiveness • Dyad relations • Service

Figure 6 Components of product value. *Source*: Wilson & Jantrania (1994)

Consumer-based studies successfully identify various perceptions of types of value, but for managers illustrate nothing about the means by which they are

> *The nature and types of consumer value constitute the essential foundation and fundamental basis for both academic study and the managerial practice of marketing.*
> Holbrook, 1999

created or the strategic dimensions of the process. It is from the strategic management literature that the seminal contribution on the strategic value creation process has been developed, based largely on the works of Michael Porter and the concept of the value chain (1980). This permitted marketers to think beyond categories of perceived value to the strategic means and processes for delivering to or enabling the customer.

This brief summary of viewpoints provides a snapshot of the state-of-the-art of contemporary knowledge about customer value. By all accounts this is quite fragmented knowledge (Woodruff, 1997; Tzokas & Saren, 1999). In order to overcome this, we turn to the concept of value propositions and attempt to integrate the value creation process with market offerings.

Value propositions

Treacy and Wiersema (1996) define the value proposition as 'an implicit promise a company makes to customers to deliver a particular combination of values'. The subsequent application of this concept has changed the focus of operations of many businesses, i.e. companies such as IBM have shifted the traditional, internally focused functions to customer-oriented, market-driven processes, looking towards a form of value delivery. In doing so, these companies have to make some fundamental decisions on segmentation and target customers' profiles (see Walters & Lancaster, 1999).

Treacy and Wiersema (1996) identified firms offering three kinds of value propositions:

1. Operational excellence. *These companies provide middle of the market products at the best price with the least inconvenience. Low price and hassle-free service.*
2. Product leadership. *These organizations offer products that push performance boundaries. The proposition to customers is an offer of the best product in the best time. Moreover, product leaders do not build their propositions with just one innovation; they continue to innovate year after year, product after product.*
3. Customer intimacy. *These organizations focus on delivering not what the market wants, but what specific customers want. Customer-intimate companies do not pursue one-time transactions; they cultivate relationships. They specialize in satisfying unique needs. Their proposition to the customer is: 'We have the best solution for you and we provide all the support you need to achieve optimum results.'*

Treacy and Wiersema's (1996) three value propositions (see box) integrate the operational delivery aspects of value with marketing issues, linked together through customers. However, based on empirical evidence, Martinez (1999) has found their categories to be limited in scope and flexibility. Firms using this analysis may miss some characteristics and competencies critical to their businesses. For example, Intel and Nike are both considered product leaders – i.e. proposition 2 above. On one hand, Intel is considered to be a product leader because it creates new products, new designs, technology and innovations year after year. Intel's capabilities reside on the research and development of microprocessors. On the other hand, however, Nike is also considered to be a product leader largely because of the successful management of its brand, image and marketing. Although Nike also conducts product development and has produced some breakthrough products, its success results more from its brand management and marketing skills.

So, here we have an example of two very different companies, with very different operations, marketing and product strategies, yet when viewed using Treacy & Wiersema's model, they share the same value proposition – that of product leaders. Martinez (1999) highlights that product leaders can come in two distinct forms. First, a 'hard' form represented by new designs, innovations, product development, etc. and, secondly, a 'soft' form, where the focus is on brand management, corporate image and marketing communications.

The value chain concept

Of the many changes that have taken place in management thinking towards the end of the twentieth century, perhaps the most significant has been the emphasis placed upon the search for strategies that will provide superior value in the eyes of the customer. One concept in particular that Michael Porter has brought to a wider audience is the 'value chain'.

Value chain activities (Figure 7) can be categorized into two types – primary activities (inbound logistics, operations, outbound logistics, marketing and sales, and service) and support activities (infrastructure, human resource management, technology development and procurement). These support activities are integrating functions that cut across the various primary activities within the firm. A firm can deliver more value to its customers through performing these activities more efficiently than its competitors or by performing the activities in a unique way that creates greater differentiation.

This concept identifies at each step in the chain and enables an analysis of how each contributes, or can contribute better, to creating customer value. Also, when the organization identifies an activity which is not contributing as well as possible to value in relation to its cost-effectiveness, then it enables managers to consider various internal or external solutions – e.g. contracting it out to be performed by

> *Competitive advantage cannot be understood by looking at a firm as a whole. It stems from the many discrete activities a firm performs in designing, producing, marketing, delivering, and supporting its product. Each of these activities can contribute to a firm's relative cost position and create a basis for differentiation . . . The value chain disaggregates a firm into its strategically relevant activities in order to understand the behaviour of costs and the existing and potential sources of differentiation. A firm gains competitive advantage by performing these strategically important activities more cheaply or better than its competitors.*
> *Porter, 1985*

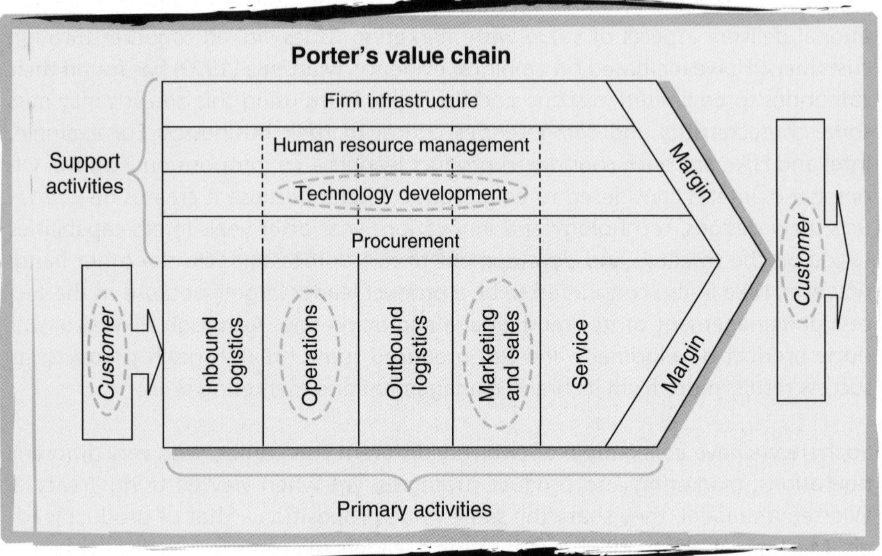

Figure 7 The value chain. *Source*: Porter (1984)

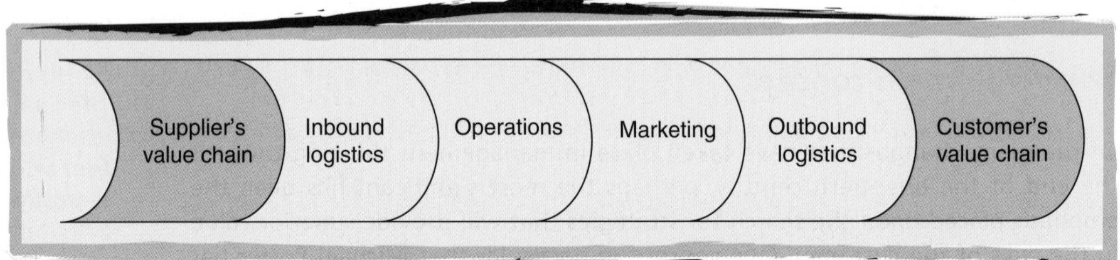

Figure 8 The extended value chain. *Source*: Porter (1984)

another firm (see Creating Solutions). Organizations to which critical tasks are outsourced must not be seen as subcontractors but rather as true partners in an *extended value chain* (Figure 8).

Some, such as Normann & Ramirez (1994), argue that there is a danger in paying too much attention to the disaggregating or breaking down of value activities in the value chain. Indeed, they *should not* be treated as separate activities to be managed but rather as an integrated and seamless process flow.

This raises the potential of a role for the consumer in value creating as opposed to the internal value focus of these 'production-orientated' models, like that of Porter. Instead, in marketing we should examine in more depth the consumer's role in terms of 'the value chain' and other models.

According to Porter's (1980) original value chain model, firms create additional margin as goods and services are exchanged along the supply (or value) chain. Each firm adds margin through value-adding activities and ultimately the buyer determines the value of the final output as 'the amount buyers are willing to pay for what a firm provides them'. Therefore, until the customer 'speaks' in the market, the value of the output is only an assumption.

In today's fast-changing environment, strategy is no longer a matter of positioning a fixed set of activities along that old industrial model, the value chain. Successful companies increasingly do not just add value, they reinvent it. The key strategic task is to reconfigure roles and relationships among a constellation of actors – suppliers, partners, and customers – in order to mobilize the creation of value by new combinations of players. . . . As a result, a company's strategic task becomes the ongoing reconfiguration and integration of its competencies and customers.
Normann & Ramirez, 1994

The customer's voice in value

Until the customer 'speaks' in the marketplace by offering a given price, the market value of the final product is only an assumption. If we take an example of a product which ultimately 'fails' in the marketplace (i.e. the customer will not buy or only pays an insufficient price beneath cost), the value added by each firm in the supply chain (e.g. suppliers of raw materials, processing, parts, assembly, manufacture, distributors, retailers) will have been based on the assumption of a successful final value judgement of the product in the market. Firms' calculated margins throughout the exchange and supply processes will have been based on this assumption. But, because this is not realized, their so-called value-adding activities did not actually *add value. Therefore, value creation can only be judged* ex-post *and the calculation of 'margins' during the production and delivery process is merely hypothetical and may or may not be realized. It is the consumer that has the crucial deciding role in determining final value. Firms' role in the system* is to create potential value that may or may not be realized by the customer.

Tzokas & Saren, 1997

This is the fundamental problem with the 'traditional' view of value, which ignores the true role of the customer according to Evert Gummesson (1997a):

> Production is viewed as value creation or value added by the supplier, whereas consumption is value depletion caused by the customer. If the consumer is the focal point of marketing, however, value creation is only possible when a product or service is consumed. An unsold product has no value, and a service provider without customers cannot produce anything.

Beyond 'speaking' in the marketplace, the role of the consumer in the 'system's' value creation process is nevertheless far from clear. In marketing theory you would expect the customer to occupy a central position, but competitive models have assumed that value is something that is produced by the firm and delivered to the customer. According to this view, value is created by organizational processes within firms and is progressively built up through exchange and collaboration between them *within the supply chain*. Piercy (1991) developed this view of the value creation by distinguishing 'value defining, value developing and value delivering' organizational processes that ultimately create customer value (see Figure 9).

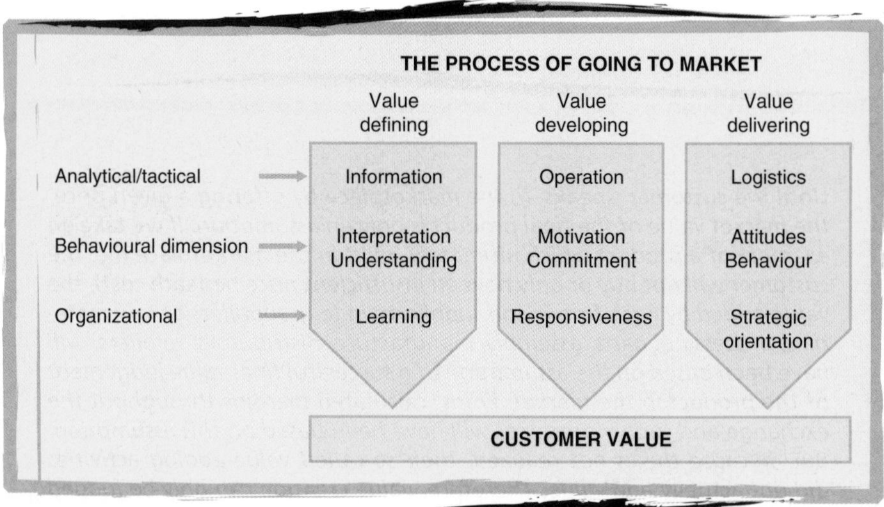

Figure 9 The dimensions of organizational processes. *Source*: Piercy (1998)

Other scholars, such as Normann & Ramirez (1994), take a contrary view of the value creation process whereby value is co-created through *interaction* between the firm and the customer, not in value chains, but value '*constellations*'. So consumers can play a key role in value creation too, not just firms, and the role of consumption, i.e. the activities, behaviours and motivations that consumers undertake when making decisions and forming perceptions about products and services, is not just to 'use up' or 'deplete' value, but is also one of value creation (see Consuming Experience).

The market has won the struggle for our national soul.
Elaine Fear, in Lloyd-Reason & Wall, 2000

The values of marketing

Fear argues that the world is now so unpredictable and unstable that the old certainties no longer serve as a guide. The dominance of ever faster-changing markets (which have 'won the struggle for our national soul') means for management that competitiveness comes from better understanding and adapting to the 'chaos' of the business environment (see Internal and external contexts).

The three 'drivers' that Riddlerstralle and Nordstrom (1999) regard as moving things forward in this 'unknown' future world are: technology, institutions and values. They argue that all three of these have important and wide-ranging impacts at different levels on individuals, companies and society. By 'values', however, they don't mean *market* values. Much more broadly than this, they cite differences internationally in *cultural* values. In China, for instance, markets are founded on the concept of *Guanxi* or trust – an alternative value system to the western market basis of legal frameworks, property rights and contracts. Obviously in different counties their cultural values affect consumers' demand for particular products, such as furnishing, food or clothing.

Values affect all our thoughts and deeds . . . artefacts and actions. Values are enormously powerful, omni-present and hugely different from place to place, person to person.
Riddlerstralle & Nordstrom, 1999

But one core 'value' underpinning the concept of marketing is the belief in choice: the right of consumers to have the freedom to choose from a selection of options in what they buy, from where and from whom; and also the corollary for sellers is the free choice of what to sell, where and to whom. So choice means lots of supplies and products on the market and the implicit assumption that more choice is always 'better' – i.e. more is a value in itself. Thus, marketing values don't just lead to more choice, they also arguably lead to *abundance and excess* and the necessary provision of *more* than consumers need or want. Battaille (1988) argues that all human systems lead to excess and waste. Thus, in this respect marketing values are merely reflecting the human condition, which always creates more than is needed and therefore produces waste. Riddlerstralle and Nordstrom (1999) provide some fascinating examples of abundant choice.

There is another related, yet competing, value that results from free markets and consumer choice. This is that the customer is *the* chooser, the one in control and the term often used is '*the* king' (no, not Elvis). This royal metaphor goes back a long way and it is deeply rooted in ideas of exchange, customer service and free market choice. As early as Shakespeare's *Merchant of Venice*, Antonio is

In 1996 there were 1778 new business books published on the American market and 20 000 new grocery product launches; Sony launched 5000 new products and in 1998 there were 30 000 new US record albums. Norway, with a population of 4.5 million, has 200 newspapers, 100 weekly magazines and 20 TV channels to choose from.

Riddlerstralle & Nordstrom, 1999

described as a 'royal merchant'. Adam Smith (1961), who was after all a moral philosopher, described the consumer as 'sovereign' in the marketplace. The royal title was also applied by Horkheimer (1967) to describe the 'courting' and 'majesty' of the customer in the pre-nineteenth century era.

In the surplus society the customer is more than king: the customer is the mother of all dictators.
Riddlerstralle & Nordstrom, 1999

Is the customer really king?

Far from today's customer being 'king', Horkheimer (1967) observed marketing now has such a powerful control apparatus ('technologies of governance') of the 'free' market that results in consumers becoming dependent on the knowledge of experts, technologies and systems that their freedom, 'inner as well as empirical', has been lost.

Underlying values can be identified by examining the words, the language that is used by proponents and writers on the subject.
Fairclough, 1995; Stern, 1990

The majesty of the customer . . . hardly plays any part any longer for the individual in relation to the advertising apparatus, the standardization of commodities and other economic realities.
Horkheimer, 1967, quoted in Schipper, 2002

Marketing has certainly generated an extensive apparatus of technologies and techniques aimed at developing brand loyalty and customer 'lock-in'. Hence the enormous amount of recent attention in marketing practice and literature to customer retention, loyalty programmes, customer relationship management and consumer 'lifetime value' (see Building Relations). This does not refer to value for the customers themselves, but for the *firm*.

Hirschman (1993) goes one step further in her discussion of the language employed to discuss the consumer in many marketing texts which, she argues, are littered with metaphors of war and combat. Market segments are 'targeted' for 'penetration'. Market share must be 'fought for' and 'won'. Customers must be 'influenced' lest they 'defect' to the opposition. Thus, consumers are worked upon until they are 'captive', although unaware of this captivity (see Internal and external contexts, 'Marketing history' subsection).

Some argue that this is nothing new. Marketing has always been concerned with the influence, if not manipulation, of consumer demand. What is different about the techniques of the new 'customer relationship management' is that the objective has shifted from sale closure to customer retention and loyalty; IT-enabled techniques are employed not only to stimulate desires and needs, but more fundamentally to develop psychological loyalty, lock-in and dependence on the brand (see Building Relations).

Is the consumer really sovereign nowadays? How much choice do customers really have? Do these terms really reflect today's marketing values?

What are marketing's values?

Desmond (1998) traced marketing's ethics from the early twentieth century when the first marketing scholars were educated in the tradition of German historicism and the social dynamics of the free market. He showed that this view of marketing as satisfying human needs through exchange is not 'value free'; it inherently contains so-called 'utilitarian' values, which, simply put, prescribe the ideal outcome as 'the greatest happiness for the greatest number'.

Ethics is the branch of moral philosophy that deals with moral judgements, standards and rules of conduct, and involves perceptions regarding right and wrong. It requires an individual to behave according to the rules of moral philosophy. The early theories studied ethics from a normative perspective, meaning that they were concerned with '*constructing and justifying the moral standards and codes that one ought to follow*' (Hunt & Vitell, 1986). More recently, positivist studies of ethics attempted to describe and explain how individuals actually behave in ethical situations.

Gaski (1999) defined ethics from the dictionary as 'standards of conduct and moral judgement or the system of morals of a particular . . . group' (p. 316). He conducted a survey to identify the normative ethical frameworks from a comprehensive review of the previous 25 years of marketing literature – i.e. what it says marketers *should and should not do*. Finding that there were surprisingly few distinct ethical recommendations, he concluded that most so-called ethical guidelines for marketers are mere restatements of other principles of bland legalistic definitions or statements of economic self-interest; there is a '. . . total redundancy and superfluity of marketing ethics . . . a vacant construct, representing nothing beyond what is already contained elsewhere' (Gaski, 1999).

Clearly, there is scope for content in marketing ethics that goes beyond the law and self-interest.
N. C. Smith, 2001

These findings, and their assumptions, have been heavily criticized by Smith (2001). While accepting that marketers should obviously act in obedience of law and their own and their company's self-interest, he argues that meeting these obligations is usually a necessary, *but not a sufficient*, condition for proper business conduct. He points out that there are circumstances where meeting ethical standards demands more of them than this because 'managers may face situations where ethics, the law and self-interest are inconsistent' (Smith, 2001).

Thus, there are serious issues concerning marketing's ethics that have been raised by those writers who have studied the values of marketing from a theoretical point of view. However, the research results, or lack of them, from those who have examined marketing practices are even more disturbing.

Marketing ethics research

One area of this research has investigated the types of ethical problems that managers face in the course of their everyday work. Empirical research on ethical beliefs in business organizations began with a well-known study of attitudes of *Harvard Business Review* readers towards business ethics conducted by Baumhart in 1961. This lists the ethical problems that business managers wanted to eliminate, including the following list: gifts, gratuities, bribes, '*call girls*', price discrimination and unfair pricing, dishonest advertising, unfair competitive practices, cheating customers, unfair credit practices, overselling, price collusion by competitors, dishonesty in making or keeping a contract, unfairness to employees and prejudice in hiring. Five of the eight most important ethical problems have to do with marketing activities. Brenner and Molander (1977) conducted a follow-up study and found the same set of undesirable practices. Findings such as these prompted Murphy & Laczniak (1981) to conclude that '*the function within business firms most often charged with ethical abuse is marketing*'.

A famous study by Chonko & Hunt (1985) looked at both the nature and extent of marketing management ethical problems and examined the effectiveness of top management actions and codes of ethics in promoting ethical behaviour. They found that bribery, fairness, honesty, price, product, personnel, confidentiality, advertising, manipulation of data and purchasing were the major ethical issues facing marketing managers.

Social values in marketing

One school of socialization theory says that individuals progress from basic moral imperatives ('don't do this, do that') to applying systematic criteria to analyse moral dilemmas and eventually further develop to using more complex, equivocal and multidimensional bases in their moral reasoning (Goslin, 1969). So the development of marketing values can also be seen to progress along a similar path in its ethical and social reasoning. Having been around as a professional discipline and as an academic subject for well over half a century, it can be argued that the moral and ethical basis of marketing theory and practice is moving towards more complex modes of analysis and understanding. Even in traditional marketing textbooks such as that of Kotler *et al.* (2001), alternative and wider values are taken into account, beyond the utilitarian, free market, managerial and consumer choice bases for decisions.

> *Kotler's societal marketing concept 'calls upon marketers to build social and ethical considerations into their marketing practices'.*
> Kotler *et al.*, 2001

There is nothing unusual in the way Kotler et al. *(2001) entitle the discussion of the product and other concepts as 'Marketing Management Philosophies', yet there are no references to philosophy.*
Lawson & Wooliscroft, 2004

Marketers are concerned with human behaviour. As the most basic motive they need to understand why customers, competitors and stakeholders behave as they do so that they can engage with and ultimately generate profits from this behaviour. The need for profits ensures that marketers study human behaviour assiduously and energetically, and their successful acquisition funds the resulting stream of marketing and academic research. As a result, the commercial marketing profession and its activities can essentially be seen as an enormous laboratory dedicated to understanding why people do as they do.

This understanding has the potential to bring enormous public benefits. A recent US review concluded that more than 50% of morbidity and premature death is directly attributable to lifestyle factors (Hastings & Saren, 2003). Major killers like AIDS, lung cancer and obesity are primarily caused by consumers' own behaviour and lifestyle choices. Furthermore, many other social ills such as crime, racism and road accidents can, at least partly, be seen as problems of human behaviour. So, marketing's understanding can be applied to social issues. The ideas and techniques used by Philip Morris to sell cigarettes to smokers can be used to unsell them, as well as encourage healthier pursuits such as exercise or safer sex (see Building Relations: Building social relationships).

Social marketing can make an enormous contribution . . . At the first level of analysis it can problematize hitherto uncontentious marketing areas through revealing underlying or hidden ambiguities and uncertainties. It can further help define the nature of some of marketing's more negative outcomes and begin to provide realistic ideas for potential solutions.
Hastings & Saren, 2003

Despite the potential to bring about these benefits – and indeed its enormous contribution to economic growth – marketing, as David Jobber (2001) reminds us, has a bad name. In common parlance it is often used as a byword for deception and exploitation, and many see it as an engine driving forward materialism and excess consumption. More specifically, individual industries come under periodic criticism from both governmental and non-governmental organizations. The litigation currently focusing on the tobacco industry and dark suggestions that the food industry is next in line provide extreme examples of this criticism.

In essence, these attacks on marketing are recognizing that it exerts a powerful influence on society, and that this influence can be negative as well as positive. Social marketing bridges this gap between the corporate sector and public welfare. It understands both worlds. As a result it has enormous potential.

Andreasen (2003) provides an excellent review of the origins and future potential of social marketing (see Building Relations: Building social relationships).

Sustainable and ecological values

> *Placing marketing in an ecological context means that it may no longer be viewed as a transaction 'meeting' customers' needs and wants, but as part of a much greater and more complex process. If ecological aspects of life could be taken into account they would give a new dimension to the formulation of marketing strategies.*
> *Kajzer & Saren, 2000*

Sustainable marketing is more than just about making products 'green' or 'environmentally friendly'. It requires a completely different way of thinking about the role of marketing and how it deals with change.

There is widespread criticism of the traditional, managerial, anthropocentric and consumerist marketing which, it is argued, must be fatally implicated in the waste, destruction and excess that many environmentalists see as the consequence of the modern market and consumption system. The traditional language of marketing employs the grammar of the mechanistic world, where matter is regarded as inert and mute, passive and exploitable (Kajzer & Saren, 2000). It speaks the language of material possession, individuality and newness, of the assumption of unlimited growth and the accumulation of waste (Sherry, 2000). The key to success is growth in sales, material output, and the primary purpose of marketing is to design strategic plans and sales forecasts to support this goal. Traditional marketing theory is predicated on the central role of the product in the exchange process and the notion of the '*product concept*' as a distinct entity and object of exchange. This has led to fragmentation of elements in the environment and treating resources as if they consisted of separate parts, to be exploited by different interest groups (Capra, 1983).

The biological business metaphor

There are several new business concepts, such as *biological business* (Clippinger, 1999), *living companies* (de Geus, 1999) and *living strategies* (Gratton, 2000). What they all have in common is the use of biological knowledge in order to create more flexible, more adaptable practices. However, many of the business theories using organism metaphors seem to be grounded in the need to make the life of the company '*sustainable*', long term and competitive, and to master human behaviour, but simultaneously ironically failing to fully include the considerations of the natural environment.

There are also 'new marketing' books, such as Fuller's *Sustainable Marketing: Managerial–Ecological Issues* (1999), that introduce notions of sustainability into marketing. Like many such authors, however, Fuller takes a very managerial approach to ecological issues. He argues that sustainability is 'a logical extension of contemporary marketing . . . Sustainable Marketing is structured around the traditional "4Ps" of marketing and explains how marketing mix decisions can and do influence environmental outcomes.' Fuller appears to think that the issues of sustainability in marketing are essentially managerial. Managers can 'bolt on', as it were, a 'green extension' to the basic marketing concept and the traditional 4Ps approach to marketing and, *voila*, marketing is sustainable!

Reading works by other advocates of sustainable marketing, however – such as Kilbourne *et al.* (1997) – there is a clear sense that nothing short of a *revolutionary reassessment* of basic marketing ideas, techniques, orientation and practice is required to achieve the undeniably radical goal of sustainability. The roles of people, society and technologies all have to fundamentally change.

Firms will have to be increasingly flexible and creative in finding new ways of doing business that are consistent with an uncertain world and the need for a commitment towards sustainable development. In some ways, change may be seen as a measure of sustainability and organizations in the future will need to embrace change and uncertainty as a vital management function (Welford, 2000). Thus, a fully sustainable view of marketing is that it not only has to take into account eco-management of resources in meeting customers' and firms' needs, but also pay greater attention to organizational–environmental configurations that are dynamic, flexible and provide space for dealing with uncertainty. Sustainable marketing requires a critical re-examination of the concept of the marketing and environment interface, and the components that make it up (see Internal and external contexts).

If the metaphor of the machine inspired managers in the industrial age, the image of living systems may inspire a truly sustainable post-industrial marketing.
Senge & Carstedt, 2001

In light of current environmental problems and marketing's contribution to them, there is a need for marketing to account for the wider context of its relationship with the natural environment of which it is part. One way to reconsider this is by examining the nature and characteristics of living ecological systems, from disciplines such as ecology and biology (Mayr, 1997), popular science (Capra, 1983), environmental management (Welford, 2000), environmental philosophy (Ferry, 1995) and design (Tsui, 1999).

The essential requirement of a more 'sustainable' approach to marketing not only concerns efficient resource management, but also learning to think in new ways, generating a new, more adaptable, marketing mindset that thrives in uncertain and complex conditions – a new dynamic approach to reconceptualizing and reorienting marketing activities that alters the way we look at products, brands, consumption, consumers and relationships, built upon ecological principles, cyclical patterns of information, that is highly flexible and easily changed.

FURTHER READING

Marketing value

Doyle, P. (2000). *Value-based Marketing: Marketing Strategies for Corporate Growth and Shareholder Value*. Wiley: Chichester.

Holbrook, M. (1999) *Consumer Value*. Routledge: London.

Norman, R. & Ramirez, R. (1994) *Designing Interactive Strategy: From Value Chain to Value Constellation*. Wiley: Chichester.

Wikstrom, S. (1996) Value creation by company–consumer interaction. *Journal of Marketing Management*, **12**, 359–374.

Marketing ethics

Gaski, J. (1999) Does marketing ethics really have anything to say? – A critical inventory of the literature. *European Journal of Marketing*, **18** (3), 315.

Hunt, S. D. & Vitell, S. (1986) A general theory of marketing ethics. *Journal of Macromarketing*, **6** (Spring), 5–16.

Ecological marketing

Fuller, D. (1999) *Sustainable Marketing: Managerial–Ecological Issues*. Sage: London.

Kilbourne, W. (1998) Green marketing: a theoretical perspective. *Journal of Marketing Management*, **14**, 641–655.

References

Alderson, W. (1957) *Marketing Behaviour and Executive Action*. Irwin: Homewood, IL.

Andreasen, A. (2003) The life trajectory of social marketing: some implications. *Marketing Theory*, **3** (3), 293–304.

Bagozzi, R. P. (1978) Marketing as exchange: a theory of transactions in the marketplace. *American Behavioral Scientist*, **21** (March/April), 535–556.

Baker, M. (1995) *Marketing: Theory and Practice*. Macmillan Press: London.

Bartels, R. (1962) *The Development of Marketing Thought*. Irwin: Homewood, IL.

Battaille, G. (1988) *The Accursed Share* (R. Hurley, trans.). Zone Books: New York.

Baumhart, R. C. (1961) How ethical are businessmen? *Harvard Business Review*, **39** (July/Aug), 6–19.

Black, A. (1984) *Guilds and Civil Society in European Political Thought from the 12th Century to the Present*. Methuen: London.

Brenner, S. N. & Molander, E. A. (1977) Is the ethics of business changing? *Harvard Business Review*, **55** (Jan/Feb), 57–71.

Capra, F. (1983) *The Turning Point*. HarperCollins: London.

Chamberlin, E. (1933) *The Theory of Monopolistic Competition*. Harvard University Press: Cambridge, MA.

Chonko, L. B. & Hunt, S. D. (1985) Ethics and marketing management: an empirical examination. *Journal of Business Research*, **13** (August), 339–359.

Clippinger, H. J. III (1999) *The Biology of Business. Decoding the Natural Laws of Enterprise*. Jossey-Bass: San Francisco.

Condra, L. L. W. (1985) *Value Added Management with Design of Experiments*. Chapman & Hall.

Crosier, K. (1975) What exactly is marketing? *Quarterly Review of Marketing*, Winter, 21–25.

Daft, R. L., Sormunen, J. & Parks, D. (1988) Chief executive scanning, environmental characteristics and company performance: an empirical study. *Strategic Management Journal*, **9**, 123–139.

de Geus A. (1999) *The Living Company*. Nicholas Brealey: London.

Deleuze, G. (1992) Postscripts on the Societies of Control. *October*, 59.

Desmond, J. (1998) Marketing and Moral Indifference. In: *Ethics and Organisation* (M. Parker, ed.). Sage: London.

Doyle, P. (2000) *Value-based Marketing: Marketing Strategies for Corporate Growth and Shareholder Value*. Wiley: Chichester.

Engel, J. F., Kollat, D. T. & Blackwell, R. D. (1968) *Consumer Behaviour*. Holt, Rinehart & Winston: New York.

Enright, M. (2002) Marketing and conflicting dates for its emergence. *Journal of Marketing Management*, **18** (5/6), 445–462.

Fairclough, N. (1995) *Critical Discourse Analysis: The Critical Study of Language*. Longmans: London.

Faria, A. & Wensley, R. (2005) A critical perspective on marketing strategy. *Proceedings of 2005 ENANPAD Conference*, September, Brasilia-DF, Brazil.

Fawcett, S. E. & Fawcett, S. A. (1995) The firm as a value-added system: integrating logistics, operations and purchasing. *International Journal of Purchasing, Distribution and Logistics Management*, **25** (5), 24–42.

Ferry, L. (1995) *The New Ecological Order*. University of Chicago Press: Chicago.

Ford, I. D. (ed.) (1990) *Understanding Business Markets: Interaction, Relationships and Networks*. Academic Press: New York.

Fuller, D. (1999) *Sustainable Marketing: Managerial–Ecological Issues*. Sage: London.

Gaski, J. (1999) Does marketing ethics really have anything to say? – A critical inventory of the literature. *European Journal of Marketing*, **18** (3), 315.

Goslin, D. (1969) *Handbook of Socialisation Theory and Research*. Rand McNally: Chicago.

Gratton, L. (2000) *Living Strategy: Putting People at the Heart of Corporate Purpose*. Pearson Education: Harlow.

Gummesson, E. (1997a) Relationship marketing as a paradigm shift: some conclusions from the 30R approach. *Management Decision*, **35** (3/4, April/March), 267–273.

Gummesson, E. (1997b) In search of marketing equilibrium: relationship marketing versus hypercompetition. *Journal of Marketing Management*, **13** (5), 421–430.

Håkansson, H. & Snehota, I. (1995) *Developing Relationships in Business Networks*. Routledge: New York.

Harker, M. (1998) Relationship marketing defined. Presented at *UK Academy of Marketing Doctoral Colloquium*, July, Sheffield Metropolitan University, UK.

Hastings, G. B. & Saren, M. (2003) The critical contribution of social marketing: theory and application. *Marketing Theory*, **3** (3), 305–322.

Hirschman, E. (1993) Ideology in consumer research, 1980 and 1990: a Marxist and feminist critique. *Journal of Consumer Research*, **19** (March), 537–555.

Holbrook, M. (ed.) (1999) *Consumer Value*. Routledge: New York.

Horkheimer, M. (1967). *Zur kritik der instrumentellen vernunft* (*Towards a Critique of Instrumental Reason*). Europäische Verlagsanstalt: Frankfurt-am-Main.

Housten, F. & Grassenheimer, J. (1987) Marketing and exchange. *Journal of Marketing*, **51**, 3–18.

Hunt, S. D. & Vitell, S. (1986) A general theory of marketing ethics. *Journal of Macromarketing*, **6** (Spring), 5–16.

Jobber, D. (2001) *Principles and Practice of Marketing*, 3rd edn. McGraw-Hill: London.

Kajzer, I. & Saren, M. (2000) The living product: a critical re-examination of the product concept. In: *The Business Strategy and Environment Conference Proceedings*, University of Leeds. ERP Environment, pp. 219–226.

Kerin, R. (1996) In pursuit of an ideal: the editorial and literary history of the *Journal of Marketing*. *Journal of Marketing*, **60** (1), 1–13.

Kilbourne, W., McDonagh, P. & Prothero, A. (1997) Sustainable consumption and the quality of life: a macroeconomic challenge to the dominant social paradigm. *Journal of Macromarketing*, **17**, 4–24.

Kotler, P. (1967) *Marketing Management: Analysis, Planning, Implementation and Control*. Prentice-Hall: Englewood Cliffs, NJ.

Kotler, P. (1972) A generic concept of marketing. *Journal of Marketing*, **36** (April), 46–54.

Kotler, P., Brown, L., Adam, S. & Armstrong, G. (2001) *Marketing*. Pearson: Frenchs Forest, NSW.

Lawson, R. & Wooliscroft, B. (2004) Human nature and the marketing concept. *Marketing Theory*, **4** (4), 311–326.

Lazer, W. & Shaw, E. (1988) The development of collegiate business and marketing education in America: historical perspectives. In: *A Return to Broader Dimensions: Proceedings of the 1988 AMA Winter Educators Conference* (S. Shapiro & A. H. Walle, eds). American Marketing Association: Chicago, pp. 147–152.

Lloyd-Reason, L. & Wall, S. (eds) (2000) *Dimensions of Competitiveness: Issues and Policies*. Edward Elgar: Cheltenham.

Martinez, V. (1999) Sustainable added value. Unpublished Masters Thesis in Technology Management, Strathclyde University.

Mattsson, L. G. (1985) An application of the network approach to marketing. In: *Changing the Course of Marketing: Alternative Paradigms for Widening Marketing Theory* (N. Dholakia & J. Arndt, eds). JAI Press: Greenwich, CT.

Mayr, E. (1997) *This is Biology, The Science of the Living World*. Harvard University Press: Cambridge, MA.

McKenna, R. (1991) Marketing is everything. *Harvard Business Review*, **69** (1, Jan/Feb), 65–80.

Merrifield, B. (1991) Value-added: the dominant factor in industrial competitiveness. *International Journal of Technology Management*, special publication on the role of technology in corporate policy, pp. 226–235.

Miles, R. & Snow, C. (1978) *Organisational Strategy, Structure, and Process*, International student edition. Stanford University Press: Stanford, CA.

Murphy, E. P. & Laczniak, G. R. (1981) Marketing ethics: a review with implications for managers, educators and researchers. In: *Review of Marketing*. American Marketing Association: Chicago, pp. 251–266.

Nonaka, I. (1994) A dynamic theory of organizational knowledge. *Organization Science*, **5** (1), 14–37.

Normann, R. & Ramirez, R. (1994) *Designing Interactive Strategy: From Value Chain to Value Constellation*. Wiley: Chichester.

Payne, A. (1995) *Advances in Relationship Marketing*. Kogan Page: London.

Piercy, N. (1991) *Market-led Strategic Change: Making Marketing Happen in your Organization*. Thomson: London.

Piercy, N. (1998) *Market-led Strategic Change: A Guide to Transforming the Process of Going to Market*, 2nd edn. Butterworth-Heinemann: Oxford.

Porter, M. (1980) *Competitive Strategy*. Free Press: New York.

Porter, M. (1985) *Competitive Advantage; Creating and Sustaining Superior Performance*. Free Press: New York.

Riddlerstralle, J. & Nordstrom, K. (1999) *Funky Business*. ft.com/Pearson: London.

Rindova, V. P. & Fombrun, C. J. (1999) Constructing competitive advantage: the role of firm–constituent interactions. *Strategic Management Journal*, **20** (8), 691–710.

Savitt, R. (1980) Historical research in marketing. *Journal of Marketing*, **44** (Fall), 52–58.

Schipper, F. (2002) The relevance of Horkheimer's view of the customer. *European Journal of Marketing*, **36** (1/2), 23–36.

Senge, P. & Carstedt, G. (2001) Innovating our way to the next industrial revolution. *MIT Sloan Management Review*, Winter, 24–37.

Shankar, A. & Horton, B. (1999) Ambient media: advertisings new media opportunity? *International Journal of Advertising*, **18** (3): 305–321.

Sherry, J. F. (2000) Distraction, destruction, deliverance: the presence of mindscape in marketing's new millennium. *Marketing Intelligence and Planning*, **18** (6/7), 328–336.

Sheth, J. N. & Gardener, D. M. (1988) History of marketing thought: an update. In: *Marketing Theory: Philosophy of Science Perspectives* (R. Bush & S. D. Hunt, eds). Amateur Marketing Association: Chicago.

Smith, A. (1961) *The Wealth of Nations*. Methuen: London.

Smith, N. C. (2001) Ethical guidelines for marketing practice: a reply to Gaski and some observations on the role of normative marketing ethics. *European Journal of Marketing*, **31** (1), 3–18.

Srivastava, R. K., Shrevani, T. K. & Fahey, L. (1999) Marketing, business processes, and shareholder value: an organizationally embedded view of marketing activities and the discipline of marketing. *Journal of Marketing*, **63**, 168–179.

Stern, B. (1990) Literary criticism and the history of marketing thought: a new perspective on 'reading' marketing theory. *Journal of the Academy of Marketing Science*, **18**, 329–336.

Tadajewski, M. (2006) The ordering of marketing theory. *Marketing Theory*, **6** (1).

Treacy, M. & Wiersema, F. (1996) *The Disciplines of the Market Leaders*. Harper Collins.

Tsui, E. (1999) *Evolutionary Architecture. Nature as a Basis for Design*. Wiley: New York.

Tzokas, N. & Saren, M. (1997) Building relationship platforms in consumer markets: a value chain approach. *Journal of Strategic Marketing*, **5** (2), 105–120.

Varey, R. J. & Lewis, B. R. (1999) A broadened conception of internal marketing. *European Journal of Marketing*, **33** (9/10), 926–944.

Vitell, S. (2001) Introduction to Special Issue on Marketing Ethics. *European Journal of Marketing*, **31** (1), 1–3.

Walters, D. & Lancaster, G. (1999) Value-based marketing and its usefulness to customers. *Management Decision*, **37** (9), 697–708.

Webster, F. Jr (1992) The changing role of marketing in the corporation. *Journal of Marketing*, **564**, 1–17.

Welford, R. (2000) *Corporate Environmental Management: Towards Sustainable Development*. Earthscan: London.

Wilson, D. T. & Jantrania, S. (1994) Understanding the value of a relationship. *Asia–Australia Marketing Journal*, **2** (1), 55–66.

Womack, J. P. & Jones, D. T. (1994) From lean production to the lean enterprise. *Harvard Business Review*, March/April, 93–103.

Woodruff, R. B. (1997) Marketing in the 21st century customer value: the next source for competitive advantage. *Journal of the Academy of Marketing Science*, **25** (3), 256.

Wooliscroft, B. (2004) Paradigm dominance and the hegemonic process. Ph.D. thesis, University of Otago, New Zealand.

Building Relations

Few businesses, or people, can do everything by themselves. Therefore, a key element in marketing is building relationships. In particular, long-term 'interactions' between buyers and sellers are important in explaining marketing behaviour and the development of markets. This section covers the role of communications, networks and institutions in establishing market relations. It also explains how marketing techniques can be used for beneficial effects on social relations, as well as negative ones. If marketing can encourage us to buy a Ferrari, it can also persuade us to drive it safely – or resist the temptation to steal one.

Relationships and interactions

Few businesses, or people, can do everything by themselves (see Marketing Contexts); therefore, a key element in marketing, indeed *the key element*, is building relationships. Increasingly companies realize that customers are their most important asset and view customer relationships as opportunities that need to be managed. The essential aim of relationship marketing strategies is of course value creation (see Marketing Contexts: Marketing values) *for both parties* through the formation and maintenance of relationships with external marketplace entities. The most important of these is usually with customers, but also with other stakeholders and partners that can influence and help companies' marketing operations.

The relationship marketing approach has grown in popularity and attention significantly in the last decade, particularly since the seminal articles in the USA by Webster (1992) and Morgan & Hunt (1994). Its roots go back to European academics in the 1970s, studying the conditions and behaviour in industrial and services marketing, notably in Sweden and Finland, where they found long-term relationships between buyers and sellers to be particularly important to each party. They concluded that these 'interactions' were also critical in explaining marketing behaviour and the development of markets. This was labelled by the industrial marketing group, IMP, as the *interaction* approach.

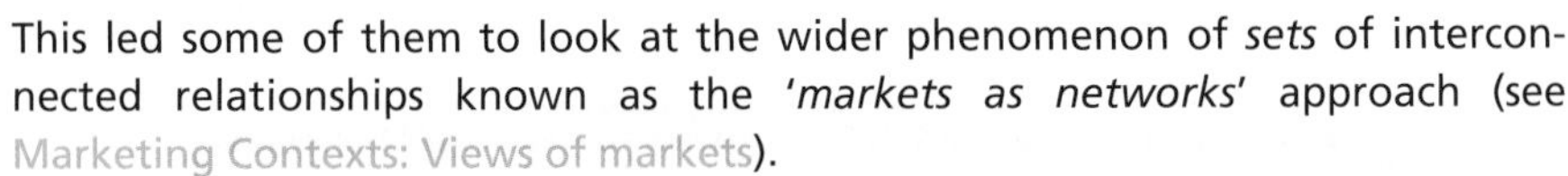

This led some of them to look at the wider phenomenon of *sets* of interconnected relationships known as the '*markets as networks*' approach (see Marketing Contexts: Views of markets).

For businesses, the possibility and need for the new relational approach to marketing has arisen for a number of reasons: more intense, often global, competition; fragmentation of mass markets through IT and communication technologies; ability to collect and analyse more data about individual customers; a generally high level of product quality that is forcing companies to seek competitive advantage in other ways; more demanding customers; and rapidly changing customer buying patterns (Buttle, 1996).

Consequently, companies have sought new ways of establishing long-term profitable relationships with customers, and ultimately, ways of maintaining these relationships in order to *retain customers* that they attract. There has been a

The interaction approach *is based on the idea that business markets aren't made up of a large number of individually insignificant customers. Nor do they consist simply of action by suppliers – who assemble a marketing mix and launch it towards a group of passive buyers, whose only reaction is to choose*

whether or not to buy. Instead the process is one of interaction between active buyers and sellers *that are individually significant to each other.*
Ford, 2004

notable shift in marketing from transactions (i.e. sales) to relationships (i.e. retention) as companies move from short-term *transaction-oriented* goals to long-term *relationship-building* goals.

The key differences between these approaches are shown in Table 1.

Table 1 Key differences between transactional marketing and relationship marketing

Transactional marketing	Relationship marketing
Focus on single sales	Focus on customer retention
Orientation to product features	Orientation to customer value
Short time scale	Long time scale
Little emphasis on customer service	High customer service emphasis
Moderate customer contact	High customer contact
Quality is primarily a concern of production	Quality is the concern of all
Limited customer commitment	

Source: Payne (2000).

There has been a shift from a transactions to a relationship focus . . . From an academic or theoretical perspective, the relatively narrow conceptualization of marketing as a profit-maximization problem, focused on market transactions, seems increasingly out of touch with an emphasis on long-term customer relationships and the formation and management of strategic alliances . . . The focus shifts from products and firms as units of analysis to people, organizations, and the social processes that bind actors together in ongoing relationships.
Webster, 1992

Grönroos (1994) spoke of the marketing strategy 'continuum', shown in Figure 10, where various types of goods and services can be placed depending upon their characteristics.

Figure 10 Marketing strategy continuum. *Source*: Grönroos (1994)

Grönroos (1994) suggests a transaction-type strategy for fast-moving consumer goods (FMCGs) and a relationship strategy for service firms. However, due to supplementary services to products, and vice versa, items may move along this continuum depending on what they comprise. For example, airlines may take you from A to B, but will offer you various in-flight products which augment the core service; on the other hand, supermarkets provide an outlet for consumer goods but provide various ancillary services such as collect by car or being helped at the checkout. Due to the proliferation of relationship marketing strategies, it is evident that contemporary firms are trying to position themselves at the right-hand, relationship-focused end of the continuum.

> ***The aim of relationship marketing is to establish, maintain and enhance relationships with customers and other partners, at a profit, so that the objectives of the parties involved are met. This is achieved by a mutual exchange and fulfillment of promises.***
> *Grönroos, 1994*

Definition and characteristics of marketing relationships

One of the most popular definitions of what is known as relationship marketing is provided by Grönroos (1994).

Note the role in Grönroos's definition of the concept of promises. He also states that: '. . . giving promises may *attract* new customers and initially *build* relationships. However, if promises are not kept, the evolving relationship cannot be *maintained* and *enhanced*.' Therefore, this definition implies other characteristics that are essential in the development of relationships, a key one being the concept of *trust*, which underlies most of the theories of marketing relationships development, including the most widely referenced paper on the subject by Morgan & Hunt (1994).

Grönroos (1994) describes trust in terms of beliefs and intentions. First, he argues that there has to be a belief in the other partner's trustworthiness that results from the expertise, reliability or intentionality of that partner. Second, he views trust as actual behaviour or a behavioural intention that reflects the degree of reliance on the other partner, thus involving a vulnerability on the part of the trustor.

So far in this chapter we have described what is meant by marketing relationships, and the characteristics of relationship marketing. The role of relationships in creating value and future developments in relationship marketing will be discussed in the next subsections.

Relationship marketing and customer value

The ability to generate and deliver value *above and beyond* the product or service is critical for today's businesses. However, it is much less clear how managers can identify what this value is *in the eyes of their customers*, and how they can develop and mobilize the necessary competencies for generating this value (see Marketing Contexts: Marketing values). It is in this task that there is significant potential of the relationship marketing approach for identifying and delivering customer value.

Trust and commitment

Commitment and trust are 'key' [to relationship marketing], because they encourage marketers to (1) work at preserving relationship investments by cooperating with exchange partners, (2) resist attractive short-term alternatives in favour of the expected long-term benefits of staying with the existing partners, and (3) view potentially high risk actions as being prudent because of the belief that their partners will not act opportunistically. When commitment and trust – not just one or the other – are present they produce outcomes that promote efficiency, productivity and effectiveness.

Morgan & Hunt, 1994

In the past the formula for identifying customer value seems to have been to listen to your customers and learn from previous mistakes. However, the rapidly changing marketing context (see Marketing Contexts) means that managers are frequently confronting totally new situations, which reduces the value of lessons from the past. Customers can only communicate existing preferences and needs, which provide very few clues or vision for the future. Technology is changing the patterns and possibilities of production and consumption (see Creating Solutions), thus creating new learning cycles for suppliers and their customers. Inter-industry competition with new players reaching across established industry sectors (e.g. supermarkets as banks; AA as insurance; mobile phone as instant camera) challenges established competitive marketing approaches. In these constantly changing conditions, experience counts for less and managers must always be learning; they must be able, as it were, to remember to forget! The Internet and E-commerce have created a new market space for buying and selling that requires different organizational and marketing competencies (see Moving Space). Information technologies have increased customer knowledge and therefore their level of expectations from their suppliers (see Creating Solutions).

These dramatic changes require marketers to reassess their understanding and calculation of what constitutes 'value' to their customers and how this value can be produced and delivered (see Marketing Contexts: Marketing values): specifically, detailed attention to customer, shareholder and employee value; appreciation of the knowledge potential underlying such relationships; mutual understanding and careful positioning of relationships provide the possibilities for firms to re-invent the future *with* their customers, employees and shareholders. This is the formula for firms to achieve sustainable competitive advantage for the future that the relationship marketing approach advocates, because while products/service can be copied easily by competitors, long-term relationships are difficult to imitate.

Future developments in relationship marketing

One study by Veloutsou *et al.* (2002) reported predictions for the development of the relationship marketing practices as a step towards the development of a system that could suggest to academics and practitioners appropriate strategies to future realities. The forecasts were based on the application of the scenario planning technique by a group of leading experts in the field (academics), who attempted to forecast the developments of relationship marketing under various scenarios. In total, 16 factors were identified as very influential in shaping the trends of relationship marketing. The first seven factors are relevant to changes in the nature of the firm's relationships with the various internal and external markets and the requirements of these markets. The remaining nine report changes in the operation and delivery processes of the relationship management chain. Table 2 lists these factors, their description and the future possibilities.

Table 2 Potentially influential factors on the advancement of relationship marketing

Factor	Description	Possibilities
Brand trust	The degree to which back-up for the branding strategy is derived more from the human element than from attributes of the product/service itself	Deriving more from the interaction with the contact personnel (human element), about equal from human element and brand attributes, more from brand attributes
Value to consumer	Precise significance to consumer of exceeding expectations	Become more important, be of similar importance, become less important
Prosumption	Involvement of consumers in design/ production of product/service	Increase, stay the same, decrease
Nature of relationships	Critical definition of the type of customer/company relationship which will determine strategy	Increase, stay the same, decrease
Parity markets/products	Lack of perceived differentiation as seen by consumers	Become more commonplace, occur as often as at present, become less commonplace
Company networks	Association of brands with networks of companies rather than single companies	Increase, stay the same, decrease
Sales as natural outgrowth of relationship management	Evolution of relationship management to the extent that the selling function becomes a natural result of the relationship	Become more likely, be as likely as at present, become less likely
Diagonal integration	IT-driven process by which firms move into new fields, achieving new synergies and economies of scope	Increase, stay the same, decrease
Global individualism	Combined effects of mass customization with global 1:1 marketing	Accelerate, move at a constant pace, decelerate
Detrimental impact of artificial relationship management	Poor implementation of relationship management programmes, which has a detrimental effect on markets	Increase, stay the same, decrease
Customization	Degree of individualized tailoring of a product/service offering	Increase, stay the same, decrease
Database marketing	Aggregating customer information for subsequent analysis	Increase, stay the same, decrease

(Continued)

Table 2 (*Continued*)

Factor	Description	Possibilities
Aggregation of customer relationship	Management of customer interactions to provide incremental value	Increase, stay the same, decrease
New media	The opportunities offered by new technology to increase personal communication with customers	Increase, stay the same, decrease
Management processes	Combining previously independent management functions to produce a synergistic effect	Become more common, happen as often as it does now, become less common
Company/customer interface	Process related to managing all points of contact between company and customer	Increase, stay the same, decrease

Source: Veloutsou *et al*. (2002).

Many people still receive what they regard as junk mail. This is directly addressed mail but which (sic) is not seen to be relevant, accurate or timely. We do indeed explore this . . . and suggest how the junk can be replaced with 'relational' . . . But we do not shy away from a critical analysis of all of this. There are plenty of examples of claimed relational interaction where rhetoric is stronger than reality.
Evans et al., *2004*

How to build relationships – the implementation of relationship marketing

Until recently, discussion on relationship marketing in several business contexts, including that of business-to-customer, has focused on the concept of *the relationship* itself – its attributes and stages (Bagozzi, 1995). However, it has paid insufficient attention to the aspect of relationship management as a *core organizational process* that extends throughout the organization and enhances the implementation of relationship marketing strategies (Sheth & Parvatiyar, 2000). The essence of such an *organizational process* is value creation through the formation and maintenance of relationships with external marketplace entities, particularly consumers, and is captured in the notion of customer relationship management (Srivastava *et al*., 1999). Easy to say, but hard to put into practice!

An operational framework to assist firms' implementation of their relationship marketing has been constructed by Payne (1995), which takes the form of a detailed planning template called 'the relationship management chain' (see Figure 11) to operationalize the six-market model (see Marketing Contexts). The focus of this template is customer value. It delineates the various managerial processes that need to be undertaken by the firm to define the value proposition, identify appropriate customer value segments, design value delivery systems and evaluate its value performance. In the model all these processes are based on the fundamental construct of customer value as the cornerstone concept in relationship marketing.

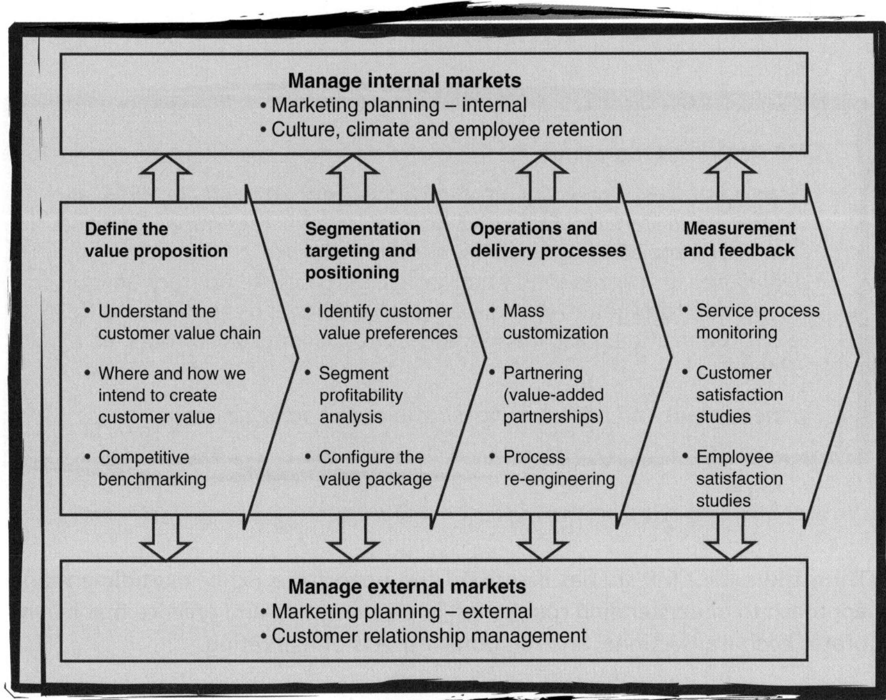

Figure 11 The relationship management chain. *Source*: Payne (1995)

With the recent development of the customer relationship management field, these techniques assist the implementation process of the relationship marketing principles. As such, they help to directly address Fournier *et al.*'s (1998) criticism that 'relationship marketing is powerful in theory but troubled in practice'. However, the success of most of these techniques depends upon the collaboration of the final customer. Therefore, to truly address the above criticism we need to understand how change in the marketplace could affect the willingness of customers to participate and willingly provide information.

Contemporary marketing practice (CMP)

Brodie *et al.* (1997) examined the extent to which contemporary organizations are carrying out relational marketing *in practice*. They investigated a number of companies across a range of industries, countries and types of markets, and concluded that many companies, whilst moving towards a relational focus, still practise transactional marketing, and many others practise both relational and transactional methods. They found the extent to which they use either or a mixture of methods depends largely on the nature of the business and the products and services on offer.

CMP Research Programme

- *Started at the University of Auckland, New Zealand, in 1996 and extended to Canada, Finland, Sweden, Ireland, Argentina, Thailand, UK, Germany, USA, SE Asia, Africa, Eastern Europe.*
- *Objective*: 'to profile marketing practice in a contemporary environment, and to examine the relevance of relational marketing in different organizational, economic and cultural contexts' *(Brodie* et al., *1997).*

Further details and papers at http://cmp.auckland.ac.nz

Thus, the early CMP studies identified the need for a richer multidimensional approach to understanding companies' implementation and practice that incorporates both transactional and relational aspects of marketing.

The next step was the development of a classification scheme that accurately reflects the different marketing practices, which uses four rather than two different aspects of marketing practice to distinguish between traditional marketing management and relationship marketing.

. . . the analysis fails to clearly identify specific types of firms which are dominated by more than one type of marketing practice, and simply highlights that* all four types of marketing are *in evidence and* practised by most firms, *to varying degrees.
Brodie et al., *1997*

Based on the 'clusters' of observations of types of marketing methods found in their wide-ranging sample of firms around the world, the CMP group's classification scheme consists of four aspects of practice:

1. Transaction marketing (TM) – managing the 4Ps to attract and satisfy customers.
2. Database marketing (DM) – using technology-based tools to target and retain customers.
3. Interaction marketing (IM) – developing interpersonal relationships between individual buyers and sellers.
4. Network marketing (NM) – positioning the firm in a connected set of inter-firm relationships.

By using research with multiple perspectives, the relative importance of different marketing practices could be examined. The implications of this approach are

Table 3 Approach to marketing by firm type

Cluster	Consumer goods (%)	B2B goods (%)	Consumer service (%)	B2B service (%)
Transactional $n = 103$	38.9	34.9	40.6	26.7
Relational $n = 98$	11.1	30.1	29.0	40.8
Pluralistic $n = 107$	**50.0**	**34.9**	**30.4**	**32.5**
Total	100.0	100.0	100.0	100.0

Source: Coviello *et al*. (2002).

illustrated in a recent article published in the *Journal of Marketing* (Coviello et *al*., 2002). The study examined 308 firms in the USA and four other Western countries to understand how different types of firms relate to their markets. What was important about the results was that there were three groups of firms. Those that have marketing practices which were predominantly *transactional*, those that have marketing practices which were predominantly *relational* and those that have marketing practices that were 'both transactional and relational', which they called '*pluralistic*'.

Each group comprised approximately one-third of the sample, and included all types of firms (consumer goods, consumer services, business-to-business goods and business-to-business services). The comparative analysis (see Table 3) does not show a dominance of a relational approach with any of the groups of firms. While there is some support for consumer service firms being more relational (service-centred logic), what is of interest is that there are many exceptions and, furthermore, that all types of firms reported in the pluralistic cluster (goods- and service-centred logic). Of the firms in the sample, this includes 50% of the B2C goods firms, 35% of the B2B goods firms, 30% of the B2C service firms and 33% of the B2B service firms. What is more challenging is that the firms that reported the pluralistic marketing practices had superior performance characteristics.

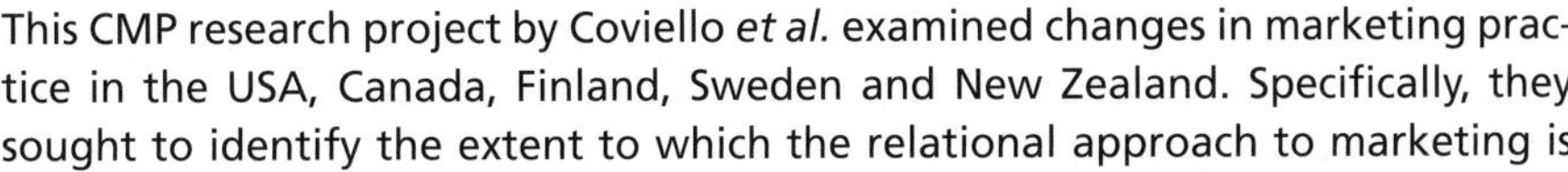

This CMP research project by Coviello *et al.* examined changes in marketing practice in the USA, Canada, Finland, Sweden and New Zealand. Specifically, they sought to identify the extent to which the relational approach to marketing is

being practised and whether it is replacing the transaction approach[1]. While results confirmed that firms were placing a greater emphasis on relationship marketing they *did not indicate there was a 'paradigm shift' from transaction marketing to relationship marketing*. Rather, their research showed that, for all types of firms (i.e. goods versus services and consumer versus business-to-business), three profiles of marketing practices were present: a transactional, a relational and a pluralistic cluster. Studies in transition economies (i.e. Russia and Argentina) suggest that Coviello *et al.*'s results are not limited to developed countries but reflect a worldwide trend (Pels *et al.*, 2004).

Building loyalty

Another way of building relationships is to build loyalty of customers to the company, brand, retail outlet or suppliers. Loyalty is not a one-dimensional concept. There are varying levels of loyalty, noted by O'Malley (1998):

1 'No loyalty'. This situation is apparent when customers are not loyal to any brand or location at all and visit stores on a random basis, dependent on time and availability.
2 'Spurious loyalty'. Viewed as a temporary loyalty. Spurious customers are often categorized as promiscuous, likely to patronize a particular outlet or brand on the basis of its promotional offers or convenience or location and are easily influenced by competing offers from attractive alternatives. As a result, it is considered relatively easy to encourage switching behaviour where spurious loyalty is evident.
3 'Latent loyalty'. Occurs when a customer has a high relative attitude towards the company or brand, but this is not evident in terms of their purchase behaviour. Whatever the explanations for latent loyalty (e.g. inconvenient locations, peer influence or stores out of stock), such behaviour does not give the consumer an opportunity to display preferential purchase actions.
4 'Sustainable loyalty'. The customer displays high repeat purchase behaviour, which is associated with a strong preference for a particular store and its facilities and services. It is said that this state is attained 'when the company has developed and communicated a proposition that clearly has long-term benefits for the consumer' (O'Brien and Jones, 1995) and where the consumer has made a conscious decision to purchase from that store on a long-term basis.

[1] The contemporary marketing practice (CMP – http://cmp.auckland.ac.nz) framework combines and compares the traditional transactional marketing literature with a synthesis of the relational literature both in North America (e.g. Berry, 1983; Morgan & Hunt, 1994; Sheth & Parvatiyar, 1995; Webster 1992) and in Europe (e.g. Grönroos, 1994; Gummesson, 1999; Håkansson & Snehota, 1995).

O'Malley (1998) argued that the role of loyalty schemes is restricted to situations where no loyalty or spurious loyalty is evident, and she doubted their usefulness beyond these stages, i.e. latent or sustainable loyalty.

An alternative approach to categories of loyalty is the seminal 'loyalty ladder' proposed by Christopher *et al.* (1991) (Figure 12), which explicitly associates levels of loyalty with different types of relationships with customers.

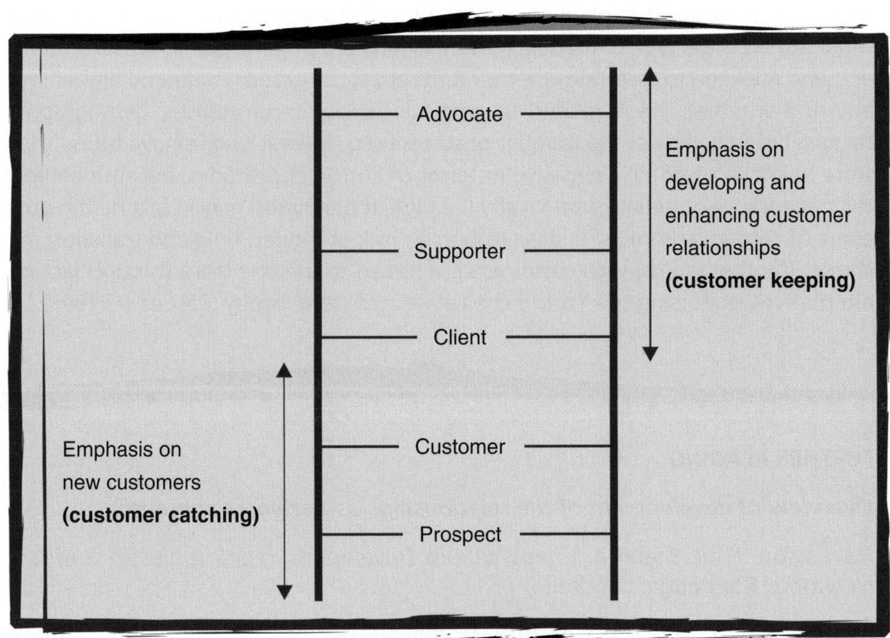

Figure 12 The relationship ladder of customer loyalty. *Source*: Christopher *et al.* (1991)

Christopher *et al.* (1991) proposed that customers move through a series of stages; they begin as 'prospects' that then become customers, regularly purchasing clients, supporters of the company, and finally active and vocal advocates for the company. This 'loyalty ladder' introduces a notion of increasing customer commitment to the firm and its offers as a customer advances up the loyalty ladder, and that customer service plays a pivotal role in achieving this progression up the loyalty ladder (Christopher *et al.*, 1991).

We know there are different types and levels, but there is no agreement about what is meant by customer loyalty. The main dispute centres on whether loyalty is an (a) attitudinal or (b) behavioural phenomenon. The behavioural perspective on loyalty usually uses a pattern of repeat purchase occasions as a measure of loyalty, particularly the so-called 'Enis–Paul' index. Dick and Basu (1994) considered that the behavioural approach to customer loyalty is problematic in that these measures make no attempt to understand the factors underlying repeat purchase. Because some degree of psychological commitment on the part of the consumer is also a necessary ingredient of true loyalty, Reicheld (1994) recommended that retention rate and share of total purchases should be used. To most, the notion of loyalty conjures up ideas of commitment, affection or fidelity (McGoldrick & Andre, 1997).

The area of loyalty that has been subjected to most research and early theories is mainly concerned with explaining customer loyalty to individual product brands and retail stores. These type of models of store loyalty are of particular interest to retailers, who are keen to ascertain whether different social groups command higher loyalty and whether this is related to particular social circumstances, demographic factors, brand loyalty or the number of stores used. Several studies have found that store loyalty is essentially negative in terms of customer attitudes, because behind the appearance of behavioural loyalty (i.e. repeat purchases) may in fact be the outcome of certain customers' limited resources, lack of money, time and transport, or choice. In other words, such customers are forced to use one store through lack of alternatives, endorsing the 'forced choice' view of store loyalty (East *et al.*, 1995).

FURTHER READING

Overview of development of the relationships-as-networks approach

Håkansson, H. & Snehota, I. (eds) (1995) *Developing Relationships in Business Networks*. Routledge: London.

Mattson, L.-G. (1999) Relationships and networks. In: *Marketing Theory* (M. J. Baker, ed.). Thomson, pp. 150–160.

Relational approach to marketing

Christopher, M., Payne, A. & Ballantyne, D. (1991) *Relationship Marketing: Bringing Quality, Customer Service, and Marketing Together*. Butterworth-Heinemann: Oxford.

Gummesson, E. (2000) *Total Relationship Marketing*. Butterworth-Heinemann.

Concept of customer loyalty

Dick, A. S. & Basu, K. (1994) Customer loyalty: towards an integrated framework. *Journal of the Academy of Marketing Science*, **22** (2), 99–113.

O'Malley, L. (1998) Can loyalty schemes really build loyalty? *Marketing Intelligence and Planning*, **16** (1), 47–55.

Reicheld, F. F. (1994) *The Loyalty Effect*. Harvard Business School Press: Cambridge, MA.

Building social relationships

Gerard Hastings

Marketing relationships: social or antisocial?

Some critics of today's marketing are drawn to the conclusion that marketing has little to tell us about social relationships – it can only affect antisocial ones (see Marketing Contexts: Marketing values). However, marketing can have two important and beneficial *impacts on social relationships*.

Firstly, marketing thinking can be applied not only to our consumption behaviour, but also to other behaviours that it might be in both our, and society's, interests to change. Our own health, for example, is heavily affected by our behaviour. If we choose to smoke a pack of cigarettes a day (minus 12 years), drink heavily (minus three years), eat junk food (minus two years) and avoid exercise (minus three years), we can shorten our lives by a considerable margin. Similarly, problems such as drink driving, racism and crime can all be devolved down to individual behaviour.

If marketing can encourage us to buy a Ferrari, it can also persuade us to drive it safely – or resist the temptation to steal one.

Secondly, improving our knowledge of how marketing works enables us to deconstruct and critique it. This can expose abuses and enable policy makers to set sensible limits, like the recent bans on tobacco advertising and promotion imposed in the UK and many other countries around the world.

Lazer and Kelley's (1973) original definition of social marketing encapsulates these two benefits:

> Social marketing is concerned with the application of marketing knowledge, concepts and techniques to enhance social as well as economic ends. It is also concerned with the analysis of the social consequences of marketing policies, decisions and activities.

The following two cases show how marketing can be successfully applied to social relations in practice.

Building relationships to combat drug abuse

NE Choices was a major drugs prevention programme which targeted 13- to 16-year-olds in the north-east of England between 1996 and 1999. It was built

around a high school drama initiative, with additional community, school governor and parent components. It aimed to change behaviour in four ways:

- reduce prevalence of drug use
- delay the age of onset of drug use
- reduce the frequency of drug use among those who use drugs
- reduce mixing of drugs (including with alcohol) by those who do use them.

The programme was heavily informed by social marketing and so had a strong consumer and stakeholder orientation. This was driven by a comprehensive programme of market research to guide the development of NE Choices, ensure it was properly delivered, and evaluate its impact both in terms of consumer satisfaction and behaviour change. It also showed that relational thinking can be just as – if not more – relevant in drugs prevention as it is when selling beans and cars.

The programme was remarkably popular with the market. Both the core customers (the young people) and the other stakeholders strongly endorsed it. The impact evaluation showed, for example, that the vast majority of children felt the programme was enjoyable (89%), thought-provoking (88%) and credible (84%), and that the drama was realistic (79%) and non-didactic (e.g. 88% agreed that 'it encouraged us to speak our own minds').

Good customer relationships were being developed:

- Meaning and messages were jointly negotiated rather than imposed.
- Customized spin-off products were carefully developed and successfully delivered to important customer subgroups.
- Comprehensive research ensured that the programme did things *with* young people, rather than *to* them.
- Innovative use was made of IT.
- This resulted in the production of a key relationship marketing tool: a comprehensive database for what is an elusive and vulnerable group.
- The young people trusted the programme and its brand, as the impact evaluation data shows.
- They also showed considerable commitment to NE Choices. For example, the last stage of research had to be conducted by mail, as a proportion of the young people had, by then, left school. The vast majority were prepared to provide contact details, and 70% completed the sensitive and complex (40-minute) questionnaire.

Furthermore, three of the strengths which emerged from the impact evaluation are known to be markers for successful knowledge, attitudes and behaviour change: reaching a range of stakeholders and settings as well as the core customers; the successful use of drama in education to engage the audience; and being non-didactic. NE Choices was not only building strong relationships with what is typically a cynical and hard-to-reach group, it was – and this will come as no surprise to the marketer – beginning to deliver on the bottom line of behaviour change.

Unfortunately, governments don't think like private companies, so although they were on to a winner, NE Choices was closed down. Philip Morris has built and honed its Marlboro brand for 50 years; the NE Choices brand was given three. Getting politicians to think in longer time frames is often difficult. Nonetheless, progress is being made. Because of the success of NE Choices, the arguments about strategic thinking mentioned above and the trust that has been built up between the (marketing) researchers and the government, the successor to NE Choices – called Blueprint – will be longer term (see website: www.drugs.gov.uk/NationalStrategy/YoungPeople/Blueprint).

Interestingly, this last point is a good example of business-to-business relationship marketing – which, as we noted above, is where such thinking originated.

Undermining abusive marketing relationships

Despite the fuzzy, feelgood factor of a label like 'relationship marketing', and the successes of programmes like NE Choices, marketing relationships can become abusive. Tobacco is a case in point. In the UK, new smokers are almost always children – 80% take up the habit before their 18th birthday. One in two of those of us who don't manage to break the habit will die as a result, and the addictiveness of nicotine (it's a match for cocaine and heroine in this department) is more than likely to defeat our attempts to quit.

The tobacco industry is heavily implicated in this toll. Study after study (Lovato *et al.* (2004) provide a good review) has shown that their advertising and promotion acts as a recruiting sergeant, capturing and retaining new smokers. This is no accident. As a now infamous planning memo by the tobacco manufacturer RJ Reynolds stated '*if our company is to survive and prosper over the long term, we must get our share of the youth market*' (cited in Pierce *et al.*, 1999).

However, social marketing, and the sophisticated understanding of relationship building it provides, has helped redress the balance and get tobacco promotion banned in the UK. Specifically, three steps were involved. We had to (i) build the evidence base of a link between tobacco promotion and youth smoking, (ii) develop good marketing relationships with politicians and other key stakeholders, and (iii) analyse the competition and destabilize their marketing relationships.

The evidence base

The tobacco industry has traditionally argued that advertising has no effect on consumption. Tobacco is a mature market, sales for it are stagnant, if not in decline, and therefore advertising cannot be increasing demand. The only effect it has is on brand switching among adult smokers.

The social marketer can approach this argument with a knowledge of segmentation and see that suggesting that there is just one homogeneous market for tobacco is naive. There are actually many markets – young smokers, roll-your-own smokers, cigar smokers and so on. Some of these may be shrinking, but others are growing. The social marketer might also deduce that advertising is likely to have varying effects on different segments. For example, established, older smokers are much more likely to be influenced by their need for nicotine than seductive messages. We know that young smokers, on the other hand, are driven by psychosocial needs – to look cool, rebellious and independent, for example – and therefore might be expected to be more susceptible to branding and other image-based appeals. The social marketer would also recognize that the issue here is integrated marketing communications, or even marketing as a whole, not just advertising. Finally, a marketer understands that IMCs are only going to be one influence (and a relatively modest one at that) on teen smoking.

All these insights help build better research to establish the evidence base: you need to focus on teenagers, a wide array of marketing practices and build sophisticated models of effect to be tested on samples that are large enough to detect small differences.

Building relationships

Politicians need hard evidence to protect themselves from tobacco industry lobbying. This is partly a matter of doing research, but also disseminating it. The first requirement is to publish in respected, scientific journals, such as the *British Medical Journal* and the *Journal of Marketing*. Data and research that appears in such outlets is unimpeachable. Secondly, there is a need to use more popular outlets, especially the quality media. This convinces the politician that the issue has public support.

Destabilizing the competition's relationships

Marketers are keen on competitive analysis. In this case the core concern is the tobacco companies' relationship with smokers, and especially young, starter smokers. Many of the anti-smoking campaigns that have run over the last 50 years can be seen as indirect attempts to undermine these, but one recent US campaign tackles the job head on. The Truth campaign has deliberately set out to attack the tobacco industry, highlighting their unscrupulous business practices and deliberate attempts to attract youngsters to the habit (see: www.thetruth.com).

Figure 13 Young people in the USA demonstrating the impact of tobacco marketing!

Redemption

In conclusion, this chapter has discussed how marketing influences human behaviour by building mutually beneficial relationships both with us, the customers, and stakeholders. These relationships sometimes become dysfunctional, typically when there is an imbalance of power. Social marketers seek to keep their commercial cousin on the straight and narrow in two ways. First, by using the same techniques and principles to influence socially desirable behaviours, such as healthy living, and second by critiquing and, when necessary, seeking controls on their more unacceptable activities.

Arguably this does little to address the fundamental flaw in marketing relationships – that they drive forward an unsustainable level of consumption. However, a recent social marketing effort – Buy Nothing Day (www.buynothingday.co.uk) – has even tried to address this very basic concern.

In essence, marketing can be seen as an amoral technology that can be used for good or ill. Provided a weather eye is kept on it, it is capable of producing socially beneficial relationships.

FURTHER READING

Andreassen, A. R. (1995) *Marketing Social Change*. Jossey-Bass: San Francisco.

Boom, P. N. & Gundlach, G. T. (eds) (2001) *Handbook of Marketing and Society*. Sage: Thousand Oaks, NJ.

Goldberg, M., Fishbien, M. & Middleton, M. (eds) (1997) *Social Marketing Theoretical and Practical Perspectives*. Lawrence Erlbaum.

Hastings, G. (2003) Relational paradigms in social marketing. *Journal of Macromarketing*, **23** (1), 6.

The role of communications

Julie Tinson

Introduction

Do you sport a David Beckham haircut? Do you style your appearance on Kylie Minogue? You may be surprised at the extent to which your views, behaviour and attitudes are replicated across an increasingly diverse populace. Marketers use celebrities and the effect they have on individuals – be it emotional, rational or both – to communicate their message. The use of celebrities (see Brand Selection) is one of the *indirect* ways in which organizations and their brands can begin to build a relationship with consumers. During the initial stages of 'courtship', organizations use celebrities they know their customers (potential and actual) aspire to be like and indirectly attract customers to the product, service, organization or brand.

> Marketing communications *provides the means by which products, brands and organizations are presented to their audience with the aim of initiating a dialogue, potentially leading to a relationship.*

The following subsections describe the use, development and effectiveness of communications for relationship building and the varying degrees of communication used throughout the buyer–seller liaison. Despite doubts about the accuracy of the marriage metaphor for market relationships, this chapter uses the analogy of a romantic relationship to explore in a step-by-step fashion the ways in which consumers are attracted to a brand through to committing to a relationship, problems encountered and possible dissolution at the end.

> Target audience *is people who, directly or indirectly, are chosen to receive communication messages.*

First encounter

In their attempts to 'seduce' consumers into a relationship, organizations use a variety of methods to communicate with their target audience. Approaches toward communications vary enormously between different cultures; thus, the means and style of communications depend partly on the country where the audience resides. As a generalization it is commonly viewed that in the USA, for example, the communication messages tend to be more 'hard sell', whereas in France consumers expect to be seduced with more 'soft sell' messages. Similarly, in the UK consumers prefer complex messages they can 'solve', which, it is argued, affords them the opportunity to feel intelligent and engages them with the message itself (Fowles, 1996). Of course, building any relationship in any country is never straightforward, and what is an attractive proposition to one person may be displeasing to another.

Q. How can organizations effectively initiate a relationship using a communications approach?
A. Initially, by using familiar language in their advertising, an organization can demonstrate an understanding of the way in which their consumers interact with one another and, by association, suggest they too understand and are acquainted with the consumer. Similarly, the use of music (the recent Levi's advertisements are a good example of this) and specific colours will all indicate an immediacy or bond with the organization and consumer.

You say it best when you say nothing at all

If a consumer's eyes meet an advertisement across a crowded room and he/she *immediately* understands the message conveyed, this might be as a result of the use and recognition of the signs or symbols used in the piece of communication. This use of signs and symbols is known as semiotics. *Semiotics* is the study of the meanings and interpretations associated with signs and symbols. An example of how we use and interpret such signs in marketing communications would be if the male and female models in an advert were depicted standing close together, the assumption most observers would make is that they were 'intimate'. Or if a solitary model were standing in the rain, this might suggest loneliness. Of course, not all cultures translate messages in the same way and organizations are beginning to differentiate their brand from that of the competitor by demonstrating they are aware of semiotics. HSBC are currently running a campaign that shows how different signs and symbols have alternative meanings in different cultures. For example, if children raise their hands in the UK it is a sign of the child trying to attract attention, but in other cultures it is a sign of rudeness.

Q. How can ads suggest meaning without words?
A. Through the use of space in the picture – for example, with greater spatial proximity implying intimacy between the people pictured closer together. Other means include: numbers – Levi's 501 suggest an established brand with longevity; time – business efficiency is often shown by a fast-moving man in a suit; clothing – Scottish people are usually depicted wearing kilts; and kinetics – sedentary lifestyles are often shown through the use of models lounging on sofas.

Not only adverts but also brands themselves usually incorporate symbolic pictures or 'logos' (see Brand Selection). For instance, McDonald's 'golden arches' symbol (the 'M') is a world-renowned logo. Whilst driving on motorways in many countries, it is usual just to see the golden arches being advertised on service station billboards, with instant recognition amongst consumers as to what the brand represents (see Consuming Experience). Not all signs or symbols have positive associations, however (this will be discussed further in the Relate subsection).

A brand is a name, term, sign, symbol, design or combination of these which is used to identify the goods or services of one seller or group of sellers in order to differentiate their offering from that of the competition.

Talking the same language

As increasing numbers of consumers become 'ad literate' – particularly young people – there is a need to make adverts increasingly abstract or creative to remain novel, innovative and challenging. So when organizations attempt to initiate a relationship with the consumer the communications approach must be engaging, inspiring and involving to convince the consumer (or groups of consumers) that they are special.

> Ad literate *is the extent to which a consumer is familiar with and can 'read' various types of advertising, the signs used and the messages they contain.*

Creativity

An example of this creativity and innovation is exemplified in the following scenario (data collated from discussions/interview with ad industry executives/senior managers). Sony Playstation was launched in 1995 when Sega and Nintendo had 97% of the market. By 1997, Playstation had taken 70% of this industry share by using a creative advertising approach. The idea was to capture the 'experience' of gaming and was to encourage consumers to think of gaming as an experience not only to be enjoyed by adolescent, male teenagers, but rather an experience to be enjoyed by a diverse consumer base. The advertisement was abstract – it used an Eskimo to open a fridge door and, as he did so, hundreds of particles flew out of the fridge, demonstrating the power and strength of the gaming experience. This approach was enormously successful in gaining a large proportion of the market share. But where could the creative concept go from here?

As over 30 million Playstation 1s had been sold across Europe, the development and launch of Playstation 2 was going to be critical for the maintenance of market share and, more importantly, encouraging consumers, through building the relationship, to buy a new model, with new features and new gaming capacity (up-selling). With competitors already producing alternative products (Microsoft and the X-Box and Nintendo with their Game Cube), Sony was reliant on the communications in order to maintain and develop the existing relationship with consumers. Sony and their advertising agency launched a 'tripartite' approach – that is, a three-pronged style of innovative communication to engage existing and potential new consumers. The experience of gaming was, as the advertising messages suggested, a powerful experience – but who was powerful? What type of experience was this? And where would the experience take place?

Three adverts in a series followed, the first of which demonstrated individuals leading a 'double life', showing a whole variety of consumers (black, white, young, old, disabled, transvestites) enjoying the experience of gaming. They, the consumers, were powerful. A second advert followed with 'Fifi' the 'model' that posited 'mental wealth' as a result of gaming. This was a stimulating experience. Finally, the *adverts* that are currently running the 'third place' suggest gaming doesn't take place at home or work – rather it takes the consumer to the 'third place'. Inspiring, engaging, abstract, complex – but these adverts speak directly to the consumers.

Internationally, the same approach has been taken, with adverts played simultaneously in 13 countries. Success has to a great extent been largely unrivalled, despite new competing products available on the market.

Advertising is the use of paid mass media to deliver marketing communication messages to target audiences.

Initiation

What is important about this scenario for building relationships through communication?

- The consumer must be attracted to the communication (impact/innovation/creativity).
- The consumer must want to be involved with the product/service/brand.
- The language/signs must be understood by the consumer. It should say, 'I know and understand you.'
- The consumer has to trust the organization to engage in the initial relationship.
- The message must be credible.

Figure 14 demonstrates the types of agencies that exist for developing different types of communication approaches. *Above-the-line* is a term used to describe

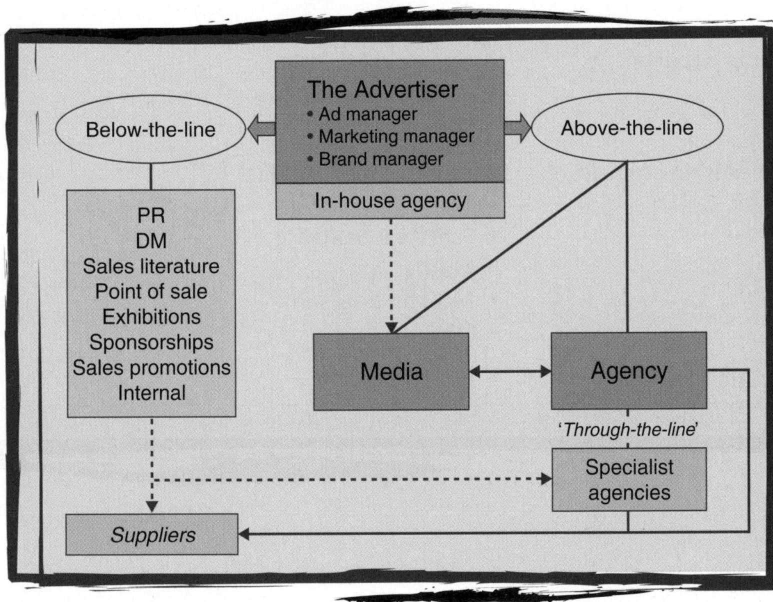

Figure 14 Advertising industry players

Table 4 Examples of major industry players

Specialist agencies	• Direct marketing – WWAV Rapp Collins – Brann – Grey Direct • Sales promotion – Carlson Marketing Group – Mosaic – DraftWorldwide – IMP Group – Haygarth Group • PR – Weber Shandwick – Momentum – Magic Hat – Fishburn Hedges
In-house agencies	• IKEA • Calvin Klein • Bernard Matthews
Media selling houses	• Granada • Carlton • Sky
Media departments	• Universal McCann • OMD Media (Omnicom) • Walker Media
Advertising agencies	• Abbott Mead Vickers • JWT • Saatchi & Saatchi • Mother • McCann Erickson • TWBA
Through-the-line	• Craik Jones

advertising promotions that employ commission-paying mass media (TV, press, cinema) and *below-the-line* is where use is made of non-commission-paying media. The use of the below-the-line term is fairly limited in the current climate, however, as it covers such a broad range of promotional activity. *Through-the-line* agencies deal with both above- and below-the-line activity. Examples of the major players are also highlighted in Table 4.

Timing

When organizations want consumers to engage with their brand, product or service, timing is of the essence and, more often, alternative communication approaches are being used to deal with the issue of timing. Advertising with regard to mortgages, associated tie-ins, insurance and finance deals are particularly prevalent in relation to timing. Messages to dissuade consumers from engaging in harmful practices are also timely (i.e. the message ought to prevent harmful behaviour).

Q. What is key to successful communication with new customers?
A. *Timing is key if a consumer is to engage with any relationship. This may be because the product is cyclical (fashionable for short periods of time) or because the consumer previously did not have the age or experience or did not have the disposable income to be able to buy.*

Ambient advertising is becoming increasingly popular as a result of its immediacy and the ability it has to *overcome timing* issues. Ambient advertising often catches consumers 'off guard' and, as a result, has a greater probability of attracting the consumer's attention and of staying in the consumer's conscientiousness. When Kelloggs launched their Nutri-Grain bar for professionals who skipped breakfast, they gave away hundreds of bars free to underground commuters as they were leaving London Underground stations going to work. The timing was perfect, because the following day, when the hungry professionals who had left home with nothing to eat wanted to buy a low-fat, nutritional product, the *problem had been solved* for them. And this of course is another key facet of communication – it resolves problems consumers may not even know they had (see Creating Solutions).

This type of communications method is often known as 'thinking outside the box'. It is particularly useful for media planning purposes, i.e. when to run an advertisement, which is the best advertising to break the product, which is the

> ***Q***. Why is ambient advertising such an important communications tool?
> ***A***. *Such is the immediacy of the ambient advertising approach that consumers can also be reminded about nuisances they were (un)aware existed. When deodorant cans replaced the hanging straps in the underground carriages, consumers were reminded how to prevent problems occurring.*

> Ambient advertising *is when the medium used for communication becomes part of the message.*

most appropriate magazine. In order to answer such questions, the most frequently used criterion is that which will provide the most *reach* – the best coverage amongst the target audience. There are numerous trade sources which will provide a holistic view of the type of media that matches the type of consumer the organization is trying to reach (e.g. BRAD, TGI and Mintel).

Different communication approaches will provide different levels of reach and often thinking outside the box produces maximum publicity. The Wonderbra campaign is the most frequently cited example of providing

> Reach *is the coverage or penetration of the potential audience and is a measure of how many members of the target audience will be reached by a medium or collection of media used in a campaign.*

maximum publicity and stretching an advertising budget to its limit; the initial budget was £330 000 with an estimated £50 m in free publicity (IPA, 1994). However, other organizations similarly manage to attract attention by using an unusual choice of media vehicle for their advertising. Yves Saint Laurent used a naked Sophie Dahl to advertise Opium and chose to put the advert on a billboard. The Advertising Standards Authority received a record number of complaints as a result and Yves Saint Laurent were given a two-year probationary period in which they had to pre-show all their billboard ads to the ASA. Thinking outside the box isn't always appropriate and won't necessarily attract the desired *target audience* to the means or content of the communication.

Q. How often is it necessary to advertise to make sure the target audience receives the message?
A. *This is known as frequency and simplistically it is acknowledged that if a member of the target audience has seen an advertisement three times (the first time to raise awareness, the second to create interest and the third to induce desire) this would be enough to encourage intention to purchase.*

Frequency *is the number of times a member of the target audience is exposed to a media/message over a specified time period.*

Figure 15 illustrates the communication process, demonstrating the two-way nature of communications from sender to receiver and back again – that is, from the organization to the target audience back to the organization. The message is encoded (creativity, engagingly, using semiotics where appropriate) and a medium is chosen to convey the message (TV advertising, billboard, direct mail). If the target audience understands the message the organization has intended to send, communication has taken place. 'Noise' is any distraction that might prevent the target audience from receiving the message, i.e. too many other advertisements. The target audience will then 'feed back' to the organization in a number of ways: (a) through doing what the message asked of them (purchasing the product, giving blood, giving up smoking); (b) taking part in *post-campaign research*. If the feedback is appropriate, the organization will consider the campaign to have been successful.

Pre- and post-campaign research *occurs when advertising is researched prior to release or after they have run. Pre-campaign testing is used more frequently, although post-campaign research allows advertising to be tested in its natural environment.*

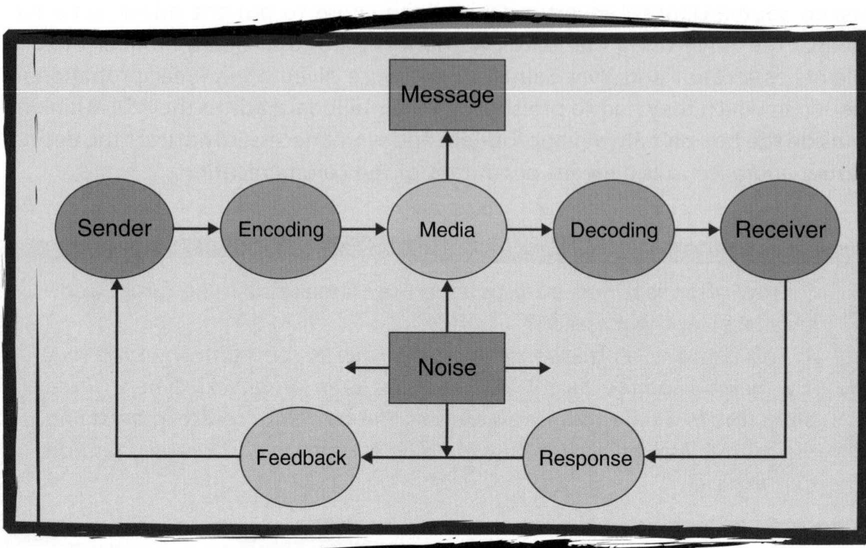

Figure 15 The communication process

Communicating with new customers

> *. . . the personal and social consequences of any medium – that is, of any extension of ourselves – result from the new scale that is introduced into our affairs by each extension of ourselves.*
> McLuhan, 1964

Communication can be used not only to whet the appetite for a relationship, but can also be used to facilitate an introduction between a brand and a new consumer. A consumer can seemingly fall into a relationship with an organization or brand, but there is generally some form of communication to ensure the consumer believes the product or service has an attractive proposition. A Virgin Vie or Ann Summers 'party' may be one such first or blind date where the host is generally a friend (or a friend of a friend) and the atmosphere jovial. As a consumer there is a feeling of safety (friends are also invited) and as the host has invited the consumer to their home, it is likely a level of trust exists between the host and consumer. It is also likely that (an) *opinion leader(s)* will be present.

> Opinion leaders *are predisposed to receiving information and reprocessing it to influence others.*

This is an extremely clever form of communication as it uses existing relationships with 'lead customers' and, to a certain extent, appropriates them. This is a very *direct* communications approach. More often than not, there is obligation to buy product(s) as the host is also a friend. Further to this, the organization has a captive audience and, as the organizer 'makes up' a 'model', she/he has a considerable opportunity to tell the attendees about the background of the organization and the brand, what the brand attributes are (meaning, value, quality, symbols) and why the consumer wants the brand in their lives. As with any first/blind date, the chemistry is essential and the longevity of the relationship is generally dependent on the first impression. The importance then of ensuring a consistent message and/or consistent approach (*integration*) is essential.

Integration *within a campaign should ensure consistency of message so as not to confuse the target audience and will provide added credibility as a result.*

Post-purchase communications

The post-purchase period in relationships is generally a time where both parties are overlooking or at least more forgiving of faults and, as such, there is an excellent opportunity to overcome teething problems. Ideally this should be a honeymoon period for both parties as the customer enjoys the benefits of their new purchase. For the seller, it is the time for building a secure relationship foundation – based on trust. As both parties are typically more forgiving at this juncture, communication is usually used to combat negative post-purchase evaluation and is more indirect in overall approach. This is particularly true of high involvement purchases (cars, holidays), where emotion and time spent deliberating choices are key factors in the decision-making and post-purchase evaluation.

Q. What is the difference between the pre- and post-purchase periods in a consumer's relationship with a supplier?
A. *The focus of the post-purchase relationship may simply rest on a few perceived user benefits.*

Another form of communications is also important at this stage. *Internal marketing communication* is critical for ensuring that employees are aware of the brand values, and even more importantly to ensure that they are able to *demonstrate* these brand values and attributes during their interactions with customers and others outside the firm, such as phone calls, deliveries, dealing with complaints or queries or service provision.

Internal marketing communication *is the extent to which brand values communicated through external communications are supported by the values shown by those inside the organization, particularly those who interact with external groups.*

Additionally, the higher the level of involvement, the greater the level of reassurance is likely to be. Volvos, for example, are known for their safety and, as such, may be considered 'boring' or 'dull' (collated following discussions/interviews with ad industry executives/senior managers). Volvo recognized the need for their drivers to consider themselves as exciting as well as safe – so their advertising approach demonstrated how safe the Volvo was in a dangerous situation (e.g. a tornado).

Q. How can advertising support consumers after the product or service has been purchased?
A. *In bouts of negative* post-purchase evaluation, *the customer would be able to support their own beliefs with the positive visual association provided by the advertising. Similarly, the advert may also encourage a potential target audience to change their attitudes and values towards the brand.*

Post-purchase evaluation *occurs once a product has been purchased and is the time when cognitive dissonance is likely to occur.* Cognitive dissonance *is when a consumer is dissatisfied with the product because it doesn't perform appropriately or when they wish they had purchased a superior product.*

Encouraging loyalty

As with all relationships, proportionately the greatest amount of time, money and effort has usually been spent on the initial 'honeymoon', i.e. post-purchase, period. But now, firms are increasingly realizing that maintaining a relationship and keeping it fresh is as important as developing it in the first place (see Building social relationships). The introduction of customer 'loyalty' cards has allowed organizations to collate and constantly update information from customers about their personal details and circumstances, income and spending, their household composition and buying behaviour. As a result, they are able to monitor what individuals consume, how often they consume it and the extent to which they are interested in *sales promotions* and special offers. They are then able to tailor promotions especially for groups of consumers (segments) in order to maximize sales and generate more repeat purchases.

Q. Does loyalty suggest that the consumers will only buy one brand or use one retail outlet?
A. Loyalty rather assumes that consumers will not shop elsewhere – but consumers are loyal for a variety of reasons (convenience, lack of choice, type of existing product prevents buying parts elsewhere, etc.). Marketers should beware of consumers' spurious loyalty (see Relationships and *interactions).*

Sales promotion *is a widely used term covering many promotional activities, but excludes advertising. It is generally associated with free offers, price deals and premium offers.*

There are outlets, such as The Bear Factory, that take building relationships very seriously. They are unique in their interactive approach to constructing the product and the 'relationship' is encouraged immediately. The shop sells soft toys but, as a consumer, you are expected to choose the type of soft toy (monkey/dog/bear), the stuffing and the 'heart'. You are encouraged to make a wish as you put the heart into the soft toy before the toy is stitched. You must choose a name for the toy and you are issued with a birth certificate once you complete the details of the individual who is to receive the toy (including their date of birth). This information is then processed and the recipient of the gift will get regular 'personal' direct mail, including reminders about the soft toy's birthday (they have an extensive product range on clothing for the toys) and birthday cards for the recipient of the soft toy. Maintaining and developing the relationship is made easy through the use of interactive purchasing and clever database marketing.

Direct marketing *refers to all communication approaches that generate a series of communication messages and responses with actual or potential consumers.*

Information and databases

Whilst a customer database holds considerably more information than an address book, the principle is the same. An address book contains names, addresses and telephone numbers of all the people known to the owner with, perhaps, some additional information on their likes/dislikes. A customer database holds information on members of a target audience including age and lifestyle. Databases can be created (using a sales promotion, for example, and collecting names and addresses of competition entrants or using existing/previous customers) or can be rented or bought (from the Royal Mail or a variety of other suppliers). Advances in information technology (see Creating Solutions) enable computerized databases to contain many levels and therefore an organization can easily retrieve their best customers, who are responsive to which type of communication approach and how often and when these customers buy the product or service (Evans, 1998). Supermarket loyalty cards are an example of database collation and management, with supermarkets tailoring relevant sales promotion for specific groups within the target audience.

Database management *is the cooperative management and upkeep of precise customer and potential customer information (in addition to competitor information market information and internal company information).*

Q. What is the benefit of database management?
A. *There is some monitoring and a proactive approach towards the relationship by the organization. If a financial services provider has given a loan to a consumer, for example, they can manage the relationship by*

monitoring repayments and by checking before completion of the loan period if the customer wants another loan or another banking product (i.e. credit card). In this way the consumer knows the organization is still interested in them and the dialogue is a way of maintaining and developing the relationship.

Q. What are the problems associated with database management?
A. *There are problems of privacy, where the consumer feels the organization is being intrusive in their communications approach. It may be a factor in customers straying from the relationship.*

Q. How committed are consumers?
A. *Temptations to switch brands or suppliers are everywhere and as a consumer it is relatively easy to be promiscuous.*

Discouraging/encouraging switching behaviour

Financial service providers who offer no or low APR on credit cards to attract new consumers often find that when they increase their rates, many of their 'new' consumers move their credit card debt to other financial service providers offering the lowest rate. These customers are sometimes pejoratively referred to a 'rate tarts' and in this scenario there is little the organizations can do to prevent this happening time and again. A tie-in may be an option, but it might dissuade genuine new customers from applying for a credit card and competition in the financial services sector is fierce.

Indeed, there are organizations that encourage switching. Virgin Mobile produced a series of advertisements highlighting the downside for customers signing mobile network contracts and discouraging impulsive long-term commitment decisions. Thus, some firms benefit from encouraging more consumer switching. For competitors who are followers rather than leaders, it is advantageous when consumers can be easily dissuaded from continuing a relationship with an existing service provider. Using communications emphasizing charm versus familiarity, charisma versus boredom and the consumer may be tempted to risk their existing relationship.

A long-term relationship will involve many changes, with the consumer modifying, adapting and becoming more experienced as time goes on. Communication approaches, alternative messages and media vehicles used must reflect the permutation in external factors (economic changes, cultural shifts), micro factors (competition, suppliers and distributors) and most importantly changes in the consumer's experiences. Coca-Cola proposed to spend £15.5 m in the UK in 2003 on their flagship brand, despite a loss of over 2% market share in the previous year. For example, consumption of soft drinks had changed significantly, with consumers realizing the benefits of drinking mineral water as opposed to high-sugar, low-fruit substitutes. Coca-Cola has not maintained its popularity, although it has purchased bottled water manufacturers after the Dasani debacle, and as such is keeping abreast of consumption changes and competition in the soft drinks arena.

Q. Why do marketing relationships end?
A. *Consumers and service providers may cite irreconcilable differences and separate for a number of reasons. Companies may become complacent about their consumers, expecting them to remain loyal even when they have failed to develop, adapt and modify their product or service. Trial purchases with other brands may have alerted the consumer to better quality, superior service, additional brand attributes or product features the current provider does not offer.*

Marks & Spencer were known for their quality brand, synonymous with the British culture, offering characteristic products known for their longevity and calibre. As a brand, Marks & Spencer were a symbol of prestige and positive attributes. Even this organization became complacent and failed to recognize a change in their target audience and the necessity to consider modifying or adapting their service provision. Whilst many of these issues have now been addressed (including a considerable spend on advertising and a clearer brand focus), the lesson was a hard one to learn. Some of the target audience is unlikely to return to Marks & Spencer as a result of the subsequent consumer discontent felt during the years of indifference towards the developing needs of the consumer, but some will have an emotional bond with the brand and will be forgiving.

Brand identity *is the position the organization wants to believe they hold in the minds of the consumer. This identity is encapsulated in the logo, signage, uniform and letterheads of an organization, and reflects enduring qualities to be aspired to.*

Many of the problems faced by Marks & Spencer and many other organizations are largely attributable to the difference between *brand identity* and *brand image*. Whilst the organization might believe consumers are loyal, the consumers may be looking elsewhere for service, as the brand identity may not be credible, reliable or comprehensive.

Brand image *is the actual perception of the organization held by the consumer. The perception rather reflects superficial qualities and existing associations. Problems occur when the gap widens between identity and image.*

Maintaining a dialogue between the organization and the customer is crucial if switching is to be discouraged and avoided. In any case, of course, some consumers will prefer the familiarity of their existing organization – i.e. 'better the devil you know'. For suppliers, it is important to leave the door open and make it as easy as possible for consumers to return to the brand, service or product if they so wish. BT use their advertising to demonstrate how easy it is to reconnect and mobile phone service providers offer consumers the opportunity to re-start their contract with their existing mobile phone number for up to six months free of charge. As it is considerably cheaper to retain an existing consumer than to find a new one, these tactics are in the interests of the organization.

In some cases the dissolution of the marketing relationship may be unavoidable. The consumer may have different needs and tastes and the organization or brand may simply be catering for a different audience. In cases where consumers have received poor service, they may leave the organization without (a) telling the organization they are leaving or (b) telling the organization why they are leaving. The best the marketer can do in terms of utilizing communications with the 'ex-customer' is to provide them with an opportunity for feedback and reflection on their reasons for leaving. Investment in evaluation is key to understanding what went wrong and how to alter marketing and operations so that other customers can be prevented from switching. The most serious implication for the firm is not just the loss of one customer, but that their own lack of understanding and insufficient knowledge of the reasons for their behaviour will fail to improve the service provision for *existing consumers*. The question then becomes: how long will they stay?

As previously explained, communication approaches must be timely in order to be effective. In the UK, for example, some universities are finding it increasingly difficult to differentiate themselves, even through branding, and it is extremely important for this 'sector' (*sic* Universities UK) to retain their existing customers (students). In order to maximize retention rates, exit interviews (as part of student retention schemes) are being conducted with consumers to find out why they are leaving university. This information (regarding service, contact, finance, personal matters and quality) is fed back into the organization, where improvements are often made for both existing students and potential recruits. This may be through the introduction of more student services or through the modules being delivered to the students who remain registered.

However, organizations are also becoming choosier about their long-term partners.

Q. How do organizations deal with consumers they do not want to have a relationship with?
A. *A process known as 'de-selection' is regularly occurring in many consumer and business-to-business markets, and organizations are very selective about the consumers to whom they offer their business. Communication approaches reflect this 'de-selection', where customers who will be less profitable are encouraged not to continue the relationship.*

De-selection *is where service providers consider which relationships are more profitable for them (or are too costly for them to continue with) and stop providing a product or service, or make the product or service too costly in order to discourage the relationship.*

Direct marketing is usually employed in the financial services sector to suggest new accounts and existing accounts become 'closed issue' – that is, they do not take on new customers for that account and lower the interest rate to maximize profit. De-selection needs to be a formal and considered process – and not merely one where customers close accounts and are not 'rescued' at the point of closure.

Greater expectations?

Having been through a relationship, are consumers more experienced?

Q. Are they more determined to make new relationships work, or are they more fickle and promiscuous as a result of their experience?
A. *The answer is as individual as consumers are and with the diversification of target audiences across consumer markets it is becoming increasingly difficult to segment the market. However, organizations continue to strive to reach their customers through communication messages and varying communication approaches – some examples of which have been outlined above.*

Reinvention

In conclusion, it may be necessary to reinvent a brand in order to make it appealing to existing or potential consumers. As the greater the distance between the producer and consumer is often the reason a relationship fails, ensuring the gap between brand identity and brand image is essential to maintaining a successful brand. Using communications to build relationships and to develop and maintain a dialogue with the consumer is key if the brand is to remain current and credible.

Skoda was a brand vilified for poor design, limited technical expertise and a lack of quality control (Piercy, 1999) and, not surprisingly, the brand image was extremely negative. However, in blind testing, consumer evaluations of value and likelihood of purchase were considerably lower when they knew the car was a Skoda. In order to address the consumer perception of the brand, Skoda needed to concentrate on both the product and the brand image. Skoda's greatest asset in its bid to reposition itself in the minds of the consumers was probably the ownership share taken by Volkswagen in 1991 (a credible, quality brand renowned for engineering) – and the resulting brand associations with Skoda. Still the brand appeal to launch the Felicia in 1995 – 'We've changed our cars; can you change your mind?' – directly addressed the issue of brand image. The company estimated that after this communications approach, 72% of first-time Skoda buyers returned for a second purchase in 1996. The success of this message is evident, although maintaining the momentum in the longer term may prove problematic.

Therefore, the significance of using communication approaches to build relationships is about narrowing the gap between the producer and the consumer. Figure 16 highlights the issues associated with brand identity and brand image, with the Skoda example demonstrating the difficulty producers have in 'getting close' to the consumer.

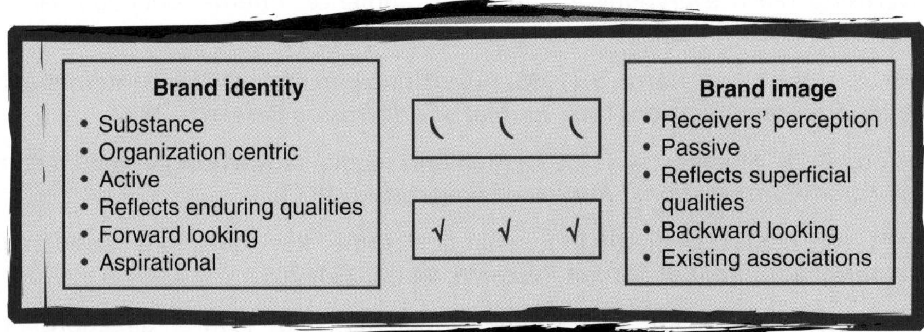

Figure 16 Differences between brand identity and brand image

This chapter has considered how effective communications and building relationships through communications can be using a direct approach (for example, a Virgin Vie party or the Bear Factory) or indirect approach (for example, the use of celebrities). Ad literacy, the extent to which the target audience is familiar with the communication messages used by organizations, was addressed through discussion of language used to familiarize the customer with the brand. The use of branding (semiotics, attributes and values associated with brands) is also a key feature of building relationships and the appropriate use of communications in order to maximize impact was also explored (Playstation). Immediacy of the communications message was considered through the description of ambient advertising. The necessity for communications to be more creative, abstract and engaging was the focus of many of the examples provided, with organizations that thought 'outside the box' used to demonstrate developments in the communications arena. Of course, effective communication messages are only really successful when married with appropriate media planning schedules – reach and importance of suitable media selection was also briefly explored. As the relationship between an organization and a customer develops it is essential to maintain a dialogue and this was particularly evident through the examples of database management.

Finally, enjoying relationships with brands as a consumer will probably be the result of considerable research on behalf of the organization. As with any relationship, knowledge is power and effective communications can only be successful as part of a two-way communications process. Organizations need consumers to assist in developing, adapting and creating a powerful experience.

Happy relationship building.

FURTHER READING

Anschuetz, N. (2002) Why a brand's most valuable consumer is the next one it adds. *Journal of Advertising Research*, **42** (1, Jan/Feb), 7.

Brace, I., Edwards, L. & Nancarrow, C. (2002) I hear you knocking . . . can advertising reach everybody in the target audience. *International Journal of Market Research*, **44** (2).

Bush, A. J., Bush, V. & Harris, S. (1998) Advertising perceptions of the Internet as a marketing communications tool. *Journal of Advertising Research*, **38** (2).

Horton, B. & Shanker, A. (1999) Ambient media: advertising's new media opportunity? *International Journal of Advertising*, **18** (3).

Lawes, R. (2002) Demystifying semiotics: some key questions answered. *International Journal of Market Research*, **44** (3), 251–265.

Meenaghan, T. (1998) Current developments and future directions in sponsorship. *International Journal of Advertising*, **17** (1).

Rudder, S. (2001) What future for ad agencies. *Admap*, May.

Schilling, M. C. M., Wood, K. & Braithwaite A. (2002) *ESOMAR, Reinventing Advertising*, Rio, November, pp. 207–229.

Suggested websites

Informative websites

www.abc.org.uk	Audit Bureau of Circulations
www.adassoc.org.uk	Advertising Association

www.asa.org.uk	Advertising Standards Authority
www.cim.co.uk	Chartered Institute of Marketing
www.dataprotection.gov.uk/ dprhome.htm	Details of latest data protection laws
www.dma.org.uk	Direct Marketing Association
www.itc.org.uk	Independent Television Commission
www.ipr.press.net/	Institute of Public Relations
www.rajar.co.uk	Radio Joint Audience Research Ltd
www.marketresearch.org.uk	Market Research Society

Journals online

www.adage.com/

www.campaignlive.com/

www.ft.com/

www.ipc.co.uk

www.marketing-week.co

www.marketing.haynet.com/

www.marketingtoday.com/

Miscellaneous

http://scriptorium.lib.duke.edu/adaccess/	Advertising history
http://sudesirek.tripod.com	Car advertising
www.geocities.com/appleads	Technology advertising
www.aber.ac.uk/media	Useful university site

Advertising agencies

www.amvbbdo.co.uk	Abbott Mead Vickers
www.bates-dorland.co.uk	Bates
www.tbwa-london.com	TBWA\London

Articles and case studies

www.warc.com	World Advertising Research Centre

The role of institutions and networks

Jaqueline Pels

In this chapter we look at the role of networks in building market relations and the various institutions that participate and support these networks.

What does the term 'network' mean?

A marketing network is essentially a set of interlinked relationships. In order to explain, let's work through *an example* of what happens when you make an Internet purchase.

Suppose you log on to Dell.com or any other website to buy a product. If it is not a standardized offer (i.e. the same item for each customer, such as a book), then you will have to help build *your own* product solution, say for a PC, where you can select different combinations of screen, stack, printer, sound, CD/DVD, extra memory, etc. This means that, through a menu selection process online, you have to provide the company with specifications of what you want so that the product can be assembled. Sometimes, when you have finished specifying your requirements and check the price, you realize that it is too expensive – so, then you go a couple of links back and alter some of the selections in your original specification in order to get the best product–price combination that you can afford. This online product–price specification process creates a dialogue between you, the customer, and Dell, the supplier. And *dialogue* is one of the *key characteristics* of a marketing relationship (see The role of communications).

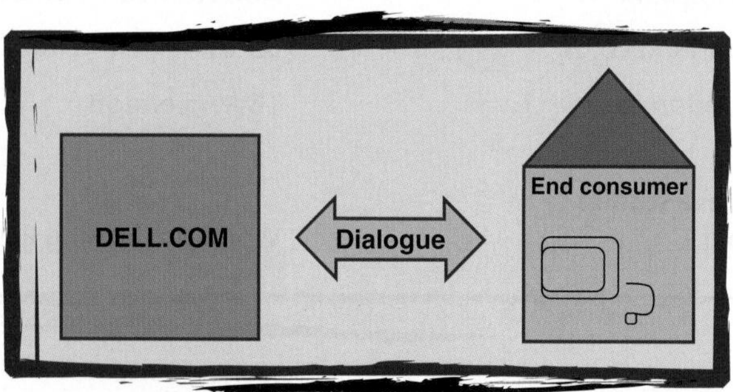

Figure 17 Dialogue between supplier and consumer

Continuing this example, if eventually you reach a satisfactory product solution and decide to buy the PC, you fill in payment details, then press 'buy' and wait for the product to be sent to you. This is the end of *your* troubles or concerns as the customer. But they now become more pressing for the supplier. From that moment of purchase, Dell or the organization from which you bought the product needs to start organizing a series of operational actions in order to ensure delivery of the product to you promptly. Your single purchase act will trigger a whole set of decisions and activities by the seller. It could be that some of the components for the computer are not manufactured in the company and that these must be shipped in from suppliers (e.g. Intel microprocessors). In this case there must be a fast and efficient *information system* (see Creating Solutions: Information technology and innovation) installed between the two firms, and *trust and commitment* between the parties must be high (see Relationships and interactions). Furthermore, once the PC is assembled it needs to reach you. Thus, contracts and agreements with external suppliers of transportation must be made. If we went into further details, this description would become more and more entangled and specific. This set of interconnected and interdependent relationships is what we call a *network* (see Figure 18).

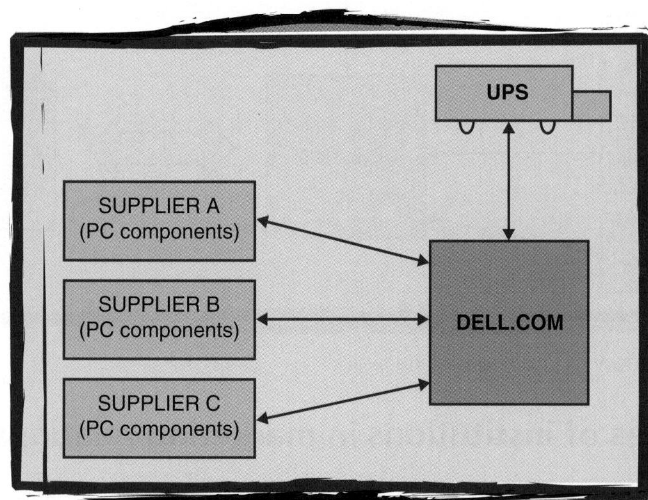

Figure 18 Example of a network

This example of an Internet PC purchase describes a small and specific network, directly involving only the supplier–manufacturer–consumer linkages. Traditionally the supplier-to-manufacturer part of the link would have been discussed under the title of 'supply' or 'procurement', while the manufacturer–consumer link would have been labelled as 'marketing'. The value of the *network* perspective is that it looks at the *whole set* of relationships involved *simultaneously* from the source of raw materials right through to delivery of the final product to customer (see Moving Space: Moving materials).

Furthermore, if were looking at Figure 18 from a wider perspective and we were able to *zoom out* further from the supplier–manufacturer–consumer link we would see many other relations (that is, dialogues) occurring with other actors. *We would be seeing the broader network*. In the Dell.com example, it implies that looking at the broader network will more accurately identify all the relationships and *institutions* involved in the supply and delivery of the product to the customer, first stimulated by the act of purchase (see Consuming Experience), understanding which are all the institutions involved in the process of: designing the most user-friendly website, defining the set of suppliers of PC components, establishing the security that will allow buyers to purchase over the Internet, guaranteeing the delivery process, etc.

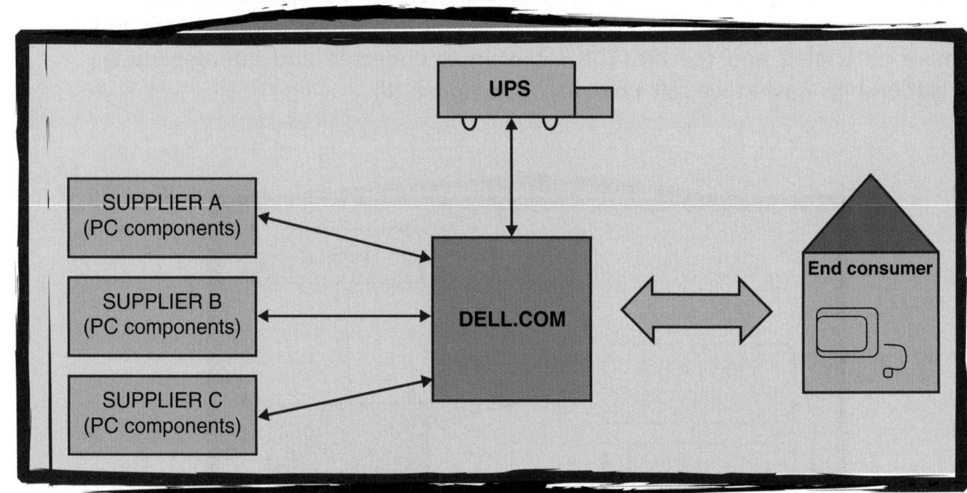

Figure 19 View of the broader network

The roles of institutions in marketing relationships

Institutions are organizations that transform inputs into outputs. There are four types of institutions: households, private firms (retailers, competitors, suppliers, etc.), public firms and government. Between these institutions, two different types of exchange can take place: (1) market exchanges and (2) relational exchanges.

In a market exchange the parties are independent and *choose* to interact with the counterpart because they perceive a benefit in engaging in this form of exchange. Once again, if we look at our Dell.com example, it is quite likely that before deciding to purchase a Dell PC the buyer has looked at and searched in other websites, and furthermore it is possible that our potential buyer has even gone to visit some offline stores. This type of exchange has strong assumptions. It believes that both the buyer and the seller are seeking to maximize their utility and that both parties/institutions have other options (i.e. other buyers – or other sellers). Furthermore, each exchange is seen as independent from previous and future market exchanges.

Relational exchanges can be broken down as follows:

1 *Level 1 relationships*. These are relationships based on primary incentives. What holds the relationship together is primarily a financial benefit. The selling firm's focus is on repeat purchase and consumers are looking for a financial advantage. This is clearly exemplified in the loyalty programmes (i.e. the frequent flyer programmes).
2 *Level 2 relationships*. These are relationships that go beyond the pricing incentives. They seek to build social bonds on top of any financial bond that may exist. What holds the relationship together is the knowledge that the actors have about each other. There is a beginning of a dialogue and both parties benefit from giving and receiving information. This is the case when we provide Amazon.com with information about a topic we are interested in (i.e. the Harry Potter saga) and Amazon.com would send us updates on the latest books, CD games, etc. related to our interests. It is important to notice that this information exchange might not lead to a sale.
3 *Level 3 relationships*. These are relationships that are solidified through structural bonds. In other words, creating special adaptations for a specific relationship that cannot be transferred to other relationships. This is the case of a consultancy firm that builds a special task force to serve a customer. The skills required to solve the problems of customer 'A' will differ from those required to solve the problems of customer 'B'; thus, the task forces will be integrated by different team members.

It is important to note that firms may choose other forms of creating value for the end consumer. They might choose to internalize some processes by doing themselves some of the activities that could be bought (i.e. the delivery system).

Choosing a relationship

Let us return to the Dell.com PC purchase example. Dell.com could choose between producing all the PC components themselves, buy them in the market or develop a relationship with certain suppliers. Dell.com's core business is not producing computers, it is offering consumers the possibility of building their own PC with the certainty that they can access the latest technology. Thus, their competitive advantage will be high flexibility at low costs.

1 If they choose option 1 (do them themselves), they would have full control of the process and would not need to adapt to another institution (the supplier);

however, costs would probably be very high as the industry is a very dynamic one and to be in the forefront of it requires indigenous investments. As we can see, the do-it-yourself option doesn't seem to be the best alternative.

2 If Dell.com chooses option 2 (the market exchange) they could obtain low costs by having the different supplier bid for each component. But let us remember that Dell.com does not sell standardized PCs, they sell tailor-made PCs, and if they are going to purchase components on a bidding system, most likely the supplier will require them to buy batches of PC components in exchange for the low prices. Unfortunately, Dell.com does not know ahead of time the specifications of the PCs they are going to sell on a particular day. Thus, to have control and be flexible they would have to have high stock and thus the cost advantage obtained in the bidding process might be lost.
3 If Dell.com chooses option 3 (the relational exchange), in order to obtain the required levels of cost, adaptation and control, the company would need a partner that sees itself as part of a larger network. This partner would understand that its own success depends on Dell.com's success and that both partners need to adapt to the end consumer's requirements. In other words, adaptation would be natural as the supplier and Dell.com would probably develop a JIT programme. Control would not be the result of strict and rigorous contracts, but of the commitment both institutions have. Finally, costs would not be dependent on volume. To find such a partner is not easy. As suggested before, the fundamental requirement for a successful relational exchange is mutuality.

Relations, exchange and networks

1 Because relationships are connected, change in one of the relationships is likely to affect other relationships. Suppose Coke suggested to Sainsbury's that they have a special in-store display. Before agreeing, Sainsbury should take into consideration how the other soft-drink suppliers will react, because if the Coke initiative is successful (and let us remember that Coke is engaging in it in order to be successful), this will affect negatively the other soft-drink firms and Sainsbury's needs to think about the big picture. On the other hand, Coke must also consider how the other retailers will react. This is called *network thinking*.
2 In the Coke–Sainsbury case the *activity* that is being connected is a promotion. We have already discussed that both Coke and Sainsbury need to consider the

impact of this activity on other institutions they are interacting with. However, they also need to coordinate this activity with other activities that they are involved with and are taking place at the same time. Probably Coke will be supporting this in-store display with some advertising; thus, the timing of both activities must match. On the other hand, it is quite likely that Sainsbury will also have some other in-store activities occurring, such as a product sampling. Sainsbury needs to make sure that these two in-store activities are harmonious (i.e. free cheese sampling and the Coke special offer) and that there are not too many in-store activities simultaneously, because these would distract purchasers. Such activities involve the technical, administrative and commercial actions of a company, which can be connected in different ways to those of another institution.

3 It is important to notice that not only activities are being connected. Actually, Coke needs Sainsbury's *resource* (the store) to reach the end consumer with its promotional activity and Sainsbury needs Coke's resource (the actual discount the promotions involves) to provide its customer with a financial benefit that will attract buyers to their stores.

So networks connect sets of institutions' activities and resources with the ultimate aim of providing a benefit (value) to end consumers. But one key question then is where and when do networks end? This is no easy question. It depends on where and what we are looking at.

- If we were thinking in very restricted terms (i.e. selling and buying of goods), then our network would be limited to the set of buyer–seller relationships the focal firm has (see Figure 17) – in our Dell.com case, just the Dell.com/end consumers network or the suppliers/Dell.com network.
- If we were thinking in more ample terms (that is, all types of exchanges), then we would have to consider a more ample and extended network, which included the customer's customer, suppliers, suppliers' suppliers, government and other institutions (see Figures 18 and 19) – in our Dell.com case, the set of suppliers/Dell.com/UPS/end consumers/other institutions.

In other words, the limits of a network of institutions that create value are variable, depending on the view and level of focus on the marketing operation. If it is a global view then obviously the network of institutions is enormous, but usually we are looking at the network involved in the supply of a specific product or associated with a specific company, or at most in one industry or business sector.

At the level of the single firm, the marketers need to understand which are their customers (both intermediaries and segments of end consumers), their suppliers (both direct and indirect suppliers), and the other institutions that may be related to a given value-creating process (the financial/stakeholders, government, business press and media, credit rating agencies, user groups, environmentalists).

In this chapter we have tried to explain how building relations can be understood in terms of the institutions involved and the network approach to analysing the links between market relationships. This means identifying the set of institutions that participate, through their activities and resources, in the marketing process. However, we have also acknowledged that these institutions might choose not to be engaged in relational exchanges and favour a more market or transactional approach (see Relationships and interactions).

Key definitions

1. A *network* is a set of interconnected and interdependent relationships.
2. *Institutions* are organizations that transform inputs into outputs.
3. A *market exchange* is the simultaneous transaction of valued goods, services and ideas between two parties (institutions) who are capable of accepting or rejecting the values offered.
4. A *relational exchange* can be based on: (i) a financial benefit, (ii) a social bond or (iii) a structural bond.
5. The fundamental requirement for a successful relational exchange is *mutuality*.
6. *Networking* implies taking into consideration how changes in one relationship may affect other connected relationships.
7. *Networks create value* by connecting institutions, their activities and their resources.
8. The *limits of a network* of institutions are subjective.

FURTHER READING

Bagozzi, R. P. (1995) Reflections on relationship marketing in consumer markets. *Journal of the Academy of Marketing Science*, **23** (4), 272–277.

Håkansson, H. & Snehota, I. (1990) No business is an island: the network concept of business strategy. In: *Understanding Business Markets: Interaction, Relationships and Networks* (D. Ford, ed.). Academic Press: London.

Möller, K. & Wilson, D. (eds) (1995) *Business Marketing: an Interaction and Network Perspective*. Kluwer Academic: Massachusetts.

Pels, J. (1999) Exchange relationships in consumer markets? *European Journal of Marketing*, **33** (1/2), 19–37.

Peppers, D. & Rogers, M. (1993) *The One to One Future*. Currency Doubleday: New York.

Sheth, J. N. & Parvatiyar, A. (2000) *Handbook of Relationship Marketing*. Sage: London.

References

Bagozzi, R. P. (1995) Reflections on relationship marketing in consumer markets. *Journal of the Academy of Marketing Science*, **23** (4), 272–277.

Berry, L. L. (1983) Relationship marketing. In: *Emerging Perspectives of Services Marketing* (L. L. Berry, G. L. Shostack & G. D. Upah, eds). American Marketing Association: Chicago.

Brodie, R. J., Coviello, N. E., Brookes, R. W. and Little, V. (1997) Towards a paradigm shift in marketing? An examination of current marketing practices. *Journal of Marketing Management*, **13** (5), 383–406.

Buttle, F. (1996) Relationship marketing. In: *Relationship Marketing: Theory and Practice* (F. Buttle, ed.). Paul Chapman.

Christopher, M., Payne, A. & Ballantyne, D. (1991) *Relationship Marketing: Bringing Quality, Customer Service, and Marketing Together*. Butterworth-Heinemann: Oxford.

Coviello, N., Brodie, R., Danaher, R. & Johnston, W. (2002) How firms relate to their markets: an empirical examination of contemporary marketing practices. *Journal of Marketing*, **66** (3), 33–46.

Dick, A. S. & Basu, K. (1994) Customer loyalty: towards an integrated framework. *Journal of the Academy of Marketing Science*, **22** (2), 99–113.

Dwyer, F. R., Schurr, P. J. & Oh, S. (1987). Developing buyer–seller relationships. *Journal of Marketing*, **51** (2), 11–27.

East, R., Harris, P., Wilson, G. & Lomax, W. Loyalty to Supermarkets. *International Journal of Retail, Distribution and Consumer Research*, **5** (1), 99–110.

Egan, J. (2000) Drivers to relational strategies in retailing. *International Journal of Retail and Distribution Management*, **28** (8).

Ehrenberg, A. & Goodhardt, G. (2000) New brands: near-instant loyalty. **16**, 607–617.

Erdogan, Z. & Kitchen, P. (1998) Getting the best out of celebrity endorsers. *Admap*, April.

Evans, M. (1998) From 1086 and 1984: direct marketing into the millennium. *Marketing Intelligence and Planning*, **16** (1), 57–67.

Evans, M., O'Malley, L. & Patterson, M. (2004) *Exploring Direct and Customer Relationship Marketing*. Thomson: London.

Fowles, J. (1996) *Advertising and Popular Culture*. Sage: London.

Ford, D. (1990) *Understanding Business Markets: Interaction, Relationships, and Networks*. Academic Press: London.

Ford, D. (2004) The IMP group and international marketing. *International Marketing Review*, **21** (2 February), 139–141.

Fournier, S., Dobscha, S. & Nick, D.G. (1998) Preventing the premature death of relationship marketing. *Harvard Business Review*, **76** (1), 42–51.

Greene, W. E., Walls, G. D. & Schrest, L. J. (1994) Internal marketing: the key to external marketing success. *Journal of Services Marketing*, **8** (4).

Grönroos, C. (1981) Internal marketing – an integral part of marketing theory. In: *Marketing of Services* (J. H. Donnelly & W. R. George, eds). American Marketing Association: Chicago, pp. 236–238.

Grönroos, C. (1990) The marketing strategy continuum: towards a marketing concept for the 1990s. *Management Decision*, **29** (1), 9.

Grönroos, C. (1994) From marketing mix to relationship marketing: towards a paradigm shift in marketing. *Management Decision*, **32** (2), 4–20.

Gummesson, E. (1987) The new marketing: developing long-term interactive relationships. *Long Range Planning*, **20** (4), 10–20.

Gummesson, E. (1999) *Total Relationship Marketing*. Butterworth-Heinemann, Oxford.

Gummesson, E. (2000) Internal marketing in the light of relationship marketing and network organisations. In: *Internal Marketing: Directions for Management* (R. J. Varey & B. R. Lewis, eds). Routledge.

Håkansson, H. & Snehota, I. (eds) (1995) *Developing Relationships in Business Networks*. Routledge: London.

IPA Case Study (1994) *The Wonderbra: How Thinking Big Ensured the Survival of the Fittest*. IPA Effectiveness Awards. Advertising Works: London.

Jackson, B. (1985) Building customer relationships that last. *Harvard Business Review*, Nov/Dec, 120–128.

Judd, V. C. (1987) Differentiate with the fifth 'P': people. *Industrial Marketing Management*, **16**, 241–247.

Kasper, H. (1998) On problem perception, dissatisfaction and brand loyalty. *Journal of Economic Psychology*, **9**, 387–397.

Kaye, R. L. (1999) Companies need to realise Internal Marketing's potential. *Business Marketing*, 1 July, 13.

Kotler, P. (1992) It's time for total marketing. *Business Week, ADVANCE Executive Brief*, **2**, 15.

Kuhn, T. (1962) *The Structure of Scientific Revolutions*. University of Chicago Press: Chicago.

Lazer, W. & Kelley, E. (eds) (1973) *Social Marketing: Perspectives and Viewpoints*. Irwin: Homewood, IL.

Lovato, C. *et al.* (2004) Impact of tobacco advertising and promotion on increasing adolescent smoking behaviours. *The Cochrane Library*, issue 2.

Lovelock, C., Vandermerwe, S. & Lewis, B. (1999) *Services Marketing: A European Perspective*. Prentice-Hall Europe.

McGoldrick, P. & Andre, E. (1997) Consumer misbehavior: promiscuity or loyalty in grocery shopping. *Journal of Retailing and Consumer Services*, **4** (2), 73–81.

McLuhan, M. (1964) *Understanding Media*. Routledge & Kegan Paul: New York.

Morgan, R. M. & Hunt, S. D. (1994) The commitment-trust theory of relationship marketing. *Journal of Marketing*, **58** (July), 20–38.

Normann, R. & Ramirez, R. (1993). From value chain to value constellation: designing interactive strategy. *Harvard Business Review*, July/August, 65–77.

O'Brien, L. & Jones, C. (1995) Do rewards really create loyalty? *Harvard Business Review*, May/June, 75–82.

O'Malley, L. (1998) Can loyalty schemes really build loyalty? *Marketing Intelligence and Planning*, **16** (1), 47–55.

Palmer, A. & Beggs, R. (1997) Loyalty programmes: congruence of market structure and success. Presented at the Academy of Marketing Conference, Manchester, UK.

Pandya, A. & Dholakia, N. (1992) An institutional theory of exchange in marketing. *European Journal of Marketing*, **26** (12), 1941.

Patton, G. C., Carlin, J. B., Wolfe, C. R., Hibbert, M. & Bowes, G. (1998) The course of early smoking: a population-based cohort study over three years. *Addiction*, **93** (8), 1251–1260.

Payne, A. (1995) *Advances in Relationship Marketing*. Kogan Page: London.

Payne, A. (2000) Relationship marketing: managing multiple markets. In: *Cranfield School of Management, Marketing Management: A Relationship Marketing Perspective*. Macmillan: Oxford.

Pels, J. (1999) Exchange relationships in consumer markets? *European Journal of Marketing*, **33** (1/2), 19–37.

Pels, J. & Saren, M. (2005) The new Ps of relationship marketing – perspectives, perceptions and paradigms: learnings from organisational theory strategy literature. *Journal of Relationship Marketing*, **3** (1).

Pels, J., Brodie, R. & Johnston, W. (2004) Benchmarking business-to-business marketing practices in transitional and developed economies: Argentina compared to the USA and New Zealand. *Journal of Business and Industrial Marketing*, **19** (6), 386–396.

Peppers, D. & Rogers, M. (1993) *The One to One Future*. Currency Doubleday: New York.

Pierce, J. P., Gilpin, E. A. & Choi, W. S. (1999) Sharing the blame: smoking experimentation and future smoking-attributable mortality due to Joe Camel and Marlboro advertising and promotions. *Tobacco Control*, **8**, 37–44.

Piercy, N. (1999) *Tales from the Marketplace: Stories of Revolution, Reinvention and Renewal*. Butterworth-Heinemann: Oxford.

Pollay, W., Siddarth, S., Siegel, M., Haddix, A., Merritt, R. K., Giovino, G. A. & Eriksen, M. P. (1996) The last straw? Cigarette advertising and realized market shares among youths and adults, 1979–1993. *Journal of Marketing*, **60** (2), 1–16.

Pressey, A. D. & Matthews, B. P. (2000) Barriers to relationship marketing in consumer retailing. *Journal of Services Marketing*, **14** (3).

Rafiq, M. & Ahmed, P. K. (1995) The limits of internal marketing. In: *Managing Service Quality* (P. Kunst & J. Lemmink, eds). Paul Chapman.

Reicheld, F. F. (1994) *The Loyalty Effect*. Harvard Business School Press: Cambridge, MA.

Reicheld, F. F. & Sasser, W. E. Jr (1990) Zero defections: quality comes to services. *Harvard Business Review*, October.

Sasser, W. E. (1976) Match supply and demand in service industries. *Harvard Business Review*, **54** (3, Nov/Dec), 133–140.

Schneider, B. & Bowen, D. E. (1985) Employee and customer perceptions of service in banks: replication and extension. *Journal of Applied Psychology*, **70**, 423–433.

Sheth, J. & Parvatiyar, A. (1995) Relationship marketing in consumer markets: antecedents and consequences. *Journal of the Academy of Marketing Science*, **23** (4), 255–271.

Sheth, J. N. & Parvatiyar, A. (2000) *Handbook of Relationship Marketing*. Sage: London.

Srivastava, R. K., Shrevani, T. K. & Fahey, L. (1999) Marketing, business processes, and shareholder value: an organizationally embedded view of marketing activities and the discipline of marketing. *Journal of Marketing*, **63**, 168–179.

Sutherland, R. (2000) This time it's personal. *Admap*, February.

Taylor, S. L. & Cosenza, R. M. (1997) Internal marketing can reduce employee turnover. *Supervision*, **58** (12), 3.

Tzokas, N. & Saren, M. (1999) Editorial Special Issue – Relationship marketing: delivering value out of bounds. *International Journal of Bank Marketing*.

Vargo, S. L. & Lusch, R. F. (2004) Evolving to a new dominant logic for marketing. *Journal of Marketing*, **68** (January), 1–17.

Veloutsou, C., Tzokas, N. & Saren, M. (2002) Relationship marketing: what if? *European Journal of Marketing*, **36** (4), 433–439.

Webster, F. E. (1992) The changing role of marketing in the corporation. *Journal of Marketing*, **56** (October), 1–17.

Consuming Experience

We are all consumers. Unless we go and live on a desert island we cannot avoid consuming and thus playing a role in the marketing process. This section looks at the role of consumers in marketing, why and what they consume, and the various ways in which consumption is related to identity. Consumer culture plays a significant part in the creation, and reproduction of people's tastes, dreams and aspirations. The concepts of consumer co-production and satisfaction are explained. We discuss the influence of consumer sub-cultures or tribes on individuals' lifestyles, possessions and values.

What is consumed?

Consumerism is often criticized for being materialistic, with an emphasis on the value and use of physical objects over non-material pursuits such as ideas, ideals and society. Yet, paradoxically, consumer culture is more and more a visual culture, in which the consumer is bombarded with multimedia images, pictorial advertisements, 'sightseeing' vacations, brightly lit shopping arcades, entertainment 'spectacles', 'eye-catching' packaging. Much consumption is visual consumption (Schroeder, 2003); therefore, it is not just materials that are consumed, but non-material images too.

Because the consumption process is more complex than it first appears, it is useful to look at the various explanations that have been proposed in order to be able to analyse from different perspectives in any given situation what it is that is being consumed.

Explanations of what is consumed

- *Materials and energy*
- *Labour*
- *Use or utility*
- *Culture*
- *Meaning and signs.*

Consuming materials and energy

It might appear obvious what the consumer consumes – physical materials that make up the products and services that they purchase and use. A car buyer consumes the car as they drive it around; we all consume the food we purchase as we eat it, or even as it sits in the fridge and rots! One definition of the product (Kotler, 1967) is '. . . anything that can be offered to a market for attention, acquisition, use or consumption that might satisfy a want or a need. It includes physical objects, services, persons, places, organizations and ideas' (see Creating Solutions). Therefore, it should be fairly clear from this wide range of the type of things that consumers consume – i.e. objects, services, people, places – and thus the physical objects that are 'used up' as they are consumed.

When you think about it, however, it becomes a little less clear what exactly it is that is being consumed in these marketing processes. One complication is that it is not only the car that is being consumed in the above example, so is petrol, so is the road surface and the road *space*, so even is the air. Often, several things are

consumed together, what are sometimes called 'complementary' products. The materials and energy in products are certainly consumed – although an ecological view would point out that they are in fact *transformed* into other forms of energy and matter, such as waste, gas, power, etc. (see Marketing Contexts: Marketing values).

It is not only these physical components that are consumed, however, because most products also have intangible features, such as service, guarantees, instructions, which we know in marketing are important for customers (see Creating Solutions). In addition, many purchases now are not primarily physical products at all – insurance, entertainment, education, health – therefore, the 'objects of consumption' cannot simply be the materials that comprise products.

Another aspect is that, from the customer's point of view, consumption is essentially an *experience*. How well they enjoyed the 'experience' of using it usually determines how satisfied the consumer is with the product. Also, in driving and even when eating, the consumer's time and some attention and effort are being 'consumed' as well. And what about the whole modern marketing phenomenon of branding (see Brand Selection): can people 'consume' a brand label simply by showing off the logo?

One way in which marketing has dealt with the multiple aspects of products that can be consumed is to think in terms of the 'total market offering'. According to the traditional marketing view, the product comprises a 'bundle of attributes' that can be analysed in terms of its constituent elements, including benefits, services and expectations, which together make up the 'total offering' to consumers (see Creating Solutions). Any or all these parts of the 'total' offering can be consumed.

Consuming labour

It may appear a strange way of looking at it nowadays, but in the eighteenth and nineteenth centuries most economists regarded the products and services that people purchased as a sort of 'jellied work', i.e. other people's labour that is solidified and stored as products. So when you purchased bread from the baker what you were buying was the *product* of all the labour activities that went into producing and delivering it, i.e. the farming and harvesting of the ingredients, the milling and milking, transporting and baking. The bread you buy is the outcome of this work and if you did not choose to buy it you would have to buy the materials and do the baking yourself. Buying the bread saves you work and this is what you pay for and consume.

This historical emphasis on the labour value of products fitted in with the times being influenced by the spirit of the Reformation, which valorized work as good in itself, as spiritually dignified, an act of homage. All this work produced 'goods', and therefore it figures that it was the work input that made them valuable.

You can still see how this labour view of consumption can be applied to today's products. For example, large parts of the labour function that were labelled as 'housework' and performed by 'housewives' or even by servants during the early twentieth century have now been incorporated in manufactured products and machinery. Home cooking has been substituted by ready-made and convenience food; home-cleaning work is mechanized by washing machines, dishwashers, vacuum cleaners, etc. Here some of the 'unpaid' house labour activities that Ivan Illich (1981) calls 'shadow work' have been in part transformed into objects of consumption within the market exchange nexus.

This example shows how consumers 'at home' use domestic appliances to perform 'housework'. They are normally consuming them in order to help minimize the amount of work they have to perform and simultaneously to save 'time'. Thus, like bread, today's products like the Hoover can also be regarded as 'jellied work'. So, despite the apparently outdated nature of the original economists' view of consuming labour, almost all products and services can still be viewed as labour-'saving', precisely because by buying them 'ready made' they save the consumer from all the work involved in making them themselves.

Apart from these more obvious examples of labour-saving devices, however, there are many other consumption aspects of products or services that are not so well explained as work substitutes. For instance, all products consist of physical materials and, whether it is bread or a car, these material elements are also required – as well as labour – to manufacture the product. For many products, the materials used to make it are much more expensive than the labour input. Whatever the proportional inputs, from the consumer's point of view, it is not so much the labour involved in manufacturing a car that is consumed, it is much more directly the physical objects – metal, rubber, glass, oil, gas – that are 'used up' over time as they drive it.

So there is a fundamental problem with the 'consuming labour' idea nowadays. The 'total market offering' for any product – a car, bread, even for a Hoover – involves more aspects than simply labour-saving; it includes the materials used to make it and features such as design, usability, storage, weight, access, effectiveness (see Creating Solutions). In other words, one of the elements that is central to consumption is its *use*. Indeed, one normally thinks of consuming a product *as* using it.

Consuming use or 'utility'

It seems obvious that consumers buy products in order to use them, and thus what is consumed is in fact the usefulness or 'utility' of the product. People pay for and judge a product's value in relation to how useful they find it, or expect it to be. When a product has been consumed, it is 'finished' and is no longer useful. Once eaten, the bread has 'lost' its usefulness; when eventually becoming unroadworthy, the car is useless, except for scrap metal. The next time the consumer is hungry or needs to drive they have to purchase a new loaf of bread or another car in order to fulfil this use. It is therefore fundamentally the 'use' of products that they are consuming. The argument here is that it is this feature of 'utility' in products that the customer uses up in the act of consumption.

People don't buy drills, they buy holes.
Kotler, 1967

In marketing we view products as 'solutions' to customer problems or needs (see Creating Solutions). Products do not normally provide these solutions simply by the act of being purchased; it is only by *using* the car or the bread that the consumer's need for transport or food is satisfied[1]. To re-emphasize an earlier point, it is more accurately the experience of the use of the product that satisfies – this is the so-called 'interactionist' approach to consumer value (Holbrook, 1999) (see Marketing Contexts: Marketing values). Whatever the nature of the consumer's satisfaction, it is nevertheless the *use* of the product that is consumed during the process. This can best be explained by looking at the origins of the concept of 'utility', which are from economics.

So central is the concept of utility to micro-economics for explaining consumer behaviour and choice between products that economic theory assumes that consumers seek to maximize their total utility from their combination of purchases. This requires a careful judgement as to the best combination of items to buy, because the law of 'diminishing marginal utility' holds that the more a person consumes of a particular good, the less utility each additional item provides. For

[1] There is of course a partial solution to the hunger 'problem' which is satisfied by the act of purchase of the bread alone. That is, the *ownership and control* of the solution that buying the loaf transfers to the customer, who can now choose to eat at any time. But until it is eaten, *i.e. used*, the bread is not consumed; it remains, if you like, in a condition of 'stored use'.

example, after a certain number of loaves of bread have been consumed, the satisfaction or utility derived from eating more bread decreases.

Thus, according to this view products are judged by consumers according to their 'utility', but it is not a static measure – even for the same product. The degree of satisfaction a consumer obtains from a product, e.g. a car, depends on how many cars you have, and how much you use them. The usefulness of the car to you also then depends on how many you have and how much you drive. Therefore, utility is not static, it *changes* with use.

There are some major criticisms of the utility concept as a basis for understanding the nature of consumption:

1 It is entirely subjective, a personal view of the product's potential to provide functional consequences by the consumer and not a property that the product inherently contains.
2 It is hard to distinguish from satisfaction, the fulfillment of a physiological or psychological need, which is something the consumer experiences (see Why consume?).
3 The price or 'exchange value' of a product may have no relation to its utility. For example, bread is much cheaper than gold, but which is more useful?
4 Even when a product is bought primarily for its functional utility, the differentiating factor between alternatives can be a 'useless' attribute, like the brand name or the colour, which are also consumed.
5 It is hard to apply this concept to the whole area of financial services, where many products are purchased in order to retain or multiply their value, not for any functional use.
6 It is hard to apply this concept to aesthetic aspects of consumption, where people's aesthetic appreciation of a work of art or sculpture is by definition entirely *unrelated* to any practical use of the object.

(Benjamin, 1936)

Consuming culture

Viewing consumption as a cultural practice opens up a whole new perspective on what is being consumed. The term culture used by sociologists covers people's common patterns of behaviour and values; it is learned and shared with other people, and that culture influences how we behave and expect others to behave (Gronhaug, 1999). When these cultural considerations are taken into account, consumer products become more than just materials, more than objects of use, their demand derives more from their role in cultural practices than in the direct satisfaction of functional or material needs; 'they are goods to speak with, goods to think with' (Fiske, 1989). A pioneering work was Douglas & Isherwood's *World of Goods* (1978); they regard consumption and consumer choices as a source of meaning for people, as a social process that helps clarify and stabilize the constantly changing cultural (or social) categories.

Consumption is not solely an individual act, it encompasses and affects the whole society and culture. This is recognized by advertisers and market researchers who take into account a wide range of social and cultural factors in order to understand consumers' behaviour and product choices (see Creating Solutions). According to Douglas & Isherwood (1978), *all* consumer needs are culturally defined. They argue that even apparently basic physiological needs like hunger are *expressed* in a particular way that is determined by the culture. For instance, 'I am dying for a Big Mac' means 'I am very hungry' in today's western culture; quite apart from language, this expression and desire would take a very different form in sub-Saharan Africa or in eighteenth century Russia.

Sociologists look at the role of consumption in making distinctions between social groups. Pierre Bourdieu, in his book *Distinction: A Social Critique of the Judgement of Taste* (1984), found that the way in which consumers classify goods differs according to social class and that their definition of 'taste' indicates closely their social class. For some products these distinctions were greater than others; these are called 'marker' goods. There were also gender differences in consumption – for example, working-class men chose steak for a special meal, whereas women chose fish.

Anthropologists have found that in all societies objects and material goods play a role in cementing social relations and people's consumption of products has a cultural function in self-expression, perceived security and attachment to society. This has been illustrated by Walendorf & Arnould (1988) in an anthropological study entitled 'My favourite things; a cross-cultural inquiry into object attachment, possessiveness and social linkage'. Products can be used by consumers to 'make a statement'; they are advertised and associated with particular 'role models' or celebrities (see Brand Selection); friends, family and peer groups influence how we view products.

Advertising appropriates cultural 'cues' in order to attach meaning to them, often drawing on well-known stories, characters and myths. Such 'mythic archetypes' have universal expression in countries' literatures and folk tales, and although these are periodically updated to suit local and contemporary conditions, they draw on a long historical lineage of common cultural meanings (Hirschman, 2000).

In a variety of ways, it is, at least partly, culture itself that people buy 'into' and consume. Not only are their choices and behaviour affected by culture, but also the meaning and values that they ascribe to the objects of consumption are reflections of both the historical and contemporary culture. This, however, begs one key question: how are these meanings and values 'transferred' from the culture to the products, and how do consumers interpret these? The obvious answer is through marketing and advertising in particular. In order to examine this question, the next subsection looks at meanings and signs as themselves the objects of consumption.

When Mark & Pearson (2001) argue that Nike is a heroic brand, they are linking these brand meanings to a long history of warrior archetypes that have populated the world's literary canon. Nike's success purportedly derives from consumers' favourable (and inherent) dispositions towards the meanings of strength, bravery, nobility and achievement of the athletic field (i.e. battlefield) encoded in its heroic brand image.
Thompson, 2004

Consuming meanings and signs

We can see that products are not consumed simply for their functional use; even a washing machine does more than wash – it carries other meanings for the consumer, such as cleanliness or comfort or prestige. Indeed, there is a strong argument that for some products the meanings are more important for consumers than their use. For example, the taste of Coca-Cola may be less important than what it stands for in the consumer's eyes, be that 'trust', 'reliability', the American Dream, 'relaxation' or whatever. The meanings that consumers interpret or ascribe to products can therefore be regarded as part of what they consume. In consumer research, this has led to increased attention to various so-called 'interpretative' techniques of analysis in order to understand these meanings and the processes by which they occur in this consumer culture. These include hermeneutics (the study of meanings) and semiotics (the study of symbols and signs).

Originating in the linguistic structuralism of Saussure (1959), semiotics proposes that the underlying structures of cultural meaning within the social environment are constituted from systems of signs. For semioticians the sign is the essential unit of meaning within language and culture. The sign has two components, the *signified* and the *signifier*, which together link words, objects and ideas to meanings and values. Almost any object, custom or artefact can be studied as part of a sign-making process, as something that signifies something from someone to someone. Applying semiotics to consumer research enables consumption to be viewed as a kind of language enabling the communication and transmission of meanings from one set of people to others. Objects of all kinds, including products, are exchanged and used to symbolize or signify all kinds of meanings within society and it is this *signification* process that is the primary focus when studying consumption semiotically.

Semioticians regard products as commodity signs and it is these signs that are exchanged, used and

> ***Brands are developed based on images, products are advertised via images, corporate image is critical for management success. Marketing is fundamentally about image management.***
> *Schroeder, 2002*

consumed. For Baudrillard (1981), traditional understandings of consumption as involving material acquisition and material commodity exchange and use are completely abandoned and these processes are subsumed under an 'economy of signs'. The symbolic perspective of consumption examines the system of signs and what they signify, or mean, for consumers. This approach has been most widely applied in advertising research (Goldman & Papson, 1996), but as consumer theory moves beyond explanations of consumption in solely economic and utilitarian terms; ideas of symbolic consumption, sign consumption and commodity signs have become increasingly applied in consumer research (e.g. Holt, 1995, 1998; Hirschman & Holbrook, 1982).

When products are analysed for their symbolic meaning as portrayed in their images, one problem is that there are several levels of the 'symbolic meaning' involved. This can refer to the product that embodies a meaning, the meaning itself that it carries, and the interpretation of the meaning by the consumer.

The act of consumption need not involve any material exchange. People can consume visually when they watch television, catch adverts, look in shop windows or recognize brand logos (Schroeder, 2002). Because consumer culture relies on images and signs so extensively, the semiotic aspects of consumption are important for marketing management in general and advertising and consumer research in particular.

FURTHER READING

Consuming culture

Douglas, M. & Isherwood, B. (1978) *World of Goods*. Allen Lane: London.

Featherstone, M. (1991) *Consumer Culture and Postmodernism*. Sage: Thousand Oaks, CA.

Consuming value

Holbrook, M. (ed.) (1999) *Consumer Value*. Routledge: New York.
(See also Marketing Contexts: Marketing values.)

How consumers consume

Holt, D. B. (1995) How consumers consume: a typology of consumption practices. *Journal of Consumer Research*, **22** (June), 1–16.

Consuming labour and work

Illich, I. (1981) *Shadow Work*. Marion Boyars: Salem, NH.

Consuming materials and energy

Kilbourne, W. (1998) Green marketing: a theoretical perspective. *Journal of Marketing Management*, **14**, 641–655.

Visual consumption

Schroeder, J. (2002) *Visual Consumption*. Routledge: London.

Why consume? Motivation and stimulation

Christina Goulding

No act of consumption takes place without some form of stimulation. This may be the result of a basic biological need, such as the pangs of hunger which stimulate the urge to eat, the stimulation of a utility need, such as a washing machine breaking down, or the stimulation of an aspirational need, as in the case of the desire for designer clothing or luxury brands. Most textbooks tend to locate the stimulation of needs within the framework of Maslow's hierarchy of needs, which proposes that we satisfy needs at different levels. At the lowest level are physiological needs such as the need for food, which must be satisfied before we can think about moving on towards more sophisticated needs. The second level deals with basic safety or security needs, while the third is concerned with love and belongingness. Moving higher up, the fourth level focuses on issues of esteem and respect, while the pinnacle, 'self-actualization', is the attainment of total self-fulfilment. However, this is a rather simplistic analysis of human motivation, and while it offers a basic framework, it has attracted a number of criticisms and so should be looked at in conjunction with other models and theories of motivation. Bernard Weiner (1992) suggests that at the very minimum a general theory of motivation should include the following:

- A theory of motivation must be based on general laws rather than individual differences
- A theory of motivation must include the 'self'
- A theory of motivation must include the full range of cognitive processes
- A theory of motivation must include the full range of emotions
- A theory of motivation must include sequential (historical) causal relations
- A theory of motivation must be able to account for achievement strivings and affiliative goals
- A theory of motivation must consider some additional common-sense concepts.

This chapter, while acknowledging that motivation underpins most human behaviour, examines a variety of other influences, including perception and the senses, memory and nostalgia, and fantasy and fiction as stimulants of consumer experiences.

'Needs' or 'wants'?

In contemporary consumer society, while there is no denying that some behaviour is survival oriented, many acts of consumption are based not so much on needs, but on wants. These wants may be induced by past experience, by exposure to information from others, or through the media. If you consider, for example, the power of television, and not just advertising, on your consumption patterns, you may be able to see certain clues and cues that have created awareness of a lifestyle, a certain 'look' or an image that has aroused a sense of desire for a particular product or service. If you consider, for example, the popular television programme *Sex and the City*, you can see the lives and lifestyles of four very different women played out in meticulous detail. The emphasis is on looks, style, careers and romance. The programme is basically a reflection of a society where women want it all, and are not afraid to strive for it: Carrie, the relationship columnist; Miranda, a partner in a law firm; Charlotte, the romantic debutante; and Samantha, the successful public relations executive. All four are looking for love, albeit of a different nature, all are independent, but most significantly, all surround and adorn themselves with the trappings of a successful contemporary lifestyle. Prada handbags, Chanel earrings and Jimmy Choo shoes form the mainstay of their wardrobes. Manolo Blahnik, although extremely successful prior to the series, has become almost iconized thanks to the constant referencing of his shoes as the ultimate accessory. In one scene, Carrie is mugged in an alley for her watch and purse, yet the thing she is most reluctant to give up are her Manolo Blahnik sandals. On the other hand, Samantha, the oldest of the group, talks openly about her botox injections and the 'impulse purchase' of a facial chemical peel. These programmes are not about advertising, but without the brands there would be no believable lifestyle, and as a consequence, anyone unfamiliar with Manolo Blahnik before viewing certainly could not claim to be after watching a whole series.

Another successful phenomenon is one that is dedicated to exposing the nation's lack of imagination and creativity in their fondness for wood-chipped walls and magnolia paint – namely, the home improvement programme. Over the last decade there has been a proliferation of these guides to 'a better home', ranging from do-it-yourself make-overs to total house transformations. Interior designers have become the new media stars as they encourage normally sane individuals to hang hammocks in their living rooms, paint their bedrooms scarlet and black to create a decadent theme, or indulge their fantasies for French rural living by distressing their furniture and painting their walls orange. Their popularity has not only changed attitudes and behaviour towards interior décor, but has also contributed greatly towards the profits of the numerous DIY stores which cater to all aspects of this new consumer obsession. Ikea, the Swedish furniture store, takes the concept of aspirational living one step further in their adverts, which started off encouraging people to 'chuck out their chintz' and progressed to the idea of 'chucking out your partner' if he or she does not complement the newly modernized and streamlined surroundings. However, as tongue in cheek as this may appear, lifestyle shopping is a fundamental part of today's consumer society, which is increasingly fuelled and stimulated by widening communications, Internet access, multi-channel television and specialist publications, to name but a few. This brings into play various forms of stimulation and subsequent reactions.

Perception and the five senses

Perceptual stimulation occurs largely through the five senses of sight, sound, smell, taste and touch. Each of these can be, and are, manipulated to some extent by marketers to create a sense of arousal, curiosity and interest in a particular product or service. As consumers, consider how the following affect you:

- *Sight*. The visual element in communication possibly offers the greatest opportunity for stimulation given the ability to play with colour, shape, size, contrast and distortion.
- *Sound*. Music is probably the most obvious example to provide with regard to the sense of hearing. It can have a positive or negative effect on mood and can be influential in determining such things as the length of stay in a particular retail environment, feelings of relaxation, irritation and the association of a particular image with a product. However, the overemphasis of particular noises or unexpected delays or silences can also stimulate curiosity.

- *Smell*. Smell can be a powerful stimulant, whether pleasant as in the case of perfume or repulsive as with rotten eggs. A common technique used in supermarkets is to deliberately accentuate the smell of baking bread across the store in order to arouse a sense of hunger and want.
- *Taste*. Taste is a sense that can lead to immense pleasure or total disgust. It is also possibly the most powerful of the senses in that it involves a combination of the others. For example, we do not just taste food, we see it, feel it, smell it and even hear it cooking. Naturally enough, however, individual tastes differ. If we consider the Marmite advertisements, the emphasis is on the fact that you will either love it or hate it. Nevertheless, the first step is to get you as the potential consumer to try the product and this can often involve free samples, tasting trials, gourmet evenings and wine tastings.

- *Touch*. Touch can be an immensely sensuous experience. The feel of silk or velvet, for example, may evoke images of luxury, indulgence and even decadence. Consequently, the packaging of certain luxury items can play an important part in communicating the personality of a product. Moreover, a tried and tested sales technique is to get the potential customer to handle the product, to become engaged with it, based on the premise that having done so the likelihood of a sale increases.

Subliminal perception

There is, however, a sixth aspect of perception, and that is subliminal perception, or messages and images that are received by the individual below the level of conscious awareness. One area that has received attention and some criticism in recent years is the use of subliminal, or possibly more accurately, subconscious, manipulation through product placements and celebrity endorsements in high-exposure films. It is probably true to say that when you watch a film your defences are down, you are relaxed and receptive to the images that you see on screen, you are drawn into the unfolding story and may not consciously notice the products that form part of the backdrop to that story. However, there seems to be some evidence of subconscious internalization of these images. For example, in the film *The Horse Whisperer*, starring Robert Redford, an Internet company 'equisearch.com' used product placement to promote their website. Although the name was only shown for a total duration of 30 seconds throughout, subsequent hits to the site more than doubled. Similarly, AOL were linked to the film *You've Got Mail*, the title of which was a direct soundbite used by the company. On a slightly different note, in Spielberg's *Minority Report*, Tom Cruise is pictured in a futuristic 'Gap' store, which provides an association between the label and the star. However, possibly one of the most convincing indicators of the power of product placement is evident in the fact that the 2002 Bond movie attracted over 160 million dollars in marketing support.

Interpretation

It is a commonly held view within psychology that individuals will look for harmony and closure in images, and will actively seek to fill in any gaps. This is largely based on what we expect to see, hear, smell, taste and feel, and also on our need for continuity. Consequently, there are many techniques used in marketing in order to stimulate a sense of curiosity and interest in the consumer. These may include the use of contrast, where a commercial is shot entirely in black and white, with the exception of a single figure shown in colour, as was the case with the Renault advert that featured a little girl in a red coat set against a black and white background, or the placing of advertisements upside down in newspapers in order to engage the viewer and encourage them to find out why. Nonetheless, it must be recognized that perception is selective – that is, as consumers you do not necessarily notice all the details of, for example, the packaging of a product which may include colour, imagery and information. Furthermore, perception and interpretation tend to differ across individuals, which complicates the process of ensuring that the message is transmitted in the manner intended by the communicator.

In addition to this, for certain products, and particularly those linked to identity expression and self concepts, the image expressed in the communication should ideally match that of the intended audience. Perfumes are an obvious illustration of developing brand personalities with a distinct market in mind. Chanel has always sought to embody the ultimate in chic sophistication with its subtle and understated numbers, Chanel No. 5, 9, 19 and so on, minimalistic frills-free bottles and the classic, instantly recognizable, intertwined double C. Yves St Laurent's 'Opium', on the other hand, is meant to convey mystery, seduction, and an illicit and dark side to the wearer's personality.

From a marketing perspective the aim is to ultimately gain a positive response and ensure that the message has a strong appeal to the consumer. Nevertheless, this is not always the case, as the classic example of 'Strand' cigarettes demonstrates.

The advert featured a man standing alone on a bridge smoking a 'Strand' cigarette, with the strapline 'You're never alone with a Strand'. However, this was interpreted as: if you are a loser and you have no friends, console yourself with a Strand. Not necessarily a self concept that most people would want to embrace and project.

The recent ban on cigarette advertising in the UK has highlighted some of the issues concerned with the influences of branding, imagery and the use of celebrities on consumer behaviour. Consider the examples in the past of advertisements which featured film stars, doctors, babies and even the 'health' benefits of cigarettes to promote tobacco. Such adverts may seem laughable in today's society, which is much more media sophisticated and aware, which itself means that communication must be based firmly on a clear understanding of the consumer perceptual process if the message is to be noticed amid the intense competition.

Provocative/offensive advertising as stimulation

It is fair to say that we live in a world of perceptual overload as marketers compete on a daily basis for your, the consumer's, attention. This has seen the rise of

a more provocative form of communication, which Stephen Brown (2001) describes as 'offensive advertising'. He provides numerous examples of advertising campaigns that were deliberately designed to shock. These include French Connection's 'FCUK' (French Connection United Kingdom) strap-line, which featured on billboards proclaiming 'FCUK me', 'FCUK fashion', etc. These adverts had the power to halt traffic and motivate thousands of individuals to write in to complain. However, despite being censored by the Advertising Standards Authority, the campaign helped to double the company's pre-tax profits and propelled them to the cutting edge of cool. Nevertheless, French Connection are by no means the only perpetrators of offensive marketing. Benetton were among the first to upset popular perceptions of what is acceptable with their images of dying Aids victims and prisoners on death row awaiting execution. Others use religion and even disgusting images of bodily fluids to attract attention and stimulate a feeling of revulsion, yet fascination. As consumers, can you deny that there is an irresistible pull towards the illicit, the repulsive or the offensive when it is wantonly displayed daring you to look? To quote from Brown, offensiveness is effective, it stands out in a world where consumers are bombarded by countless messages, most of them safe and sanitized and serious. Essentially it works because:

- It stands out 'from the crowd'
- It is efficient – it necessitates a second look
- It is cheap and often attracts the attention of a news-hungry media, thus generating more free publicity
- It is easily emulated.

In a parody of the 4Ps, Brown (2001) offers a classification of offensive marketing entitled the '4Cs', which differentiates between the various types of offensive communication:

- *Carnal*. This involves sexually explicit or sexploitative campaigns, such as the shirt maker Van Heuston's proposal that 'a man is not a man without fifteen and a half inches to play with'. Or even Pot Noodle's current campaign, which portrays its consumption as something degenerate, disgusting and perverted.
- *Corporeal*. Refers to bodily fluids, faecal matter and unnatural functions. For example, Supernoodles' contention that plates should be licked clean rather than washed.
- *Creedal*. This consists of offences against religious beliefs, illustrated in Benetton's nun kissing priest poster.
- *Cultural*. Images that offend the canons of aesthetic good taste. Stella Artois's campaign which depicted bottles of beer being opened on 'top of the range' durables such as a Gibson semi-acoustic guitar is an example of this.

Of course, there is no suggestion that all advertisements are destined to adopt an offensive stance if they are to fully register in your minds, although the rise in the phenomenon does raise some interesting questions regarding our level of retention and information processing, particularly in relation to what we remember.

Memory

In discussing the perceptual process, it is important to consider the nature of memory and the relationship to perceptual stimulation. As with motivation, there are a number of conceptual descriptions of memory, which range from habit formation and control, Jungian psychoanalytical perspectives of the collective unconscious, to human conditioning associated with the behavioural school. However, the most common interpretation of memory within consumer research is to view it as an information processing mechanism which works on a number of levels.

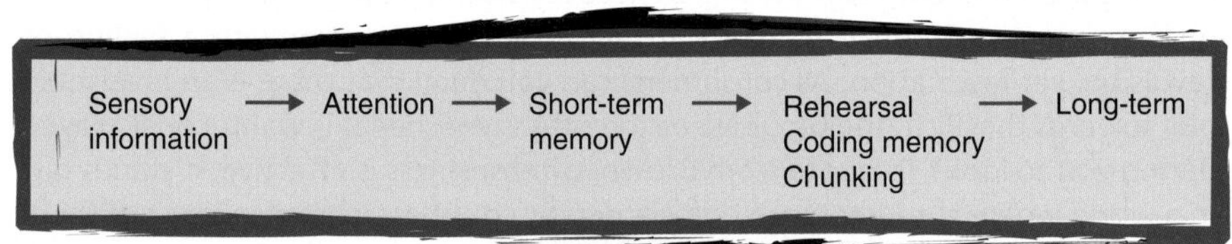

Figure 20 Different levels of memory

The first level involves some sort of sensory input or information which is noticed, but may be dismissed instantly. If the information is of interest it passes through into the short-term memory, which has a limited storage capacity and basically deals with the problem in hand. For example, consider going into a shop to purchase a number of items that you have not written down. You may well mentally repeat the list until you have paid for the items, after which time the information is no longer of any use and may be forgotten. However, should the information be of future value, you will employ techniques such as chunking, which involves breaking down information into manageable units, as you possibly do with telephone numbers, and rehearsal or repetition. This allows the information to pass into the long-term memory, where it is retained and retrieved at a later date.

If you consider the process involved in revising for an exam the stages become clearer. For example, the stimulus may be a textbook which is read and the information temporarily stored in the short-term memory. In order to retain information, notes are taken and synthesized using key words, colours or symbols, which are then re-read and rehearsed, allowing them to register in the long-term memory, hopefully to be retrieved during the exam. Obviously, the aim of marketers is to attract attention through the stimulus induced through their communication, provide information and ensure that consumers retain that information for future action. As we have seen, offensive marketing campaigns are one way of doing this. People certainly remember the images, discuss them and, according to the resulting sales figures, act upon the information. Another aspect of memory that is used to stimulate a desire for products is that of nostalgia.

Nostalgia – a subcategory of memory

Memory and nostalgia differ on one fundamental level. When we look back objectively at certain times or events in our lives, we remember both the good things and the bad associated with that particular period. When, however, we reflect nostalgically, we remember only the positive features. Nostalgia therefore is a kind of filter mechanism that acts as a kind of memory without the pain. The nostalgic reaction can also be stimulated through any one of the senses. The sight of a photograph taken on holiday can instantly transport you back to that time, the unexpected smell of a perfume once worn by someone close can conjure up an image from the past, as can the playing of a particular song. The taste of food associated with childhood can summon up scenes of earlier days, in the same way that handling a possession that holds fond memories can bring to life images of happy times.

It is little wonder, therefore, given the positive nature of nostalgia, that it has been used in marketing to create favourable product images and consumer experiences. These can range from re-inventing popular classics, such as the Volkswagen Beetle, in a new turbo-charged form, whilst still retaining a familiar shape reminiscent of the 'flower power' generation, or Coca-Cola's reintroduction of its classic glass bottle (Brown, 2002), to advertisements such as Levi's small-town 1950s American commercials, which projected an aura of innocence and safety. There are also a number of retail outlets dedicated to presenting an 'olde worlde' image, such as 'Past-Times' and 'Laura Ashley'. In addition, the leisure industry has been quick to recognize the power of the 'untainted' past and acted accordingly. Breweries, for example, have spent millions 'theming' and 'pastizing' hundreds of their public houses, while the heritage industry is busy offering trips back in time to enable visitors to experience anything from Viking settlements to industrial Victorian working towns. However, nostalgia, due to its selective nature, relies heavily on fantasy and to a degree fiction, which are two powerful stimulants for the consumer experience.

Fantasy and fiction as consumer stimulation

Essentially we might characterize consumer experiences and stimulation on the basis of whether individuals are 'cognition', 'novelty', 'sensation' or 'fantasy' seekers (Table 5).

Table 5 Characterization of consumer experiences

Novelty seeking	Safari holidays, latest/alternative fashions, exotic foods
Sensation seeking	Skiing, horror films, paragliding, bike/motor racing
Fantasy seeking	Literature, novels, magazines, romantic films
Cognition seeking	Information-seeking consumers, high interest in advertisements, product evaluation reports

Of course, as complex consumers you may move from one state to another depending upon your situation and context. However, some of you will have a greater or lesser propensity to engage, for example in fantasy or novelty seeking, while others may be more rational and logical. There is a growing view that certain aspects of consumer behaviour are characterized by hedonism, by fantasy and the quest for romance (Campbell, 1987). Indeed, the power of the romantic fantasy as a stimulant is evident across many consumer product offerings and experiences. If we take, for example, the transformation industry, which may include cosmetics, the anti-ageing industry, gyms, the market for health foods and aesthetic cosmetic surgery, all of which hint at the promise of eternal youth, there is some support for the notion that many of us hold close the desire to become a better, more perfect 'other' (Belk, 2001). Much of this, however, is a fantasy, based on a propensity to believe the many testimonials which appear in countless infomercials, detailing stories of balding men whose hair has grown back after applying a miracle lotion, or the before and after pictures of the middle-aged woman whose wrinkles have been dramatically reduced, thanks to the latest technology in skin care. Two elements are prevalent in these cases – promise and hope – two ingredients that are found in abundance in popular magazines, especially those aimed at women, and in popular romantic fiction.

According to Stevens *et al.* (2001) the romantic discourse is important, particularly when advertising to women. An analysis of soap operas, romantic fiction and women's magazines offers a rich source of fantasy and escape that seldom bears any resemblance to the reality of their everyday lives. Indeed, it is often the complete contrast and lack of realism that holds the attraction, allowing them to look, dream and sometimes purchase. The mixture is usually one of showing a different, and better, life whilst at the same time striking a balance between information and entertainment, and practical realism and escape. Russell Belk (2001) distinguishes between different types of consumption fantasies, classifying them as:

- *Hopeful fantasies*. Here individuals engage in fantasies in the hope that they will translate into reality. For example, women who read bridal magazines from an early age in anticipation that one day they will actually be able to consume the products – the dress, reception, hairstyles and so on – depicted in their pages.

- *Hopeless fantasies*. With hopeless fantasies the images shown in magazines may appear totally out of reach of the viewer, evoking in the process more pain than pleasure. This is often the case in beauty magazines, where incredibly thin, flawless models are used to promote products aimed at the average person, whilst being in no way representative of them.
- *Enchanted illusions*. Here readers of, for example, specialty magazines are seeking imagination-inspiring consumption in which they can believe. They read to find out about new things they can want, whether they be based on beauty, sport or health.

Stephen Brown takes a slightly different tack in his analysis of contemporary popular novels, and those of Judith Krantz in particular. Krantz is responsible for the 'sex and shopping' novels *Scruples* (1978) and *Scruples Two* (1992). These are basically raunchy, romantic fiction which charts the rise from rags to riches of an ugly duckling, who of course turns into a beautiful swan, inheriting along the way a fortune that she uses to open a specialty clothes store called 'Scruples'. The books contain the usual mix of highs and lows, misfortunes and fortunes, love and deceit, the obligatory gratuitous sex, and of course a happy ending. However, Brown makes the interesting observation that, although works of popular fiction are routinely dismissed as atrociously written and mindlessly consumed, on closer analysis it is impossible to ignore the pervasiveness of marketing phenomena and consumption behaviours. National brands, such as Coca-Cola, designer labels and famous celebrity names are present within the pages, along with discussions of specialty retail operations and the intricacies of the mail-order business. However, their main appeal is that they offer an insight into the lives and lifestyles of the impossibly rich, which brings us back to the start of the chapter, which discussed images in the media as stimulants. So whether it is the contemporary *Sex in the City* style television programme or the popular novel that is consumed, the mix of fantasy, aspirational lifestyles, hedonic consumption and education in the form of showing the viewer what is possible and how to achieve it, are all significant influences in today's consumer society.

Key terms

- *Perception*. Information gained through the stimulation of the five senses.
- *Subliminal perception*. Messages or images received below the level of conscious awareness.

- *Provocative/offensive advertising*. Images used to attract attention and stimulate a strong response through offending socially accepted norms.
- *Memory*. The process through which we internalize and retain information, from sensory input, short-term retention, coding, rehearsing and chunking, through to long-term memory and later retrieval.
- *Fantasy*. The stimulation of the imagination through the use of images, stories and scenes that result in a temporary escape from reality.

FURTHER READING

Motivation

Weiner, B. (1992) *Human Motivation: Metaphors, Theories and Research*. Sage: London.

Sensations and perception

Singer, J. L. (1993) Experimental studies of ongoing conscious experience. In: *Experimental and Theoretical Studies of Consciousness* (G. R. Bock & J. Marsh, eds), Ciba Foundation Synopsium 174. Wiley: Chichester.

Zucherman, M. (1979) *Sensation Seeking*. Lawrence Erlbaum: Hillsdale, NJ.

Experiences and behaviour

Csikszentmihalyi, M. (1992) *Flow: The Psychology of Happiness*. Rider Press: London.

Hirschman, E. (1984) Experience seeking: a subjectivist perspective on consumption. *Journal of Business Research*, **12** (March), 115–136.

Attracting attention

Brown, S. (2002) FCUK consumer research: on disgust, revulsion and other forms of offensive advertising. *European Advances in Consumer Research*, **5**, 61–65.

Memory

Baddeley, A. (1976) *The Psychology of Memory*. Basic Books: London.

Houston, J. P. (1981) *Fundamentals of Learning and Memory*. Academic Press: New York.

Nostalgia as stimulus

Brown, S. (2001) *Marketing: The Retro Revolution*. Sage: London.

Holbrook, M. B. (1993) Nostalgia and consumption preferences: some emerging patterns of consumer tastes. *Journal of Consumer Research*, **20** (2), 245–256.

Holbrook, M. B. (1998) Rocking the ages. *Journal of Macromarketing*, **18** (Spring), 72–77.

Stern, B. (1992) Historical and personal nostalgia in advertising text: the fin de siecle effect. *Journal of Advertising*, **XXXI** (4, Dec), 11–22.

Role of fantasy as stimulus

Belk, R. (2001) Speciality magazines and flights of fancy: feeding the desire to desire. *European Advances in Consumer Research*, **5**, 197–202.

Scott, L. (2002) Barbie genesis: play, dress and rebellion among her first owners. *Gender, Marketing and Consumer Behaviour*, **6**, 151–166.

Stevens, L., Brown, S. & Maclaran, P. (2001) The joys of text: women's experiential consumption of magazines. *European Advances in Consumer Research*, **5**, 169–173.

The role of consumers

We are all consumers. Unless we go and live on a desert island we cannot avoid the consuming and we all play an important role, or roles, in the marketing process as consumers.

The important thing to note is that the consumer's role is not passive, but active.

The role of the 'prosumer'

Certain aspects of consumers' activities can actually contribute to production, i.e. they play a role in making things as well as consuming them. Traditionally, in marketing, even though one would expect the consumer to occupy a central position, it was generally assumed that a product was something that was produced by the firm and offered to the customer, whose role in the market was then to purchase it (or not) and consume it. A number of writers now take a contrary view of the marketing process whereby products, or 'market offerings', are *co-created* by the firm and the customer/consumer (e.g. Normann & Ramirez, 1993).

This has led to the idea of looking at the consumer as a co-producer that has been applied in marketing through the notion of the 'prosumer', whereby certain production or marketing activities are devolved by suppliers to consumers. A basic example is where some children's toys (and some for adults) are deliberately designed and aimed at engaging the user and stimulating their own entertainment. These might include 'Meccano' kits, which have to be constructed before use, toy soldiers which have to be painted (and imaginatively activated) by the consumer, and self-assembly model railways. At another level, the 'Ikea' phenomenon, which has been so successful in revolutionizing how people shop for furniture, involves the transfer of 'self-service' to the shopper from the retailer, including loading and delivery. In addition, the 'job' of the customer also involves the assembly of the furniture from flat-pack, an operation that would otherwise be performed by the manufacturer.

The consumer's role as part-worker, however, is not confined to the realm of tangible consumption. The recent public obsession with 'reality' television whereby the audience are not only invited to vicariously view the unfolding events, but actively encouraged to determine the outcome and fate of the 'victims' through telephone voting, is a further example of consumer involvement in the production process of their own and others' so-called entertainment.

Four characteristics of services are usually given: intangibility *(as opposed to tangibility of physical goods),* perishability *(cannot be stored) and* heterogeneity *(hard to standardize); it is the fourth characteristic* – inseparability *(or simultaneity) – that more distinctly captures the essence of services. It states that services are partly produced and marketed at the same time by the same people, that the customer is partly involved in the production and delivery process and that the customer partly consumes the service during its production.*
Gummesson, 2000

Some marketing activities have to be 'prosumed' in the sense that they have to be produced and consumed at the same time, together, and the consumer is therefore involved in their production. This is the case notably for most services, which are characterized by 'inseparability' of production, exchange and consumption. For services such as airlines, hairdressers and restaurants, the interaction between the front-line staff and the customer directly affects the perceived quality of service; the service 'experience' can be enhanced not only by the 'service provider' performing well, but also by customer-input factors such as their knowledge, effort and attention.

For advanced economies, services now constitute far more of the national output, labour and value than manufactured products. Some authors have begun to argue that services are so important in marketing that the whole subject should be based on them, not on physical goods. Vargo and Lusch (2004) proposed that a 'new dominant logic' for marketing is emerging based on a service-centred perspective. Their key propositions included that 'all economies are service economies', that 'the enterprise can only make value propositions' and that 'the customer is always the co-producer'. This involves a shift in emphasis from a goods-centred logic that is based on tangible resources, embedded value and exchange transactions to one that focuses on intangible resources, relationships between buyers and sellers, and the *co-creation* of value.

This does not just apply to services, however. A number of writers, such as Normann & Ramirez (1993), take a similar view of the entire value creation process in marketing, whereby value is co-created through interaction between the firm and the customer, not in 'value chains', but in value '*constellations*'. They see consumers playing a key role in value creation, not just firms, and the role of consumption, i.e. the activities, behaviours and motivations that consumers undertake when making decisions and forming perceptions about products and services, is not just to 'use up' or 'deplete' value, but is also more fundamentally one of value creation (see Marketing Contexts: Marketing values).

Needs are in reality the fruits of production.
Galbraith, 1967

Baudrillard (1970) regards consumption, not as the 'mirror' opposite of production, and more than merely an extension, but as an *integrated part of the production process* – and thus consumers as indistinguishable from workers. It is in his analysis of the history of the industrial system that Baudrillard (1998) traces the 'genealogy of consumption' as a socio-economic and epistemic phenomenon:

> The system of needs is the product of the system of production . . . In this way it produces the system of needs, the productive/demand force as a

> rationalized, controlled and integrated whole . . . Needs are nothing but the most advanced form of the rational systemization of production at the individual level, one in which 'consumption' takes up the logical and necessary relay from production.

In addition, for services generally, economic and cultural values are intertwined and, indeed, advertising as a professional service provides a good example of the mutual interconnectedness of cultural and economic values that are both produced *and* consumed during the process (Du Gay, 2001).

Consumer identity

There are various ways in which consumption is related to identity for consumers.

Firstly, there is the economic and social identity, which everyone has as a consumer in the marketplace. When considering making purchases, then buying, using and evaluating them, we become a consumer – we take on a consumer identity. Playing the 'role' of consumer gives us certain expectations about behaviour and confers on us certain rights and responsibilities. We will discuss this aspect in more detail under 'consumer performance' (see later in this chapter).

Secondly, some people use consumption to *display their identity* to others. Such 'conspicuous consumption' behaviour of buying, using, and showing off products and brands can be used to 'say something' about the person's identity (see Brand Selection).

Thirdly, at another level, consumers can be doing more than displaying their identity through products; they can be *creating* their own perceived self by *identifying with* the objects and symbols of their consumption – i.e. 'You are what you consume.'

Displaying identity

Consumer goods are used to signify social status as demonstrated through the choice of a particular selection of goods that classifies the consumer according to various socio-economic hierarchies – such as their wealth, knowledge, social position, taste, refinement. It is not simply the display of the material possessions themselves that is important, nor simply economic capability or the price paid. According to Bourdieu (1984), modern consumption is primarily concerned with the establishment and maintenance of 'distinction' or difference between social classes and status groups. The maintenance of difference thus not only implies a competitive relationship between consumers who perceive themselves to inhabit different groups and identities, but also has the effect of 'bonding' consumers more closely within these subcultures and social communities (see Consumer culture and subcultures). By seeking to align themselves with certain group norms, consumers must share with the others in that group such things as their common consumption ambitions and adopting similar behaviours and lifestyles.

The notion that consumer goods are employed to signify social position and their use by individuals to demonstrate their taste and distinction is not a particularly modern phenomenon. Several classic anthropological studies have shown that the primary function of material culture is not the satisfaction of 'needs' but the role in social rituals and the establishment of social hierarchies both within and between groups (e.g. Mauss, 1966). It was Veblen (1899) who first detailed the modern 'conspicuous consumption' behaviour of the *nouveaux riches*, and the manner in which certain types of goods and services were employed by them as registers of their new social position. The success of early department stores as centres for taste and fashion was largely a consequence of the vast appetite for status symbols among the newly emerging affluent middle class in the nineteenth century (Laermans, 1993).

Creating identity

An important theme within consumer research aims to understand 'the co-constitutive, co-productive ways in which consumers, working with market generated materials, forge a coherent, if diversified and often fragmented sense of self' (Arnould & Thompson, 2005). Consumers are viewed as identity seekers and makers, and it is the marketplace that is the primary source of 'mythic and symbolic resources' through which people construct 'narratives of identity' (Belk, 1988; Holt, 2002).

> *The emotion-laden experiences of the consumer: irrational, incoherent and driven by unconscious desire . . . able to build a* DIY self *through consumption, yet suffering an expansion of inadequacy through adverting.*
> *Elliot, 1999*

For Bauman (1988), individual freedom in modern society takes the form of 'consumer freedom', through which the individual is able to invent and create their own self-identity. People are free to use consumer goods to 'become' any of their 'possible selves'; they can be *creating* their own perceived self by *identifying with* the objects and symbols of their consumption. This is one aspect of human behaviour that 'actor-network theory' (Callon, 1999) deals with from a sociological perspective.

People may identify themselves with objects of consumption in many forms in their everyday life. If 'lifestyle' TV programmes and magazines are to be believed, for many people these are often consumer objects such as their home, possessions, decoration, furniture, clothes, garden, car, and jewellery. Of course, the

most intimate physical manifestation of one's identity is the body and so in this respect are the use of products and services to make it look better and 'improve' one's 'self-image'. Identity is therefore also often related nowadays to body image and thus to the consumption of particular beauty, health care and cosmetic products. People's identities and 'self-esteem' are so closely associated with their bodies that it can strongly motivate their choice of food consumption, diet, sports, fitness, medical and surgical products aimed at affecting or changing their body image.

The body is, after all, the site of *all* consumption. There has been a growth in interest on the part of consumer researchers in the nature of the body, identity and symbolic consumption (e.g. Thompson & Hirschman, 1995), and in particular the role of the '*embodied self*' (Featherstone, 2000; Mauss, 1979/1936), which includes body modification such as cosmetic surgery (Schouten, 1991) and body art (Goulding & Follett, 2001; Velliquette & Bamossy, 2001). The field of body modification provides a wealth of possible case studies for understanding the degree of consumer involvement in the production, creation and consumption of a new, highly visible 'identity'.

Creating identity: the case of tattoos

One popular form of body adornment which has a long and well-documented history is that of tattooing. Perhaps as a consequence of celebrity role models sporting tattoos, and shifts in fashion towards body adornment, including body piercing and tattooing, acquiring a tattoo is now seen as part of contemporary popular culture and is a global multi-billion pound industry (DeMello, 2000). However, the tattoo, the 'object' that is purchased, is unique both in its concept and practice, and has very few comparisons, largely due to the permanency of the act. Whilst information search is a key aspect of many service encounters, the nature of tattooing probably provokes a greater degree of investigation, time and involvement. Tattoos are permanent. They are considered by most recipients to be works of art, to be created by 'artists' upon a canvas, the body. They are both public and private statements about the individual's identity, and, significantly, the act involves an often-extended period of pain and potential risk of infection. This brings into question the role of trust due to the very high risk and high degree of involvement by the consumer.

Goulding & Follett, 2001

For some people, whatever personal problems they may face – whether it is loss of community, lack of self-esteem, unhappiness or boredom – they can be 'solved' by adopting a particular consumer lifestyle and constructing a 'better' self through the products and services associated with it (Elliot & Wattanasuwan, 1998). Some argue that the 'freedom' to construct their identity through consumption is in fact quite limited by the 'structuring influence of the marketplace' and that while consumers can pursue personal goals through the market they are in fact 'enacting and personalizing' from a choice of 'cultural scripts' or lifestyles, many of which are set by marketers (Arnould & Thompson, 2005).

Consumer culture and subcultures

Many contemporary commentators have pointed to marketing as one of the key cultural architects of our time. They suggest that marketing since the 1950s has come to play a significant role in the creation and reproduction of taste, dreams and aspirations (Ewen, 1988), needs (Packard, 1957), selves and identities (Elliot, 1999), desiring consumers (Bauman, 2001), morality (Grafton-Small & Linstead, 1989), materiality and hedonism (Pollay, 1986), and sign systems (Baudrillard, 1981). In today's consumption society, a new and powerful social and professional group has emerged, called 'the new intellectuals' by Featherstone (1991), who are engaged in the production and distribution of symbols, taste and ideal lifestyles, and work within the fields of marketing, advertising, fashion and design. The abundance of marketing messages and signs for which the so-called 'culture industries' are responsible in everyday life may even qualify marketing professionals for carrying the label of the 'ministers of propaganda of the consumer culture'.

Although the power and influence of the marketing profession is undoubtedly very great in creating the cultural language and 'setting the scene' for consumers (Svensson, 2004), one criticism of the argument and observations above is that they *understate the role of the consumer* in determining their own culture. For example, Elliot (1999) pointed out that 'consumers do not passively accept marketing communications but may actively renegotiate the meaning subjectively and construct their own interpretations'. This view of the culturally active consumer has been supported by other studies of 'marketplace' cultures, which according to Arnould & Thompson (2005), 'in contrast to traditional anthological views of people as culture bearers, consumers are seen as culture producers'. Many of these studies use ethnographic methods of research.

Ethnographic studies of consumer cultures

The roots of ethnography lie in cultural anthropology, with its focus on small-scale societies, and the original central concept remains paramount today; that is, a concern with the nature, construction and maintenance of culture. Ethnographers aim to look beyond what people say to understand the shared system of meanings we call 'culture'. Pettigrew (2000) argues that consumption represents a phenomenon that can be effectively addressed with the use of ethnographic techniques, based on the understanding that the social meanings found in material possessions can be viewed as cultural communicators. These include, for example, Arnould & Price's (1993) 'river magic', Hill's (1991) study of homeless women and the meaning of possessions, and Schouten & McAlexander's (1995) longitudinal study of the new 'biker' culture in the US.

Goulding, 1999

Subcultures may be defined as sites of praxis, ideologically, temporally and socially situated where fantasy and experimentation give way to the construction, expression and maintenance of particular consumption identities.
Goulding et al., *2002*

The study of subcultures, their activities, power relations, hierarchies and constitute identities has a long tradition of analysis within the discipline of sociology. In the UK several studies have focused on youth subcultures as a form of resistance to cultural domination (e.g. Hall, 1976) on youth subcultures in Britain, Hebdidge (1979) on the mods of the 1960s). Other authors have regarded music-based youth subcultures as 'the culture industry's commodification of dissent' (Frank & Weiland, 1997).

Beyond 'sites of resistance', subcultures are also a form of consumer culture at the micro level. They are responsible for the creation of micro-markets and the products and services to meet these demands. They have opinion leaders, innovators and imitators of the latest trends in specialized clothing, jewellery and accessories. Examples of contemporary subcultural groupings include heavy metal music fans, gay consumers, motorcycle gangs, white river rafters, skydivers, *Star Trek* followers, the rave music scene, Goths, surfers, freerunners, etc.

Marketing and consumer researchers have more recently begun to focus on the material artefacts and consumption practices that underpin, support and define the very existence of many subcultures and the consumption experiences of those involved. These look at how consumers forge feelings of social solidarity and create self-selected, sometimes transitory and fragmented, (sub)cultural worlds involving the pursuit of common consumption interests. Much of this work is based on Maffesoli's (1996) concept of the 'neo-tribe' (see Cova & Cova, 2002).

The concept of the neo-tribe

Maffesoli (1996) argues that traditional bonds of community between individuals have been eroded and the free market ethos promotes a continual quest for personal autonomy and difference. Consumers, however, find such conditions lonely and alienating; therefore, they form looser groupings of shared interests and engage in joint activities and rituals based on lifestyle choices and leisure pursuits. The neo-tribe provides affectual bonds between people based on leisure activities, cultural pursuits, religion and intellectual interests. The process of feeling emotions together provides an 'emotional glue' that creates a reconnection between people who are otherwise disparate in today's individualistic society. Members are bound together by a process called 'proxemics', which develops from being close to someone because you share the same space/sentiment – surfing, driving the same car. Marketing has recognized these tribes and advertising addresses them directly – and tribes recognize themselves in these messages and images.

Other terms used to describe these are:

- Consumption world
- Subculture of consumption
- Consumption microculture
- Brand community.

Brand communities are groups of consumers who merge together around brands. They are based on some form of product or label that provides a shared meaning and common interest for that group of people. They are essentially an imagined community whereby physically distanced people are united by their attachment to the brand. The members' use of brand is public and visible and serves as a badge that signifies membership within the community of interest.

There a number of themes that emerge from these studies of different consumer subcultures:

- Subcultures provide a platform for the construction of alternative identities.
- Tribal aspects of consumption are pervasive, fostering collective identifications grounded in shared beliefs, meanings, myths, rituals practices and status hierarchies.
- Myth, play and fantasy are important aspects of experiential and 'carnivalesque' consumption.

Brand community
. . . a specialized, non-geographically bound community, based on a structured set of social relationships among admirers of a brand . . . [They] are legitimate forms of community, but communities of a particular stripe, and of their time. These communities may form around any brand but are most likely to form around brands with a strong image, a rich and lengthy history, and threatening competition.
Muniz & O'Guinn, 2001

- Subcultures are made up of diverse groups of people – not gender or class based. It's possible to be a bank manager in the week and a biker at the weekend.
- There are different levels of commitment which reflect the individual's identity.
- People need to escape from their 'everyday life'.
- Subcultures are based around product constellations, places, events and services. Businesses emerge to serve the wants and needs of participants.

Consumer subculture studies

Schouten & McAlexander (1995) – US bikers
Belk & Costa (1998) – mountain men
Miklas & Arnould (1999) – Goths
Kozinets (2001) – Star Trekkies
Goulding et al. *(2001) – dance culture*
Kates (2002) – gay consumers.

In its concern with performance, marketing reveals itself as an inherently dramatistic discipline – it scripts, produces and directs performances for and with consumers and manages the motives consumers attribute to the decision to perform. From this perspective, consumers behave as if they were audiences responding to or participating in performances . . . Consumers may be said to choose products, but they consume performances.
Deighton, 1992

Consumption as performance

In a groundbreaking article, Deighton (1992) pointed out that the word 'performance' often occurs in accounts of consumption, but it is seldom brought into the foreground of the discussion or analysis. He gives examples of several different types of uses:

- Consumers attend performances that are staged for them, such as sports events, music concerts, religious services, theatre, college lectures, circuses.
- Consumers participate in performances that require them to play an active role. In many service markets consumers have to play their part in the 'performance' of the service operation, such as restaurants, weddings, workshops, sales demonstrations (see Grove & Fisk, 1983).
- Consumers perform with products, such as clothes, using them as props in performances which they enact to influence others – and it is the others who actually consume the performance.
- Products perform for consumers as they use them. Detergents perform by cleaning. A product is the 'frozen potential for performance'. The marketer's purpose in designing and delivering the products is to direct their performance well.

In all these examples performance is the core element in the consumption experience. Deighton (1992) suggests that it might be argued that frequently it is performances, not products, that are the objects of consumption. Many consumer transactions involve performances, not possessions. Yet, marketers have in the past tended to study things – products, consumers, adverts, demands, distribution channels – not events (Vargo & Lusch, 2004).

Like other aspects of social interaction, consumption events are improvised around what Schank & Abelson (1977) call 'situational scripts', in which:

- The situation is specified (eating in a restaurant)
- Several players have roles to perform (cook, waiter, customer, cashier, owner)
- The players share an understanding of what is to happen (show to table, give menu, choose items, take order, serve food, eat meal, ask for bill, pay bill, leave tip).

Situational scripts are not subject to much change, nor do they provide the apparatus for handling totally novel situations. Thus a script is a predetermined, stereotyped sequence of actions that defines a well known situation.
Schank & Abelson, 1977

The situational script does not have to be written out word for word; the consumption event is 'scripted' only in the sense that once each 'actor' knows the roles to be played, then they can improvise the performance accordingly. It is a structure that delineates the sequences of events in a particular situation.

The notion of performance is a useful way of looking at consumption because it encompasses and unites many of the concepts inherent within the consumption experience. All performances take place within a setting or on a stage. One of the phenomena associated with consumer communities or subcultures (see subsection above) is that important places are transformed and resignified, and this may apply equally to the 'rendezvous' of mountain men in the USA (Belk & Costa, 1998) or the annual Gothic festival at Whitby, normally a quiet fishing village in NE England. For Goths, Whitby has emotional attachments due to its connection with the Dracula myth, and a perceived authenticity, resulting from the Abbey, which is a tangible reminder of the vampire's arrival in Britain (Goulding *et al*., 2002).

Performances are imbued with certain characteristics. These include a setting or a stage on which the performance takes place, stories or plays with scripts which are acted out, by actors and stars who take on supporting and key roles, props and costumes and the creation of a spectacle.

Performances depend on stories, plays, narratives or myth. The vampire myth is the cornerstone of the Gothic movement and is played out and reconstructed during the festival. However, other leisure-based communities are also often predicated on either 'real' or fictitious myth – for instance, the 'mountain men' (Belk & Costa, 1998), the 'easy rider' myth that feeds the biker culture (Schouten & McAlexander, 1995), or the science fiction-based story that has inspired and seen the *Star Trek* phenomenon develop and grow (Kozinets, 2001). Myths allow for fantasy and escape, which are central to both performance and observation of performance. This performance allows for the construction and enactment of alternative identities through the adoption of temporary roles. Thus, individuals may shed their everyday identities and become 'actors' for a temporary period in time.

Most consumption communities are rooted in material culture, whereby the costumes and accessories that support the performance also serve to differentiate the individual. These props convey meaning and are heavily encoded and symbolic. They act to extend the 'self' (Belk, 1988) and imbue the individual with dramatic persona. Finally, performances involve spectacle and can be acted out in a carnivalesque atmosphere (Bakhtin, 1984) that provides the opportunity to reverse the codes and norms of everyday behaviour.

Implications of viewing consumption as performance

1. *The role of place, space and time in consumer experience is reconceptualized and adds depth to our understanding of temporally and spatially situated consumption (see Moving Space).*
2. *The role of myth, play and fantasy and their role in contemporary consumption (Thompson, 2004) offer insights into the complex nature of fantasy construction and alternative realities.*
3. *The idea of the consumer as 'actor' and leading to a reformulation of the construction of consumer identities, from 'we are what we have' (Belk, 1988) to 'we are what we do' (Deighton, 1992).*
4. *The role of props and the nature of material culture have the potential to strengthen our understanding about the commodification process.*
5. *The modes of symbolic consumption and the relationship between individual, group and object, which links to the ideas of actor-network theory (Latour, 1987; Appadurai, 1986).*
6. *The nature of spectacular consumption (Peñazola, 2000), which appears to be growing in importance as society becomes more insatiable for the novel, the thrilling and experiences that are far removed from the everyday.*

Consumer satisfaction

Satisfaction is closely related to the consumption performance and in a sense follows on from it. Following purchase of the product, service or event the customer will normally evaluate its performance in some way, unless they are completely non-judgemental. In traditional marketing this is what determines the customer's satisfaction, or not.

Most of the theory and measures of customer satisfaction come from services marketing, including the famous SERVQUAL scale for rating service quality. This employs a comparison of customer expectations of service performance with their evaluation of its actual performance to indicate confirmation or disconfirmation of expectations. It is this level of dis/conformation of expectations that is taken as the measure of quality and/or satisfaction.

SERVQUAL rating scale – technique for measuring service quality

- *A multiple-item scale that measures customers' perceptions and expectations so that the size of the gaps can be identified*
- *Based on five criteria: reliability, responsiveness, courtesy, competence and tangibles*
- *Respondents indicate the extent of their agreement/disagreement to a series of statements according to a numerical scale (typically a 1–5 or 1–7 Likart scale).*

Parasuraman et al., 1985

Despite its roots in service quality, it should be noted, however, that the concept of satisfaction is not exactly the same as quality. Strictly, quality is an attribute of the product/service performance and satisfaction is the customer's perceived gratification from their experience of it.

The similarity nowadays of the measures of product/service quality and customer satisfaction has compounded the difficulty in distinguishing the two concepts, especially since the two are often used interchangeably. For example, Holbrook (1999) writes:

> One admires some object or prizes some experience for its capacity to accomplish some goal or perform some function. Such a utilitarian emphasis on the appreciation of instrumentality relates closely to the *concept of satisfaction* based on comparison of performance with expectations and appears to *constitute the essence of what we mean by quality.*

A further confusion is that both quality and satisfaction are related to loyalty and sometimes used synonymously with value (see Marketing Contexts: Marketing values). Another complexity which is noted by Oliver (1997) is that quality is an input to value, but quality is also an input to satisfaction through

customers' comparison of performance to expected quality standards. The essential problem is that all these terms are related to each other and 'embedded in a web of consumption constructs'.

Although consumers may accurately be described as 'satisfied' or 'dissatisfied' with a product or company performance, there is considerable confusion as to the meaning and multiple uses of this and related concepts. The use of the term consumer satisfaction, therefore, should always be treated with caution and in particular the measures employed should be strutinized carefully in order to reveal exactly what the customer is being asked to evaluate. Even when the customers' rating is broken down into key components, their rating of, say, 'how satisfied are you with the delivery service', may be based on various interpretations of 'satisfactory' delivery in terms of different elements of process and/or outcome, which may not be apparent in the questionnaire results, such as on-time delivery, early delivery, order completeness, staff help, ease of packaging, etc.

One of the key points to remember is that both quality and satisfaction are personal judgements about things, events and feelings. Because often it is different 'actors' in the product and consumption performance that are making the evaluation, it is quite possible for the quality ranking of a product or service to diverge significantly from customer satisfaction ratings – for example, in the case of high-quality glassware which nevertheless does not meet the consumers expectations, use requirements nor their aesthetic appreciation. Equally, I am satisfied with the performance of my medium-quality personal computer, which is perfectly adequate for my use of it – and indeed for my ability to use it. An MBA programme may not be rated as high quality, but students are very satisfied with it. These differences are partly due to the fact that quality can be ascribed to a product or service by both producers and consumers, whereas *consumer satisfaction is entirely subjective and evaluated by customers alone*.

> ***Those who are at a disadvantage in exchange relationships where that disadvantage is attributable to characteristics that are largely uncontrollable by them at the time of the transaction.***
> *Andreasen, 1975*

Disadvantaged consumers

Not all consumers are equal – and some are more unequal than others. The voice of the customer is louder for some. Even in the USA and the UK there are many people who are unable to fully participate in the consumer society because they have little discretionary spending or choice. Some of this is due to low incomes; however, consumer disadvantage may take several forms, including lack of access to markets, information and education, availability of finance and credit, exploitative practices of business, and other personal factors such as immobility or illness.

Equally, the problems faced by poor consumers go beyond the resource scarcity and meagre consumption opportunities. From his extensive studies of the poor and the wider 'culture of poverty' in which they are said to exist, Hill (1991, 2002) found that their plight is exacerbated by living in an inescapable consumer culture – for example, by the role of the media, which all too effectively communicates the standards and opportunities for material accumulation in society through television, movies and music, demonstrating the vivid contrast between their culture of poverty and the consumer abundance that surrounds them. Not only are they materially deprived, but they are thus unable to fully participate in the so-called 'semiotic democracy' that Fiske (1987) suggested is provided by television and other mass communications.

A further cause for concern regarding disadvantaged consumers is the role and emphasis of consumption in the process of identity, self-esteem and connectedness to other consumers (see Consumer identity and Consumer culture and subcultures). Consumers who are unable to fully participate in consumer choice are also potentially further handicapped by their exclusion from the symbolic and cultural aspects of consumption.

Of course, marketing itself cannot liberate all consumers from such deprivations. Many of these problems have wider public policy implications. Marketing practices can, however, attempt to alleviate some of the disadvantages faced by the worse off consumers, even in small practical ways by economical quantities and packaging, advice on economical uses, encouragement of healthy eating by retailers. At a strategic level, marketers can adopt corporate social responsibility, the 'triple bottom line', social marketing, business ethics and consumer education policies (see Marketing Contexts: Marketing values).

FURTHER READING

Prosumer co-production

Normann, R. & Ramirez, R. (1993) From value chain to value constellation: designing interactive strategy. *Harvard Business Review*, July/August, 65–77.

Vargo, S. L. & Lusch, R. F. (2004) Evolving to a new dominant logic for marketing. *Journal of Marketing*, **68** (January), 1–17.

Wikström, S. (1996) The customer as a co-producer. *European Journal of Marketing*, **30** (4), 6–19.

Consumer identity

Belk, R. W. (1988) Possessions and the extended sense of self. *Journal of Consumer Research*, **15**, 139–168.

Elliot, R. & Wattanasuwan, K. (1998) Brands as resources for the symbolic construction of identity. *International Journal of Advertising*, **17** (2), 131–144.

Goulding, C., Shankar, A. & Elliot, R. (2002) Working weeks, rave weekends: identity fragmentation and the emergence of new communities. *Consumption, Markets and Culture*, **5** (4), 261–284.

Consumer culture and subcultures

Arnould, E. & Thompson, C. J. (2005) Consumer culture theory: twenty years of research. *Journal of Consumer Research*, **31** (4), 841–849.

Cova, B. & Cova, V. (2002) Tribal marketing: the tribalization of society and its impact on the conduct of marketing. *European Journal of Marketing*, **36** (5/6), 595–620.

Schouten, J. & McAlexander, J. (1995) Subcultures of consumption: an ethnography of the new bikers. *Journal of Consumer Research*, **22** (1), 43–61.

Consumer performance, satisfaction and disadvantage

Deighton, J. (1992) The consumption of performance. *Journal of Consumer Research*, **19** (December), 362–372.

Hill, R. P. (2002) Consumer culture and the culture of poverty: implications for marketing theory and practice. *Marketing Theory*, **2** (3), 273–293.

Oliver, R. (1997) *Satisfaction: A Behavioural Perspective on the Consumer*. McGraw-Hill: New York.

Richins, M. L. (1994) Valuing things: the public and private meanings of possessions. *Journal of Consumer Research*, **21** (3), 522–533.

References

Andreasen, A. (1975) *The Disadvantaged Customer*. The Free Press: New York.

Appadurai, A. (1986) *The Social Life of Things*. Cambridge University Press: Cambridge.

Arnould, E. J. & Price, L. L. (1993) River magic: extraordinary experience and the extended service encounter. *Journal of Consumer Research*, **20** (June), 24–45.

Arnould, E. and Thompson, C. J. (2005) Consumer culture theory: twenty years of research. *Journal of Consumer Research*, **31** (4), 841–849.

Baddeley, A. (1976) *The Psychology of Memory*. Basic Books: London.

Bakhtin, M. (1984/1965) *Rabelais and his World* (H. Iswolsky, trans.). Indiana University Press: Bloomingdale.

Baudrillard, J. (1970) *The Mirror of Production*. Telos Press: St Louis.

Baudrillard, J. (1981) *For a Critique of the Political Economy of the Sign*. Telos Press: St Louis.

Baudrillard. J. (1996) *The System of Objects*. Blackwell Verso.

Baudrillard, J. (1998) *The Consumer Society: Myths and Structures*. Sage: London.

Bauman, Z. (1988) *Freedom.* Open University Press: Milton Keynes.

Bauman, Z. (2001) *Community: seeking safety in an insecure world*. Polity press: London.

Belk, R. W. (1988) Possessions and the extended sense of self. *Journal of Consumer Research*, **15**, 139–168.

Belk, R. W. (1995) Studies in the new consumer behavior. In: *Acknowledging Consumption* (D. Miller, ed.). Routledge: London.

Belk, R. (2001) Speciality magazines and flights of fancy: feeding the desire to desire. *European Advances in Consumer Research*, **5**, 197–202.

Belk, R. & Costa, J. A. (1998) The mountain man myth: a contemporary consuming fantasy. *Journal of Consumer Research*, **25** (December), 218–252.

Benjamin, W. (1936) The work of art in the age of mechanical reproduction. *Zeitschrift fur Socialforschung*, **V**, 1 (H. Zorn, trans.).

Bourdieu, P. (1984) *Distinction: A Social Critique of the Judgement of Taste*. Routledge: London.

Bourdieu, P. (1987) The forms of capital. In: *Handbook for Theory and Research for the Sociology of Education* (J. G. Richardson, ed.). Greenwood Press: New York.

Bourdieu, P. (1994) *Distinction: A Social Critique of the Judgement of Taste*. Routledge: London.

Brown, S. (1998) *Postmodern Marketing 2: Telling Tales*. International Thomson Business Press: London.

Brown, S. (2001) *Marketing: The Retro Revolution*. Sage: London.

Brown, S. (2002) FCUK consumer research: on disgust, revulsion and other forms of offensive advertising. *European Advances in Consumer Research*, **5**, 61–65.

Callon, M. (1999) Actor-network theory – the market test. In: *Actor-Network Theory and After* (J. Law & J. Hassard, eds). Blackwell: Oxford, pp. 181–195.

Campbell, C. (1987) *The Romantic Ethic and the Spirit of Modern Consumerism*. Blackwell: Oxford.

Cova, B. & Cova, V. (2002) Tribal marketing: the tribalization of society and its impact on the conduct of marketing. *European Journal of Marketing*, **36** (5/6), 595–620.

Csikszentmihalyi, M. (1992) *Flow: The Psychology of Happiness*. Rider Press: London.

Deighton, J. (1992) The consumption of performance. *Journal of Consumer Research*, **19** (December), 362–372.

DeMello, M. (2000) *Bodies of Inscription; A Cultural History of the Modern Tattoo Community*. Duke University Press: Durham.

Douglas, M. & Isherwood, B. (1978) *World of Goods*. Allen Lane: London.

Du Gay, P. (2001) *Servicing as Cultural Economy, in Customer Service: Empowerment and Entrapment* (A. Sturdy *et al*., eds). Palgrave: Basingstoke, pp. 200–204.

Elliot, R. (1999) Symbolic meaning. In: *Rethinking Marketing* (D. Brouwnlie *et al*., eds). Sage: London, pp. 112–125.

Elliot, R. & Wattanasuwan, K. (1998) Brands as resources for the symbolic construction of identity. *International Journal of Advertising*, **17** (2), 131–144.

Ewen, S. (1988) *All Consuming Images: The Politics of Style in Contemporary Culture*. Basic Books: New York.

Falk, P. (1994) *The Consuming Body*. Sage: London.

Featherstone, M. (1991) *Consumer Culture and Postmodernism*. Sage: Thousand Oaks, CA.

Featherstone, M. (ed.) (2000) *Body Modification*. Sage: London.

Firat, F. & Dholokia, N. (1998) *Consuming People: From Political Economy to Theatres of Consumption*. Routledge: New York.

Firat, F. A. & Venkatesh, A. (1995) Liberatory postmodernism and the re-enchantment of consumption. *Journal of Consumer Research*, **22** (December), 239–267.

Fiske, J. (1987) *Television Culture*. Routledge: London.

Fiske, J. (1989) *Understanding Popular Culture*. Unwin Hyman: Boston.

Frank, T. & Weiland, M. (eds) (1997) *Commodify Your Dissent: The Business of Culture in the New Guilded Inn*. Norton: New York.

Galbraith, J. K. (1967) *The New Industrial State*. Hamish Hamilton: London.

Gergen, K. (1991) *The Saturated Self: Dilemmas of identity in Contemporary Life*. Basic Books: New York.

Giddens, A. (1991) *Modernity and Self Identity: Self and Society in the Late Modern Age*. Cambridge Polity Press: Cambridge.

Goffman, E. (1959) *The Presentation of Self in Everyday Life*. Doubleday: New York.

Goldman, R. & Papson, S. (1996) *Sign Wars: The Cluttered Landscape of Advertising*. Guildford Press: Surrey.

Goulding, C. (1999) Consumer research, interpretive paradigms and methodological ambiguities. *European Journal of Marketing*, **33** (9–10), 859–873.

Goulding, C. & Follett, J. (2001) Subcultures, women and tattoos: an exploratory study. *Gender Marketing and Consumption* (Association for Consumer Research), **6**, 37–54.

Goulding, C., Shankar, A. & Elliot, R. (2002) Working weeks, rave weekends: identity fragmentation and the emergence of new communities. *Consumption, Markets and Culture*, **5** (4), 261–284.

Grafton-Small, R. & Linstead, S. (1989) Advertisements as artefacts: everyday understanding and the creative consumer. *International Journal of Advertising*, **8** (3), 205–218.

Gronhaug, K. (1999) The sociological basis for marketing. In: *Marketing Theory* (M. Baker, ed.). Thomson Learning: London, p. 111.

Grove, S. J. & Fisk, R. P. (1983) The dramaturgy of service exchange: an analytical framework for services marketing. In: *Emerging Perspectives on Services Marketing* (L. Berry, ed.). American Marketing Association: Chicago, pp. 45–49.

Gummesson, E. (2000) The marketing of services. In: *Marketing Theory* (M. Baker, ed.). Thomson Learning: London, pp. 216–230.

Hall, S. & Jefferson, T. (1975) *Resistance through Rituals: youth sub-cultures in post-war Britain*. Routledge: London.

Hebdidge, D. (1997/1979) Subcultures: the Meaning of style. In: *The Subcultures Reader* (K. Gelder & S. Thornton, eds). Routledge: London.

Hill, R. P. (1991) Homeless women, special possessions, and the meaning of home: an ethnographic case study. *Journal of Consumer Research*, **18** (December), 298–310.

Hill, R. P. (2002) Consumer culture and the culture of poverty: implications for marketing theory and practice. *Marketing Theory*, **2** (3), 273–293.

Hirschman, E. (1984) Experience seeking: a subjectivist perspective on consumption. *Journal of Business Research*, **12** (March), 115–136.

Hirschman, E. C. (2000) *Heroes, Monsters and Messiahs: Movies and Television Shows as the Mythology of American Culture*. Andrew McMeel: Kansas City, MO.

Hirschman, E. C. & Holbrook, M. B. (1982) The experiential aspects of consumption: consumer fantasies, feelings and fun. *Journal of Consumer Research*, **9** (September), 132–140.

Holbrook, M. B. (1993a) Nostalgia and consumption preferences: some emerging patterns of consumer tastes. *Journal of Consumer Research*, **20** (2), 245–256.

Holbrook, M. B. (1993b) On the new nostalgia: 'These Foolish Things' and echoes of the dear departed past. In: *Continuities in Popular Culture: The Present in the Past and the Past in the Present and Future* (R. Browne & R. Ambrossetti, eds). Bowling Green State University Popular Press: Bowling Green, OH.

Holbrook, M. B. (1998) Rocking the ages. *Journal of Macromarketing*, **18** (Spring), 72–77.

Holbrook, M. (ed.) (1999) *Consumer Value*. Routledge: New York.

Holbrook, M. B. & Schindler, R. (1994) Age, sex and attitude toward the past as predictors of consumer's aesthetic tastes for cultural products. *Journal of Marketing Research*, **XXXI** (August), 412–422.

Holt, D. B. (1995) How consumers consume: a typology of consumption practices. *Journal of Consumer Research*, **22** (June), 1–16.

Holt, D. B. (1998) Does cultural capital structure American consumption? *Journal of Consumer Research*, **25** (June), 1–25.

Holt, D. B. (2002) Why do brands cause trouble? A dialectical theory of consumer culture and branding. *Journal of Consumer Research*, **29** (June), 70–90.

Houston, J. P. (1981) *Fundamentals of Learning and Memory*. Academic Press: New York.

Illich, I. (1981) *Shadow Work*. Marion Boyars: Salem, NH.

Kates, S. (2002) The protean quality of subcultural consumption: an ethnographic account of gay consumers. *Journal of Consumer Research*, **29** (3), 383–399.

Kates, S. (2003) Producing and consuming gendered meanings: an interpretation of the Sydney Gay and Lesbian Mardi Gras. *Consumption, Markets and Culture*, **6** (1), 5–22.

Kotler, P. (1967) *Marketing Management: Analysis, Planning and Control*. Prentice-Hall: Englewood Cliffs, NJ.

Kozinets, R. V. (2001) Articulating the meanings of Star Trek's culture of consumption. *Journal of Consumer Research*, **28** (1), 67–88.

Kozinets, R. V. (2002) Can consumers escape the market? Emancipatory illuminations from Burning Man. *Journal of Consumer Research*, **29** (1), 20–38.

Laermans, R. (1993) Learning to consume: early department stores and the shaping of modern consumer culture (1860–1914). *Theory, Culture and Society*, **10**, 79–112.

Latour, B. (1987) *Science in Action: How to Follow Scientists and Engineers Through Society*. Open University Press: Milton Keynes.

Lipovetsky, G. (2003) La société d'hyperconsommation. *Le Débat*, No. 124, (March/April), 74–98.

Maffesoli, M. (1996) *The Time of the Tribes: The Decline of Individualism in Mass Society*. Sage: London.

Mark, M. & Pearson, C. (2001) *The Hero and the Outlaw: Building Extraordinary Brands through the Power of Archetypes*. McGraw-Hill: New York.

Mauss, M. (1966) *The Gift: Forms and Functions of Exchange in Archaic Societies*. Cohen-West.

Mauss, M. (1979/1936) *Body Techniques in Sociology and Psychology* (B. Brewster, trans.). Routledge and Kegan Paul: London.

McRobbie, A. (1995) Recent rhythms of sex and race in popular music. *Media, Culture and Society*, **17** (2), 323–331.

Miklas, S. & Arnould, S. (1999) The extraordinary self: Gothic culture and the construction of the self. *Journal of Marketing Management*, **15** (6), 563–576.

Muggleton, D. (2000) *Inside Subculture: The Postmodern Meaning of Style*. Berg: Oxford.

Muniz, A. & O'Guinn, T. C. (2001) Brand communities. *Journal of Consumer Research*, **27** (March), 412–432.

Normann, R. & Ramirez, R. (1993) From value chain to value constellation: designing interactive strategy. *Harvard Business Review*, July/August, 65–77.

O'Donnell, K. & Wardlow, D. (2002) Fairy tales can come true, it can happen to you: women's transformational myths in an infomercial. *Gender, Marketing and Consumer Behaviour*, **6**, 167–180.

Oliver, R. (1997) *Satisfaction: A Behavioural Perspective on the Consumer*. McGraw-Hill: New York.

Packard, V. (1957) *The Hidden Persuaders*. Penguin: New York.

Parasuraman, A., Zeithaml, V. & Berry, L. (1985) A conceptual model of service quality and its implications for future research. *Journal of Marketing*, **49** (4), 41–50.

Peñaloza, L. (2000) The commodification of the American West: marketers' production of cultural meanings at a trade show. *Journal of Marketing*, **64** (October), 82–109.

Richins, M. L. (1994) Valuing things: the public and private meanings of possessions. *Journal of Consumer Research*, **21** (3), 522–533.

Saussure, F. de (1959) *Course in General Linguistics*. McGraw-Hill: New York.

Schank, R. & Abelson, R. (1977) *Scripts, Plans, Goals, and Understanding: An Inquiry into Human Knowledge Structures*. Lawrence Erlbaum: New Jersey.

Schouten, J. (1991) Selves in transition: symbolic consumption in personal rites of passage and identity reconstruction. *Journal of Consumer Research*, **17** (March), 412–425.

Schouten, J. & McAlexander, J. (1995) Subcultures of consumption: an ethnography of the new bikers. *Journal of Consumer Research*, **22** (1), 43–61.

Schroeder, J. (2003) *Visual Consumption*. Routledge: London.

Scott, L. (2002) Barbie genesis: play, dress and rebellion among her first owners. *Gender, Marketing and Consumer Behaviour*, **6**, 151–166.

Seebaransingh, N., Patterson, M. & O'Malley, L. (2001) Finding ourselves: women, breast augmentation and identity. *Gender, Marketing and Consumption* (Association for Consumer Research), **6**, 15–16.

Singer, J. L. (1993) Experimental studies of ongoing conscious experience. In: *Experimental and Theoretical Studies of Consciousness* (G. R. Bock & J. Marsh, eds), Ciba Foundation Synopsium 174. Wiley: Chichester.

Smith, A. (1961) *The Wealth of Nations* (E. Cannan, ed.). Methuen: London.

Stern, B. (ed.) (1998) *Representing Consumers: Voices, Views and Vision*. Routledge: London.

Stern, B. (1992) Historical and personal nostalgia in advertising text: the fin de siecle effect. *Journal of Advertising*, **XXXI** (4, Dec.), 11–22.

Stevens, L., Brown, S. & Maclaran, P. (2001) The joys of text: women's experiential consumption of magazines. *European Advances in Consumer Research*, **5**, 169–173.

Svensson, P. (2004) *Setting the Marketing Scene; Reality Production in Everyday Marketing Work*. Lund Business Press: Lund.

Thompson, C. J. (2004) Marketplace mythologies and discourses of power. *Journal of Consumer Research*, **31** (June), 162–180.

Thompson, C. & Hirschman, E. (1995) Understanding the socialized body: a poststructuralist analysis of consumer's self conceptions, body images and self care practices. *Journal of Consumer Research*, **32** (September), 139–153.

Unger, D., McConocha, M. & Faier, A. (1991) The use of nostalgia in television advertising: a content analysis. *Journalism Quarterly*, **83** (3), 345–353.

Vargo, S. L. & Lusch, R. F. (2004) Evolving to a new dominant logic for marketing. *Journal of Marketing*, **68** (January), 1–17.

Veblen, T. (1899/1995) *The Theory of The Leisure Class: An Economic Study of Institutions*. Penguin: London.

Velliquette, A. & Bamossy, G. (2001) The role of body adornment and the self reflexive body in life-style cultures and identity. *European Advances in Consumer Research*, **5**, 21.

Walendorf, M. & Arnould, E. J. (1988) My favourite things; a cross-cultural inquiry into object attachment, possessiveness and social linkage. *Journal of Consumer Research*, **14**, 531–547.

Weiner, B. (1992) *Human Motivation: Metaphors, Theories and Research*. Sage: London.

Zucherman, M. (1979) *Sensation Seeking*. Lawrence Erlbaum: Hillsdale, NJ.

creating solutions

Marketing creates solutions by providing products, services and other 'market offerings'. The question is 'solutions to what?' It is market offerings *as solutions* that we are concerned with in this section; how they are created, what problems or opportunities they solve, how to identify them, how to understand them, how marketers organize for them and the consumers' role in solutions. Technology, innovation and new product development provide the basis for solutions to many consumer and marketing problems. Here we explain how information technology, organizational processes and market research help to ensure that the 'voice of the customer' contributes to creating solutions.

Solutions to what?

Marketing creates solutions by providing products, services and other 'market offerings', but then the next question is 'solutions to what?' The traditional marketing answer is to 'customer' needs and wants. This is one type of problem that people seek to solve through marketing. In any market exchange, however, with any market offering, there are *two* sets of problems or needs that are relevant – i.e. those of buyers *and sellers*. Both customers and marketers may have problems which they attempt to solve through the market, one by buying an 'offering', the other by making it available and selling it.

We can view market offerings as solutions to customers' problems or marketers' problems, or both. Banks introduced automated teller machines (ATMs) as a 'solution' to customers' need for 24-hour access to cash and less waiting time. But ATMs also solved the banks' problem of the cost of maintaining staff and facilities in high street and other expensive locations. The introduction of ATMs solved both customers' and marketers' problems.

One type of problem can often lead to another. A customer's need for a new product becomes the marketer's problem to find a solution and provide it. A marketer's problem, such as finding customers for a new product, leads to the customer's problem of hearing about it, understanding its use and considering whether to try it. Of course, in the later case you may say it is less of a problem, more an opportunity for the consumer. But this simply depends on how one looks at it. One customer's opportunity to buy or not to buy may be regarded by another as an evaluation and decision 'problem'; also, one marketer's opportunity to sell may be a sales 'problem' for others. So, problems and opportunities are two sides of the same coin. The term 'problem' is used here to refer to the needs, wants, objectives, targets and requirements that buyers and sellers seek to solve by engaging in an exchange of some market 'offering'.

It is *market offerings as solutions* that we are concerned with in this chapter; how they are created, what problems (or opportunities) they solve, how to identify them, how to understand them, how marketers organize for them and the consumers' role in solutions.

Product solutions

The obvious way in which marketing 'creates solutions' is by making and selling products and services. In marketing we can view products as 'solutions' to customer

The way in which marketing has dealt with the multiple aspects of 'solutions' that can be created for customers is to consider not only physical products and services, but to think in terms of the 'total market offering'. According to this view, the market offering comprises a 'bundle of attributes' that consists of all of its constituent elements, including benefits, services and expectations, the materials used to make it, its 'intangible' attributes, such as service, guarantees, instructions, image, design, reputation and functional features including usability, storage, weight, access, effectiveness, etc., all of which together make up the 'total offering' to customers.

problems or needs. Products do not normally provide these solutions simply by the act of being purchased; it is only by *using* the car or the bread that the consumer's need for transport or food is satisfied. Indeed, more accurately from the customer's point of view, consumption is essentially an *experience*. How well they enjoyed the 'experience' of using it usually determines how satisfied the consumer is with the product. Many purchases now are not primarily physical products at all – insurance, entertainment, education, health. Therefore, the 'objects of consumption' can be viewed very broadly covering, for example, objects, materials, services, people, places, ideas, information – and even images, identities, cultures and myths (see Consuming Experience).

[One definition of the product is] anything that can be offered to a market for attention, acquisition, use or consumption that might satisfy a want or a need. It includes physical objects, services, persons, places, organizations and ideas.
Kotler, 1972

Traditional marketing theory was predicated on the central role of the product in the exchange process and the notion of the 'product concept' as a distinct entity and object of exchange. In the next subsection we explore what is meant by the idea of a 'product' in order to reach greater understanding of the marketing process. It is important to recognize that marketing theory does not, and never has, regarded the product simply as the physical object of exchange and consumption.

In Kotler's view there are five levels of the product (see Figure 21). The *core* benefit is defined as the problem-solving capacity that the customer is buying, e.g. 'the purchaser of a drill is really buying holes'. The *generic* product is the basic version of the tool, beyond which are added the 'attributes that buyers normally expect' of the product, such as in this case leads, plug, instructions of use, etc. The *augmented* product provides additional features that distinguish one producer's offer from competitors' versions of the product, a two-speed drill with multiple settings and anti-vibration casing, for instance. The final level is more abstract, the *potential* which any product represents for future transformation and development – perhaps computerised drill settings or an online drilling solutions service as part of the product package. So, according to the traditional marketing view, the product can be analysed in terms of these constituent elements, including benefits, services and expectations, which together make up the 'total offering' to consumers.

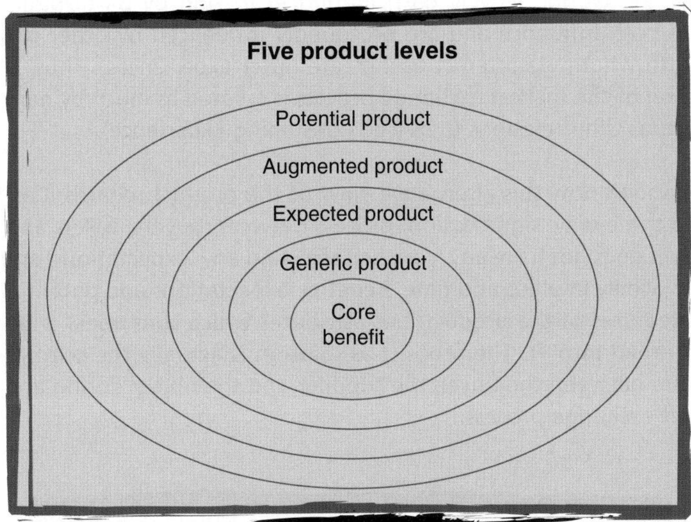

Figure 21 Product levels. *Source*: Kotler (1972)

However, products are consumed for many different attributes, not only their functional properties (see Consuming Experience: What is consumed). Customers do not perceive product value in solely functional, product or any one-dimensional terms. For example, Wilson & Jantrania (1994) separated product-related aspects of value creation from vendor-related types and distinguished economic from non-economic components of value (see Marketing Contexts: Marketing values – Figure 6).

The field of 'relationship marketing' (see Building Relations) also recognizes that the market exchange process involves much more than the basic exchange of products for money in order to satisfy the parties' needs. Market exchange of products takes place in the context of and encompasses wider social and business relationships and networks. Therefore, the product concept should not be regarded as a separate entity, as 'the object of exchange', which can be broken down into its 'five level' parts.

According to this *relational* view, the product cannot be separated in this fashion from its customer–supplier context and treated as a separate entity that can be deconstructed and understood in terms of its basic elements. On the

contrary, the *product itself cannot be separated* from the relationships between the three actors in the market exchange process – i.e. buyers, suppliers and the material objects involved.

The reason for this interlinking of products and people is that people are not distant observers of the world separated by an invisible glass window from other people and material objects. So consumers and producers are not disconnected from the world of objects and products 'out there'. On the contrary, we all exist as part of the world, actively participating *in it*. And by participating in the world, we both influence and are profoundly influenced by other people and objects with whom we interact and create 'inter-experiences'. Thus, the social construction of the market exchange process is created as much by our relations to products as their relations to us (see Consuming Experience).

Figure 22 shows how this alternative view of the product regards it as the outcome of a three-way 'signification' process between buyers, sellers and objects. The product does not have any 'core benefit', and any 'expectations' and 'potential' differ widely in place and time. Benefits, expectations and potential are not inherent features of the product, but attributes which consumers and suppliers ascribe or 'read into' it. The product-as-solution is actually the *outcome* of the relationship between the buyer, the supplier and the object during and beyond the market exchange process.

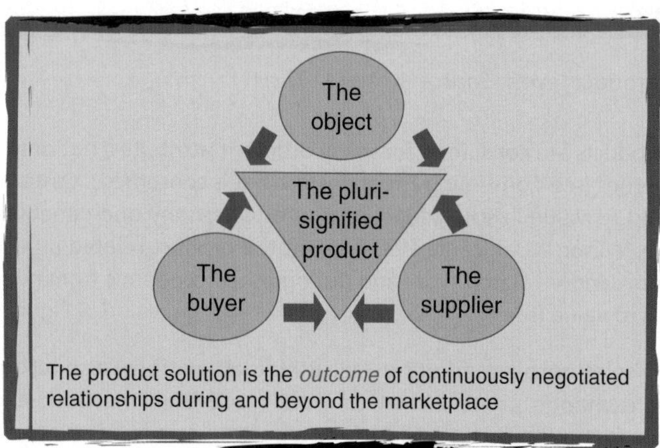

Figure 22 The 'signified' nature of the product. *Source*: Saren & Tzokas (1998)

So products do not remain the same, for different parties involved, during their lifetime. According to the product life cycle (PLC) theory, which plots sales of a product over its lifetime, typically products develop through four stages in their life – introduction, growth, maturity and decline (see Figure 23). During their life they adapt, are improved, developed and spread more widely amongst consumers.

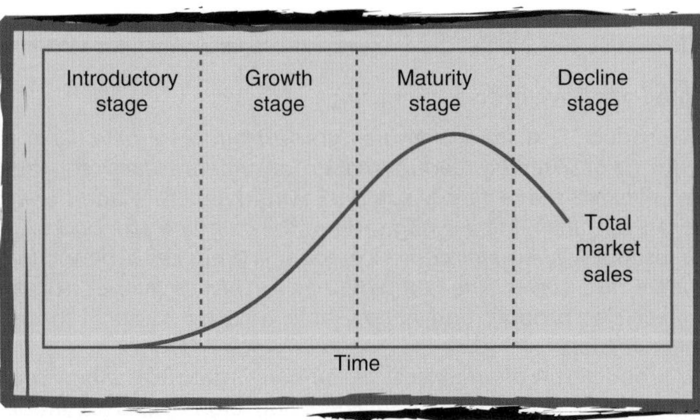

Figure 23 Product life cycle

All industries were once growth industries . . . The history of every dead and dying growth industry shows a self-deceiving cycle of bountiful expansion and undetected decay.
Levitt, 1960

Products are constantly changing as producers adapt and develop them (product innovations), find better ways of producing them (process innovations), and as different consumers use them in different ways and view them in different ways (re-signification). Take a product like Scotch whisky, at the mature stage of the PLC. In Britain sales of the traditional spirit are falling, as it is viewed by some young people as 'an older person's drink'. In other parts of the world, such as Spain, Japan and South Africa, it is fashionable amongst all groups of drinkers. Manufacturers of whisky cannot alter the basic component, but are constantly searching for new packaging, labelling, advertising 'innovations', in order to influence the way in which potential and existing customers view the product – i.e. 're-signify it' (see Brand Selection).

Are diamonds forever? The PLC suggests all products eventually die. *Why do products die?* Usually for one or a mixture of the following reasons:

1 Technological advances leading to obsolescence
2 Competition
3 Consumer tastes change
4 Supply of material limited
5 Government regulation.

Markets therefore require a constant supply of new products in order to replace dying ones and to cater for new needs of customers and suppliers. The degree of 'newness' can vary enormously, however, and the term 'new product' is applied to mean very different things.

New products have different meanings of 'new'

- New product 1. *A snack manufacturer introduces a new, larger pack size for its best-selling savoury snack. Consumer research for the company revealed that a family-size pack would generate additional sales without cannibalizing existing sales of the standard size pack.*
- New product 2. *An electronics company introduces a new miniature compact disc player. The company has further developed its existing compact disc product and is now able to offer a much lighter and smaller version.*
- New product 3. *A pharmaceutical company introduces a new prescription drug for ulcer treatment. Following eight years of laboratory research and three years of clinical trials, the company has recently received approval from the government's medical authorities to launch its new ulcer drug.*

Based on examples from Trott (2005)

In order to clarify the multiple uses of the term, one method of classifying new products is by the degrees of newness to the market and newness of the product (Ansoff, 1979). Booz, Allen & Hamilton (1982) divide new products into six convenient categories:

- 'New to the world' products
- New product lines (new to the firm)
- Additions to existing lines
- Improvements and revisions to existing products
- Cost reductions
- Repositionings.

As we noted above, there are always two types of problems being solved with a product offering in a market, those of consumer and producer. Firms need new products too and they face enormous costs and effort in order to develop and market them; all the more so the more 'new to the world' the product. The manufacturing issues in adding new product improvements or achieving cost reductions can also be considerable (e.g. R&D costs in aerospace and pharmaceuticals industries). It follows therefore that firms and the business literature tend to adopt a classification of new products which reflects the needs and solutions of the suppliers.

The new product development (NPD) process is normally viewed as comprising a series of activity or decision 'stages' as follows:

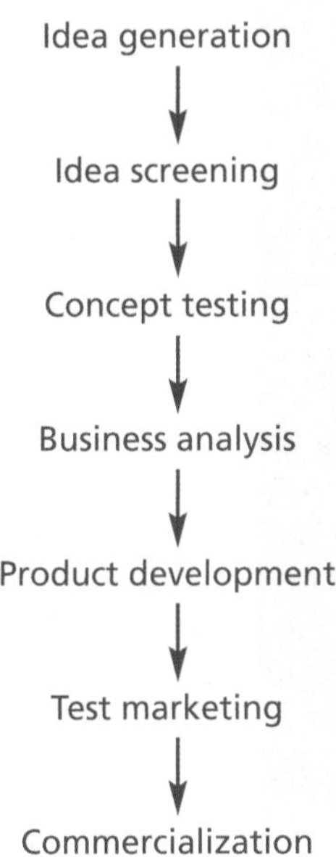

This type of linear 'stages' approach to NPD has been criticized for not accurately reflecting firms' existing practices or the ideal methods. In particular, it does not allow for, nor illustrate, the following five features which often occur during the NPD process:

1. *Recursive processes* – going back and repeating an activity again.
2. *Simultaneous processes* – conducting two or more stages at the same time.
3. *More attention to early stages* – focusing on the initial stimulus, motivation and idea selection.
4. *External activities* – elements conducted outside the firm or with partners.
5. *Technical and organizational variations* – firm-specific processes and behaviour.

Because the creation of new products is such a major issue for companies, it is entirely logical that the models of the NPD process, whatever sequence they follow, tend to focus on corporate activities, decisions and processes. They help companies to plan and organize their NPD, to identify R&D requirements and the role of technology in developing new product solutions (see 'The role of technology' section below). What they need also is to also take a products-as-solutions approach *from the customers' perspective*, i.e. to build in the links at each stage to customer problems and the corresponding customer information required in order to develop solutions. The aim should be to permit the 'voice of the customer'

to be introduced at key points in the NPD process (Griffin & Hauser, 1995).

Even the conventional categories of product newness fail to take a products-as-solutions approach from the customers' perspective. In the Booz, Allen & Hamilton classification of newness of products above, for example, it is clear that these are predominantly producer issues that are addressed – new lines, additions to lines, cost reductions – with only repositioning being a market issue, and primarily one for the marketer. Although this classification may help point to new product requirements for the company's portfolio, it does not clarify the priorities for the development of new product solutions to customer, as well as producer, problems.

In order to apply the product-as-solution perspective from the consumer point of view, then the key question to ask is 'what are the customer problems being solved' by new products and how can these best be categorized? In order to answer this question, the marketer has to understand the nature of the customer problems, to access and 'listen to' the voice of the customer, and to ensure that such information and knowledge drives the innovation structure and not the other way round (see Information for innovative solutions).

The role of technology

Technology provides the basis for solutions to many consumer and marketing problems. It is used to develop new and improved products, better services, production and delivery methods, and information systems (see Information technology and innovation). Few of these solutions involve great advances in new technologies, however. Many do not require any 'new' technology at all, but new products and solutions are created by *combining* existing, 'tried and tested' technologies *in new ways*. Even 'low-tech' products (beer, wine) can be manufactured better applying high-tech methods and 'no-tech' services (hairdressing) utilize technology to improve support materials (e.g. colouring).

We are often told that technological change is accelerating, but not all products or markets are based on 'high-tech' solutions. Some industries face a problem of lack of innovation. This can be either because, like steel, fibres and petrochemicals, they have reached a point of technological maturity or where they have achieved market saturation with few opportunities for growth or only replacement demand, such as automobiles, white goods, TV, radio.

These circumstances encourage firms to restrict their innovation to incremental improvements in the same core technologies. They are unlikely to be able to justify major technological solutions unless perhaps they can adapt new developments from outside their industry and apply it to their product solutions without the major R&D investment costs and time scale. This, however, requires managers to have the ability to monitor their external environment widely enough to spot technological opportunities, having the ability to visualize their application in their own business and having the organizational skills to adapt the technologies and bring them to fruition.

It is in these tasks that technology and marketing need to combine in order to create market solutions. In the BBC 2005 Reith lectures, Professor Lord Alex Broers, of the Royal Society of Engineers, argued that technology companies should be led by marketers, 'those who understand what customers want' (BBC Radio 4, 2005).

Ideas about marketing and technology do not fit easily together in most enterprises. Organizing and planning marketing operations assumes that markets are predictable and there exists a set of carefully defined ambitions for the company, normally called 'strategy'. Technological change does not fit comfortably within such a framework – it is unpredictable and can arrive with stunning speed from fields far outside managers' or companies' expertise.

Furthermore, technology is usually described and evaluated from a purely technical perspective, which only specialists have the knowledge and language to understand, and it is regarded as the responsibility of R&D specialists in laboratories. The potential offered by a technology and the implications for the company, its products and its customers is less easily demonstrated, understood and implemented than for other marketing opportunities – exporting, new distributors, advertising.

Technology by itself is rarely a solution. The NPD and innovation field is full of examples of new products that employed exotic technology but failed to achieve customer acceptance.
Wind & Mahajan, 1997

So technologies are required to develop new solutions and better market offerings, often through new product development, but technology does not fit easily into marketing planning or strategic thinking.

In examining the failure of technology-based products, one of the major reasons seems to be the pioneers' failure to recognize the importance of the social and economic context of the innovation. People do not buy technology, they buy products and services that deliver specific benefits and solve certain problems. The technology is the facilitator that enables the development of the products and services and helps shape customers' needs and wants.

Therefore, understanding the social, cultural and economic context in which consumers will use the technology – i.e. how it will be bought, transported,

stored, consumed and discarded – is critical to the design of effective new products and services.

Defining technology application areas

- What: *the application or need to be solved*
- How: *the technology required and its potential*
- Who: *the customer to be served and their perceptions of the technology.*

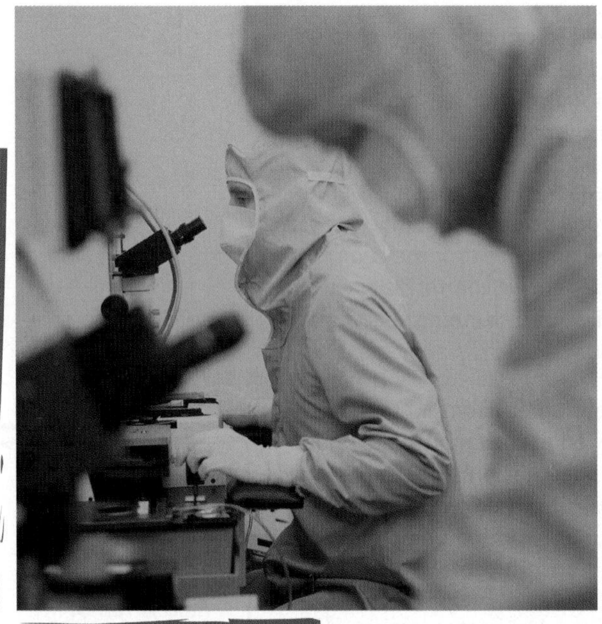

For example, when a new technology-based product (video phone) is being developed, the market research should seek to ascertain not only 'what the demand is', 'how many units will be sold', but more fundamentally how the *consumer* 'understands' the technological function of the video phone. By analysing common perceptions of how certain technologies work, companies will be able to direct their NPD efforts with a deeper knowledge of how the customer really understands the technology involved. This may appear unnecessary at the development stage – or even at any stage! How many car drivers understand the technological workings of the vehicle? How many computer users understand the technology involved? The answer is not that the consumer must or should fully understand the technology, but to find how then they perceive it to work, which helps design it into products in order to make it easier for customers to see the benefits and make full use of it. This will help both the functional design aspects and the eventual communication of the innovation to customers, both of which have been found to critically affect the rate of acceptance or 'diffusion' of new products in the market (Rogers, 1962).

For instance, no study has addressed what the consumer believes is happening, stage by stage, when they give their credit card details to an Internet service provider. How do they imagine the information is stored? Who do they believe processes the transaction? What do they visualize when they hear the terms 'secure site' or 'database'? Internet service providers have become a multibillion dollar industry, yet take-up on using credit cards over the Internet has remained low.

If they found out how the consumer envisages the operation of the technology then the Internet marketing firm would in a better position to develop service and technical innovations that fit with the consumer's conceptualization of a system that they do not necessarily understand technically. They would also be better able to develop effective marketing communications to directly address any customer's concerns about security, reliability and quality with regard to their system.

One way in which consumers try to understand the working of technologies that they don't understand is through visualization and metaphors to 'picture' it (Schroeder, 2002; Sherry, 2000). We know that it is more than the technical functions of products that consumers use and that the symbolic meanings they ascribe are important (see Consuming Experience: What is consumed?). So, even the technical functions of products themselves are also often understood and expressed by consumers in terms of the symbolic and 'imagery' – e.g. 'building' a website', 'surfing' the Internet.

These metaphors and images are used and new ones developed by suppliers for the communication of technology to consumers, using terms such as 'the marriage of TV and communications', 'lovable networks' and 'electronic highway' (Dobers & Strannegard, 2001).

FURTHER READING

Braun, E. (1998) *Technology in Context, Technology Assessment for Managers.* Routledge: London.

Ford, D. & Saren, M. (2001) *Marketing and Managing Technology*. International Thomson Business Press.

Griffin, A. & Hauser, J. (1995) The voice of the customer. In: *New Product Development: A Reader* (S. Hart, ed.). Dryden Press, Chap. 13.

Hart, S. (ed.) (1995) *New Product Development: A Reader*. Dryden Press.

Hisrich, R. & Peters, M. (1992) *Marketing Decisions for New and Mature Products*, 2nd edn. Maxwell Macmillan.

MacKenzie D. & Wajcman, J. (eds) (1999) *The Social Shaping of Technology*, 2nd edn. Open University Press: Buckingham.

Sherry, J. (2000) Place, technology and representation. *Journal of Consumer Research*, **27** (2), 273–278.

Twiss, B. (1992) *Managing Technological Innovation*, 4th edn. Pitman: London.

Information technology and innovation

Mairead Brady

Introduction

Developments in technology, particularly since 1980, have affected the information-gathering process for marketing and innovation. Information technology has revolutionized the data-gathering processes and possibilities, enabling firms to capture, analyse and distribute market information more rapidly, more widely and more economically. It also enables solutions to be designed for, and in some cases by, individual customers themselves (see Consuming Experience). This chapter outlines the roles and applications of information technology (IT) for creating innovative solutions.

What is information technology?

There are many different perspectives, or aspects, to IT. There have been definitional issues with IT since Leavitt & Whisler (1985) first introduced the term.

Various perspectives include:

> ***Information systems do not deliver benefits, but can only facilitate improved business performance if used in the proper manner.***
> *Ward* et al., *1996*

1 IT as a social construction
2 IT as an information provider
3 IT infrastructure – hardware and software
4 IT as business processes and systems.

With respect to the social construction of IT, individuals, due to their levels of knowledge, have their own views and definitions (MacKenzie & Wajcman, 1999; Koppes *et al.*, 1991), depending on the purpose of the definition (Braun, 1998) and their subjective vantage point (Hitt & Brynjolfsson, 1996).

For the purpose of this chapter, IT is viewed as a collective term for a wide range of software, hardware, telecommunications and information management techniques, applications and devices (Leavitt & Whisler, 1985; Porter & Millar, 1985; Willcocks, 1996). Marketers should not be looking at the technology itself, or at IT spend, but on better management of IT and improved IT skills in order to reap the benefits from IT.

The focus on IT must be on the human element of IT, how people use the outputs of IT and how they contribute to the inputs to IT (Bloomfield *et al.*, 1994; Davenport, 1994, 1997). This is of particular importance in the marketing department, as this is a people-based department. People are different and it is people that will make the difference. They are adaptive and flexible, while IT is static.

The use of information technology to its full potential means using human beings to their full potential.
Walsham, 1993

IT and marketing

This is the dawning of a new era for marketers, who are only slowly embracing and utilizing a wide range of ITs in marketing. Marketers have not yet exploited the IT available and yet a range of new and potentially more innovative and useful ITs are on the horizon. Marketing is only at the embryonic stage of exploiting many of the ITs available. Most commentators have assumed that marketing practice has been rocked by major IT innovations and that IT in marketing has transformed marketing practice. The reality is that empirical research has shown that marketing practitioners have struggled to embrace IT applications (Brady *et al.*, 2002; Leverick *et al.*, 1997; Bruce *et al.*, 1996). There are many reasons why many of the ITs are only slowly developing or being utilized within marketing practice. Marketing has been the slowest of the management functions to embrace IT internally and externally marketers are waiting for the diffusion of technology through the population.

Of all the management disciplines, marketing is the one where human emotions, values and personal goals all interact together in the most heady brew.
Holtham, 1994

Within marketing, there have been limited attempts to classify ITs (see Brady *et al.*, 2002). The major difficulty is that there are hundreds of IT applications and a myriad of Internet- and telecommunication-based IT applications targeted at marketing, which could be classed as IT usage in marketing (see Holtham, 1994; Leverick *et al.*, 1997; Marchall, 1996). The sheer range of IT systems and software that can be classed as IT usage in marketing is extensive. There are over 200 software products targeted at marketing and sales. For the purpose of this chapter we will use an adaptation of the Brady *et al.* table (Table 6) in order to highlight the innovations from an interactions perspective.

Information managers must begin thinking about how people use information, not how people use machines.
Davenport, 1994

Even though Table 6 does categorize and list the main ITs currently available, there is no full and distinct list of marketing-related ITs. There are two main orientations of the numerous ITs in marketing and they can be classified in relation to their dominant focus as follows:

- *Information* – focuses include research, analysis and planning (see Moving Space).
- *Interactions* – focuses include communications and connections (see Building Relations).

Table 6 Contemporary marketing practice and information technology component

Information (research, analysis and planning)	Interactions (communications and connections)
Analysis and planning	***Communications***
Marketing planning systems	Internet
Marketing modelling	Website design packages
Executive support systems	– Website security
Decision support systems	– Interactive website applications
ERP (enterprise resource planning)	– E-commerce applications
Knowledge management systems	Intranets
Pricing software	Extranets
Project management software	Electronic data interchange (EDI)
Promotion tracking software	Email
Media spend analysis packages	Video conferencing
Logistics systems	Call centre
Geographical information systems	CATI
Customer profitability analysis	Automatic call distribution
PRISM clusters – databases	Computer telephony integration
Forecasting software	Helplines
Performance tracking software	Voice mail
Databases	Spam blocking systems
Centralized customer database	Voice-activated software
– Integrated with sales	Mobile communication devices
– Integrated with call centre	Computer links with suppliers
– Integrated with Internet	Computer links with customers
– Integrated with point of sale	Self-service technologies
Data consolidation and display	– Integrated TV and Internet: TiVo
Data mining	– Internet technology
Data warehousing	***ATMs***
Data visualization and analysis packages	Vending machines
GQL – Graphical Query Language	Hand-held scanners
SQL	Biometrics
Data profiling	Mobile phones
Research	Sales related
Internet	Customer relationship management
Marketing information systems	Sales force automation packages
Data analysis packages	
Geographic information systems	**Mobile phones**
Demographic online systems	Laptops

(Continued)

Table 6 (*Continued*)

Information (research, analysis and planning)	Interactions (communications and connections)
Internet survey – design and application	Networked computers
Online mailing lists	Telemarketing
Web analytical technologies	Customized sales force systems
Monitoring and tracking software	Point-of-sale information systems
Nielsen information database	Customer applications
Customer relationship management	***Point of sales***
CRM software	EPOS
Customized front-office and back-office systems	Production technology – customization
Marketing evaluation software	
Contact management software	
EPOS	
Planagram, spaceman category management	
Personalization/customizations	
Bar codes – scanning	

Source: adapted from Brady *et al*. (2002).

Of course, it is not so clear-cut and well defined as the table suggests and there are ITs which can and do overlap between the two. So an IT can be predominantly for communication but can supply information for research and analysis.

There are three major issues.

Firstly, many marketing ITs are not specific to the marketing department. So, though consumers may consider that the IT they are utilizing is a marketing IT, this may not be so. Two examples of this clearly indicate the difficulties in this area:

- The ATM machine we utilize was designed to suit the abilities and specification requirements of the IT department, with little or no input from the marketing department. Research has shown that this is often the reality within companies (Scarbrough, 1998).
- The killer application for the mobile phone is text messaging, with several million text messages being sent daily in the UK alone. This application was not designed or even noticed by marketers when they first launched the mobile phone. This application was developed as an internal communication line between engineers!

Secondly, many ITs are industry specific. If we take the example of scanner technology, this is only applicable to products with bar codes. Or we can look at shelf space technology (see Moving Space) and note that again this is industry specific. Other software needs to be customized for companies. All companies are unique and customization of software for the marketing department was very popular during the 1980s and 1990s and remains so.

Thirdly, legacy systems are a major issue within companies. Many businesses have legacy databases dating back to the 1970s which had a dominant finance and/or production focus. These systems are now being utilized by marketing with varying degrees of success.

Consumer interactions – consumer awareness of ITs

Within the range of ITs available to the consumer, some are very visible (like the Internet) while others, though hidden, are part of the consumers' understanding of IT in marketing (like the database) and others are completely hidden from the consumer (forecasting software). Many of the more information-based IT applications could not operate without consumer input, though consumers are generally not aware of them (see Moving Space), particularly many of the tracking, monitoring and surveillance systems. Many of the interaction ITs are ones that consumers engage with. Of interest in this chapter are the self-service technologies and external communication and connection IT-based applications. The many challenges facing marketers in assimilation information-based IT are documented in the Moving Space section. From an interactions perspective we will look at some of the major innovations in this area and the diffusion of innovation model, utilizing the mobile phone as a core example. Much of the information in the following subsection will date. In 50 years time people will laugh at much of this discussion and review. As Barnes (1993) observed, technology is expected, accepted and disposable, so most consumers will not think twice about many of the issues we are discussing here.

Exploiting innovation – the diffusion of innovation

If we look at the mobile phone and diffusion of that technology, we can see clearly that it is only in the period 2001–2002 where the late majority was reached and SMS and other marketing usage could effectively and efficiently commence. Despite much of the hype about new technologies we must be aware of the diffusion process for technological innovations (see Figure 24).

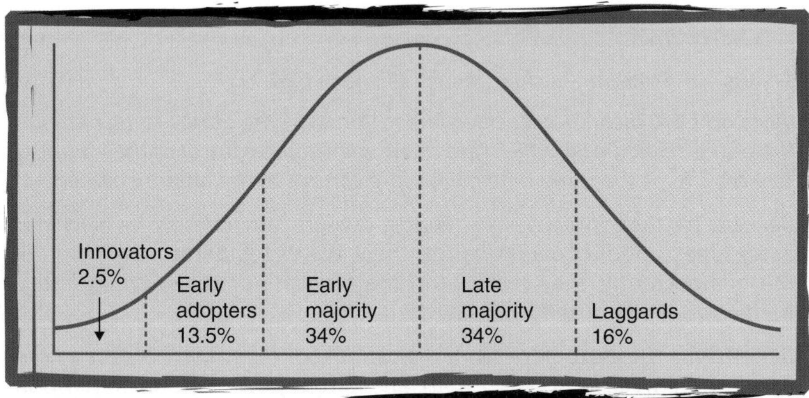

Figure 24 The diffusion of innovations. *Source*: Rogers (1983)

Software is increasingly determining the nature of the experiences customers, employees, partners and investors have with a company, its products and services and its operations. Therefore positive software-mediated experiences are critical for retaining customers, motivating employees, collaborating effectively with partners and communicating with investors.
Prahalad & Krishnan, 1999

Consumer perceptions of innovations in IT

Though marketers talk of innovations in IT as very positive developments, many consumer reactions are not so positive. In some ways innovations in marketing and information technology have resulted in new challenges for consumers and marketers. McKenna (1999; www.mckenna-group.com) noted that: 'The cold impersonal sameness of technology and the high-touch human uniqueness of marketing seem eternally at odds.'

The use of IT by practitioners can have a myriad of impacts on customers. Some customers will view an IT as a relationship marketing device, while others will consider it an insult to them and as a negative development. This links to the concept of the mismatch of customer and company perspectives of the relationship.

The consumer perspective – self-service technologies

Consumers often want 'right here, right now, tailored to me, given to me the way I want IT' and sometimes the only way to do this is through IT! In many ways companies can be seen to be utilizing IT to let the consumer satisfy themselves better. But for all the benefits, are self-services technologies better for the consumer? A recent study into self-service technologies was carried out by Meuter *et al*. (2000).

There is a trade-off for the consumer who self-serves. Rather than the company providing an employee to service consumer requirements, consumers now can

E-Suds – the simple washing machines goes high tech

IBM and USA Technologies have joined forces in the States to test market the e-suds technology, which gives consumers more control of their laundry services and at the same time gives more control to the laundry owners.

Benefits for the company – the laundry owners can monitor the machines at all times, conduct maintenance, check water temperature and so on. More importantly, they can control the purchase of the washing detergent and softener used by the customer.

Benefits for the customer – from the comfort of their own home they can monitor their washing rather than having to wait for each cycle to finish (Power, 2002).

Q. Can you think of any negative aspects to this service?
A. *Going to the laundry can be a very social process.*

do this themselves. So consumers can be seen as virtually an unsalaried staff member for the company. Think about Internet banking, booking a holiday online, self-scanners in supermarkets or ATM machines. In all these examples, you the consumer do the work. Think of the stages in the online booking of a holiday. The barriers and the benefits to online shopping have been well articulated in both the academic and business press. One view must be how to capture some of the particular shopping aspects online. How does online shopping cope with squeezing of the pan of bread to check that it is fresh? Or how does it cope with impulse shopping, a crucial part of shopping from both the company's and the customer's perspective?

Many services have added an online or self-service provision. Some examples are:

- Delivery services which allow for tracking of parcels by consumers (see, for example, www.FedEx.com and www.UPS.com)
- Online airline ticket booking (see, for example, www.ryanair.ie) which enables online booking of flights
- Online banking (see, for example, www.aib.ie).

The big worry from the consumer perspective is that the use of technology means a lack of service, no human interaction, that their every action is tracked and that ultimately the technology that was supposed to provide freedom just adds more restrictions and greater control.

Also, humans are humans and all the technology in the world does not necessarily change behaviour. As Henry (2000) states:

> Learning drawn from the understanding of human need for intimate social interaction, group acceptance and conformity to group norms . . . question the viability of groups of virtual communities and a significant expansion in the range of media programming content.

Solutions through IT – innovations through IT

Enhanced production technology – the customization option: made to order not to sell

A major innovation which can be operationalized for a mass market is the development of production technology in the product area, which relates to the make to order or make to sell concept. Through the availability and use of information systems and changing consumer expectations, companies can now make to order rather than to sell. Gone are the days of inventories and stockpiling. Do you remember car parks full of new cars at airports waiting for sales to occur? The policy now is to wait until the consumer orders and then start to manufacture. Enhanced margins through customization, modularity, intelligence and organization have developed from this technology (Venkatraman & Henderson, 1998). A good example of this has to be the Dell Computers business model (see www.Dell.com).

The advantage for the customer is the perceived customization. You can choose the colour of your car (from a defined range), you can choose interior colours, etc. (see www.volkswagen.com). There is some level of what Prahalad & Ramaswamy (2000) refer to as co-creating and personalization of the experience, encouraging choice and flexibility (see Consuming Experience).

Interactive products

We now have products with which we can interact, products that are in some ways intelligent products. For example, though the car is obviously a product, the General Motor company now provide various services which mean that the company can extend the level of services and interact with the consumer. Should a consumer lock their keys into their car, with the use of a monitoring and geographical positioning system the company can remotely unlock the doors anywhere in the world!

Numerous children's toys have interactive devices with dolls which can answer questions and toys that utilize voice recognition software and react to a child's voice.

Remote delivery

We have always had some version of remote delivery – The Sears Catalogue was first introduced in the nineteenth century as a mail-order catalogue. The advent of IT has meant a wider range of products and services can be delivered remotely or alternatively we can avail ourselves of these services through remote bookings. Products that have an information content can be delivered through IT applications and one of the dominant platforms used is the Internet platform. One example is a newspaper which can now have dual delivery of content both in the paper and online versions (see, for example, www.ft.com).

The new world of television – product placement gone mad courtesy of Bluetooth technology

Marketers have often thought of targeting a specific person with advertising (see Building Relations). IT could now allow them to do so. Blue Screen Technology is a super technology that is underused at the moment. Blue boards are starting to appear at sport stadiums. How they operate is that the billboard advertising relates to the broadcasting location. So if a World Cup match is played in Korea between England and Germany, when the game is broadcast in the UK the billboards have advertisements in English related to the English market and when it is broadcast in Germany the German commercials can be seen.

TiVo – creating solutions

What is TiVo? The latest in control of your television. The television is the dumbest piece of equipment in your house. The toaster is more intelligent. Now comes TiVo to improve its intelligence. As it stands in most households, the television can only accept the television programmes as they are provided by the television stations. Now with TiVo consumers have control. They can decide what to watch and when. See www.tivo.com/1.0.asp for more information.

The road ahead

The road ahead is full of potentially more exciting and challenging ITs. It is very hard to decide which ITs will be developed and which marketers and consumers will embrace. What we can say is that the technology is available, it is when it can satisfy a need or improve a service or create efficiencies and so on that it will be utilized.

We are still at the early stages of assimilation of IT into marketing practice. Remember a lot of these developments are generational issues. We will be amazed over the next few years at the range and ability of IT. Remember all the IT in the world does not make marketers better marketers; what marketers need to do is to understand and exploit the IT to improve their marketing practices. Ultimately, it is the technologies that will provide benefits for the company and the customer which will be embraced and adopted.

Ask not what IT can do for you, but what you can do for IT.

FURTHER READING

Galliers, B. & Baets, W. (eds) (1998) *Information Technology and Organisation Transformation, Innovations for the 21st Century*. Wiley Series in Information Systems: Chichester.

Leverick, F., Littler D., Wilson, D. & Bruce, M. (1997) The role of IT in reshaping of marketing. *Journal of Marketing Practice: Applied Marketing Science*, **3** (2), 87–106.

McKenna, R. (1999) *Real Time Marketing*. Harvard Business School Press: Cambridge, MA.

Meuter, M., Ostrom, A., Roundtree, R. & Bitner, M. (2000) Self service technologies: understanding customer satisfaction with technology based service encounters. *Journal of Marketing*, **64** (3), 50–64.

Porter, M. J. & Millar, V. E. (1985) How information technology gives you competitive advantage. *Harvard Business Review*, July/August, 149–160.

Prahalad, C. & Krishnan, M. (1999) The new meaning of quality in the information age. *Harvard Business Review*, **77** (5, Sept/Oct), 109–139.

Reichheld, F. & Schefter, P. (2000) E-Loyalty – your secret weapon on the web. *Harvard Business Review*, **78** (4), 105–113.

Information for innovative solutions

Information constitutes the basic tenet of the traditional marketing concept as it is expressed in terms of 'market orientation', which is the strategic posture adopted by a firm that methodically collects and disseminates information about its customers and competitors and takes decisions that are directly based upon this information (see Kohli & Jaworski, 1990). In addition, information figures prominently in the new product development literature (e.g. Li & Calantone, 1998), because designing and making innovative solutions requires information. As you would expect, the better the quality of information, the better the innovation, the better the potential solutions. Conversely, creative solutions require innovation, sometimes 'radical', sometimes 'incremental'. Solutions to customer and marketing problems must be based on knowledge and information, and innovation is necessary in order to make new solutions happen.

It is through market research that the building blocks of knowledge are gathered as a key input for innovative solutions in marketing. The term 'market research' covers a wide range of information-gathering techniques and processes.

The precise role and use of marketing research by innovative firms is unclear. In some cases it is not employed at all when competitive pressures to be first to market with the latest technology do not allow time for firms to conduct marketing research. Sometimes the cost involved is prohibitive or situations with market and technological uncertainty mean that customers can't articulate their needs and requirements, so marketing research is inappropriate. For highly innovative new products, potential customers often cannot see the benefits, thus cannot 'want' something which they cannot imagine, so less reliance can be placed on conventional market research information. Initial market tests for the Sony Walkman indicated little demand for the new product, which was subsequently an enormous market success.

The delusion of data

If you've got all the data then you've got all the answers.
But data is not enough. You need to understand customers – their situations, lifestyles, attitudes, needs. (Humby, 2004)

Sultan and Barczak (1999) investigated the degree to which technology firms use market research in the new product development process. They found that these companies were using less structured, more qualitative methods (see 'Researching markets') to gather customer information for developing new products, and were disseminating this information and using it to design products and, to a lesser extent, for developing marketing strategies.

Thus, understanding the social–cultural–economic context in which the new product or new technology will be used (as well as bought, transported, stored consumed, and discarded) is critical for the design input for successful innovations (see Solutions to what?, 'The role of technology' subsection). This has significant implications for marketing research and requires the application of various types of qualitative research methods, including those based on anthropology, that can produce actionable results.

Information for innovation comes from lead users in both business and consumer markets that are encouraged to get 'close to the company' in order that marketers can better hear 'the voice of the customer'.

An alternative method for gathering information about customers is von Hippel's (1978) proposal that 'thoughtful use of lead users can help to address the problem of market research in areas of new technology'. This highlights the importance of relationship building (see Building Relations) with customers who have bought new products early in order to gather marketing information to develop solutions for the many customers who, unlike the lead users, are reluctant to commit to technologies they do not properly understand and that have not yet been substantially 'proven' in practice. This can be achieved by building sufficient customer references within an industry or better marketing communication of the innovation, so that the more cautious customers will be willing to risk implementation of what they may regard as an 'immature' new product or service offering.

Ultimately, customers exhibit their behaviour through buying. The aim is to understand the different types of behaviour.

To address some of these issues, Aaker *et al.* (2001) proposed that 'concept' testing is conducted with potential customers as a market research method during the early stage of the product development process. At this stage the product does not yet

exist, so the technique involves gathering respondents reactions to the concept of the new product, which can take the form of pictures, verbal descriptions or a 'mock-up' model of the innovation. This is used extensively by automobile manufacturers, who often reveal their 'concept cars' at motor shows and utilize the prototype models for gathering customer reactions. There are several problems associated with this technique:

- Respondents may read the concept statements or see artists' impressions without considering the environment in which the new product will be used
- Participants are usually presented with only a small amount of information
- For some new products, consumers prefer to learn through trial and error rather than reading
- These limitations can be restrictive when testing radical 'new to the world' products, because concept statements do not permit the replication of respondents' actual information search and processing.

Commercial knowledge is not truth, but effective performance: not 'what is right' but 'what works' or even 'what works better'.
Demarest, 1997

We must distinguish between information for innovation and scientific knowledge. Scientific knowledge denotes knowledge as 'truth' and represents the output of scientific methods (i.e. experimentation and facts), which cannot be disputed. Market and commercial knowledge does not take the same form, nor can such unequivocal claims be made of it. Demarest (1997) suggested that commercial knowledge is closer to what the French call '*bricolage*': the provisional construction of 'a messy set of rules, tools and guidelines that produce according to the expertise and sensitivity of the craftsman'. This distinction is significant because it explains and allows for different and competing views of market knowledge and information. Thus, information for innovation is necessarily imprecise, imperfect and incomplete.

The design of market research for information and knowledge on innovation needs to address the following questions: *where* to look for knowledge, *what* to look for and *how* to look for it (Tzokas & Saren, 2004).

In the next subsection this is discussed from the professional market researcher's point of view by Andy Barker of Research International.

Researching markets – it's qualitative Jim but not as we know it

The world of commercial qualitative research has undergone significant evolution in recent years. The manic growth of the early 1990s has given way to market maturity in this decade. This maturing, coupled with an extremely high degree of competition in the UK qualitative market in particular, has led to unprecedented methodological innovation on the supply side and innovation in how qualitative information is obtained and used on the client (demand) side. The net effect of this has been, to some extent, the blurring of what 'qualitative' means.

With this in mind, the themes that are of particular interest are the following:

- Developments in the supply side, such as an obsession with ethnography and ethnographic approaches; the gradual shift from the psychological model of qualitative research to a behavioural model; the development in thinking about consumer identity.
- On the client or demand side, the evolutions worthy of note include the increase in direct consumer experience or immersion; the meteoric rise to top billing of the concept of 'insight'; the growth of innovation needs.

Professional perspective – the supply side

Anyone who has attended market research industry seminars over the last few years will have noted the increasing allusion to ethnography as the 'method of the moment'. Commercial qualitative practice has finally caught up with the rhetoric and an ever-greater amount of work with at least an ethnographic flavour is proposed, sold and conducted.

However, we should define our terms here. What the academic reader (or indeed the professional ethnographer or sociologist) might consider to be ethnographic enquiry (e.g. detailed, painstaking participant observation studies mapping entire subcultures and tribes – see The role of consumers) once passed through the necessary commercial filters of time and budgetary pressures becomes something more like a safari into consumer land. Social scientists might be travellers through the world of consumer reality, whilst commercial researchers are inevitably tourists visiting consumers in their natural habitat, camcorders and tape recorders in hand, spending a day in their world but back in the Hilton by nightfall.

But in spite of this important distinction between academic and commercial ethnography, it must be said that ethnographic approaches, however bastardized, can produce insights which would otherwise be very hard to get from traditional qualitative methodologies such as focus groups.

For example, there are things which consumers might not consider it relevant to talk about in groups, but which might be visible even in a relatively short-lived encounter with consumers in their 'real life' context. This is especially true given the low involvement nature of many categories where FMCG (fast-moving consumer goods) brands operate, from washing detergent to ready meals.

A further thematic development in qualitative research is the noticeable shift from getting deeper and into consumers' minds and instead getting closer and closer to their lives. This broader approach is a welcome development and is based on a number of factors. Firstly, it is a result of a philosophical recognition of a changing conception of the consumer mind from stable, constant, consistent to fragmented, changing, unstable. Indeed, there is a strong recognition that the consumer 'mind' is really only meaningfully formed at particular fleeting moments of consumption and that these are hard to access/replicate by more and more probing. Some other methodological approach is required.

On a more pragmatic level this new approach, involving understanding the behavioural context of consumers as well as their psychological motivations is based also, I suspect, firstly, on a frustration with consumers' post-emotionalization of their behaviour when called on to reveal their innermost motivations, in focus groups, concerning brand choice in a category with very little meaning to them; and, secondly, on the commercial imperative to offer something different to clients.

This shift in interest from understanding just what people think to what they do tends to manifest itself, in methodological terms, as a move to observation of behaviour as a supplement to standard qualitative research activity. Pre-tasking is increasingly common and is often about getting consumers to record their real life behaviour before a formal research session in order to inject a dose of behavioural reality into otherwise, by definition, 'artificial' focus groups.

Less common is a shift from analysis of the individual consumer as the master/mistress of his/her actions to the provision of an account of the cultural dimensions of consumer behaviour. This can be seen in semiotic analysis (which is, after some years of in principle popularity, enjoying more widespread commercial application) and which, roughly speaking, analyses brands, advertising, packaging, etc. as cultural objects rather than understanding consumers' opinions of them *per se*.

The model of 'the consumer' has changed

As detailed earlier, within the qualitative research world the model of the consumer has largely changed from one where he/she is a passive recipient of marketing, with a stable and constant set of opinions, attitudes and responses, to a model which takes account of consumers' multiple consuming identities (see Consuming Experience). Qualitative methodologies of questioning or analysis have grown up and evolved which deal with this philosophical issue.

Once again there is a practical issue here and it concerns the increasing difficulty of matching messy consumer reality (as reported by consumers or observed by

ethnographically orientated researchers) with the ideal world of tidy consumer segmentation. In short, consumers often demonstrably resist pigeon-holing and so it makes sense to develop models and methods that make sense of this.

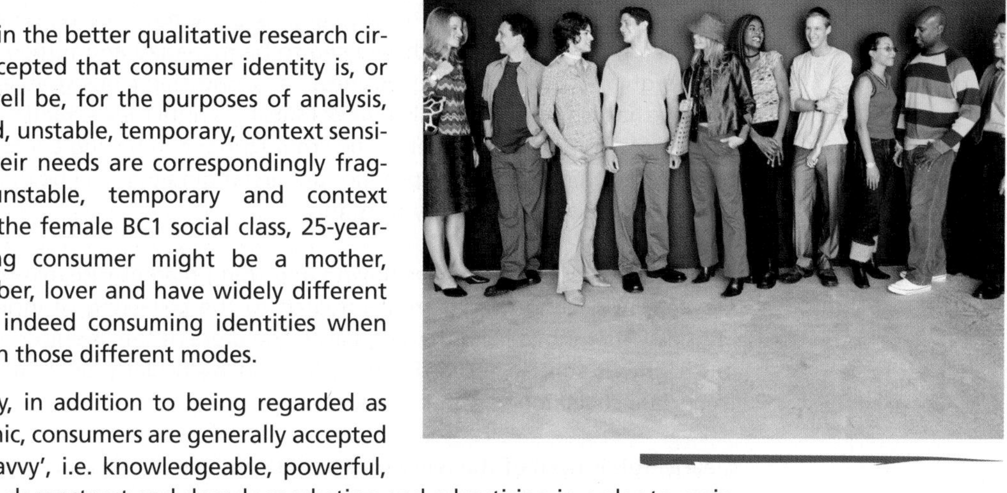

Therefore, in the better qualitative research circles it is accepted that consumer identity is, or might as well be, for the purposes of analysis, fragmented, unstable, temporary, context sensitive and their needs are correspondingly fragmented, unstable, temporary and context sensitive – the female BC1 social class, 25-year-old working consumer might be a mother, driver, clubber, lover and have widely different needs and indeed consuming identities when operating in those different modes.

Interestingly, in addition to being regarded as schizophrenic, consumers are generally accepted as being 'savvy', i.e. knowledgeable, powerful, and able to deconstruct and decode marketing and advertising in order to maintain an active, participatory relationship with brands. This idea is not without its critics and research with consumers has tended to suggest that they might not feel as savvy as analysis would have them be (see Consuming Experience).

In methodological terms this often translates to changes in the balance of power in the research situation, with consumers no longer ambushed in groups as the real purpose of the session emerges from the camouflage of a general chat about the product category. In addition, respondents are routinely 'given the marketing problem' assuming that they are in a position to solve it directly. Again, this approach is not without its critics.

Client perspective – the demand side

We have outlined changes on the supply side of the commercial qualitative market, but what changes are happening on the demand side – how are clients' needs and behaviours changing the way qualitative market research is defined and used?

First and foremost, consumer immersion is the new game in town. All over the world, marketing directors and consumer insight professionals (once called market research managers) are mixing with carefully selected, screened and scrubbed consumers for their hit of authentic consumer reality.

This is, on many levels, a very positive development because research buyers and users can be out of touch with the consumers they strive to understand and a day

spent with the Joneses can be 'worth', in insight gleaned, far more than a $500K global usage and attitude study.

However, the suburban garden path of immersion does not necessarily lead to insight and research buyers and users need to be trained in how to interact with real people, how to actively observe and listen. What is more, once they have gathered their observations these need to be managed and turned into insight that might be useful for the business. It is one thing being able to observe directly that schoolchildren microwave Mars bars until they explode as a snack to keep them going between returning from school and having a 'proper' dinner, but another thing entirely to produce understanding that will be the beginnings of a leverageable opportunity from this.

A further theme in companies buying and using market research has been the move from getting insight from research to the collecting of insights for the business. That move from the singular to the plural is the linguistic signifier of a much bigger shift in research generally, and particularly qualitative research, from data collection to insight generation.

Clearly, this is born of the need that businesses have to innovate and this innovation in turn needs to be focused on genuine, unmet consumer needs. These needs, in an increasingly crowded and fragmented marketplace (especially in categories with a frightening number of brands, variants, products, etc.), are often relatively niche and can amount to different perspectives (or angles) on a problem rather than entirely new needs. These are expressed in terms of consumer insights, i.e. bite-sized expressions that offer a manageable route into consumers' lives in a particular category.

Thus, 'insights' have now become a valuable commodity in businesses and research agencies are increasingly charged with providing insights rather than 'truth'. That is not to say that these two concepts are incompatible, rather there is a difference in emphasis from obtaining a holistic, accurate, objective picture of consumer behaviour, motivations, etc. in a given category to providing useful insights about consumers in the category.

In addition, businesses are investing large sums of money in programmes aimed at generating and managing insights in the business, from databases to specifically designed methodologies for turning data into insights (see Information technology and innovation).

Mainstream research on the supply side has not yet responded to this shift, which has opened up a lucrative door for para-consultancies to walk through. This has led to the emergence of a new category of super-consultancies who infiltrate client businesses on a multi-platform basis and offer a range of services from design and marketing consultancy to qualitative research. The vacuum left

by the wholesale abandoning of the advertising agency planner has also contributed to this.

Therefore, businesses have become adept at buying, generating and in some cases storing insights. However, many are still grappling with the question of what to do with all these insights, i.e. how to turn them into consumer/business propositions. Companies that are better at this have shifted emphasis and structure from the traditional relationship of marketer–researcher–agency planner–research company to an emergent structure of marketer–consumer insight manager–research company partner–planner.

From insights to innovation

We discussed earlier that the need for insight which turned into the rush for insights was driven by the need to innovate in an increasingly crowded global marketplace. However forward looking the practitioner, like it or not, research is inherently backward looking – it can only predict, with any degree of certainty, the past. But within the newly constituted research market there is an increasing emphasis on future solutions.

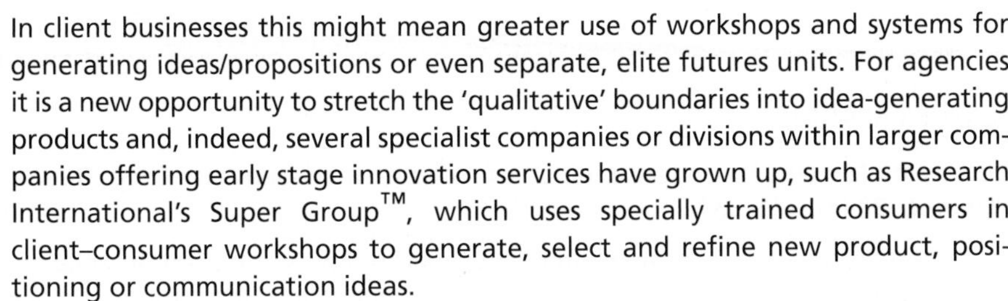

In client businesses this might mean greater use of workshops and systems for generating ideas/propositions or even separate, elite futures units. For agencies it is a new opportunity to stretch the 'qualitative' boundaries into idea-generating products and, indeed, several specialist companies or divisions within larger companies offering early stage innovation services have grown up, such as Research International's Super Group™, which uses specially trained consumers in client–consumer workshops to generate, select and refine new product, positioning or communication ideas.

Interestingly, the role of the consumer in this type of 'qualitative research' is not considered to be a worthy subject of research, it is something between creative partner and spokesperson for the less creative, less articulate great unwashed mass of everyday consumers. In this mode of research, 'respondents' are no longer asked to 'respond' as such, they are asked to create, they are used as a highly skilled resource; they have one foot in consumer reality, but their heads planted firmly in the clouds!

As often happens, we can observe the trickle through of these approaches into more mainstream qualitative work with the often theatrical, invariably exciting and often highly profitable methods increasingly requested and inserted into more everyday consumer qualitative research.

Summary

In order to illustrate the trends over time, we can map the developments of qualitative research 'discourse' from its residual codes of deep exploration through a currently dominant focus on eclecticism to the emergence of a pragmatic set of approaches aimed at gaining insights in partnership with companies (Table 7).

Table 7 Development of the qualitative research 'discourse'

Residual	Dominant	Emergent
Exploring the mind	Exploring the brand	Exploring behaviour
Deeper and deeper	Wilder and wackier	Closer and closer
Academic analysis	Creative presentation	Part of the business
Some rigour	Models of thinking	Pragmatism
Expertise/name	Experience based	Knowledge based
Strong ethics	Loose ethics	Partnership
Guru domination	Boutique domination	Relationships

FURTHER READING

Demarest, M. (1997) Understanding knowledge management. *Long Range Planning*, **30** (3), 374–384.

Li, T. & Calantone, R. J. (1998) The impact of market knowledge competence on new product advantage: conceptualization and empirical examination. *Journal of Marketing*, **62** (4), 13–29.

Moorman, C. (1995) Organizational market information processes: cultural antecedents and new product outcomes. *Journal of Marketing Research*, **32** (3), 318–336.

Nonaka, I. (1991) The knowledge creating company. *Harvard Business Review*, **69** (6), 96–104.

von Hippel, E. & Thomke, S. (1999) Creating breakthroughs at 3M. *Harvard Business Review*, **77** (5), 47–57.

Organizational processes and capabilities

Emmanuella Plakoyiannaki

Processes, capabilities and creation of solutions

The purpose of marketing has always been to attract and retain customers, however widely they are defined. This core objective requires that the firm is constantly developing and delivering solutions that meet customer needs and wants. To accomplish this goal, firms emphasize three important elements that reflect marketing practice – namely, organizational processes, capabilities and culture.

Organizational processes play a key role in the creation of customer solutions, since they enable firms to integrate tasks, resources and activities with the purpose of delivering a superior value offering with respect to changing customer needs. *Organizational capabilities* are deeply embedded into processes and relate to the capacity of the firm to deploy resources (e.g. knowledge, skills and people) in order to deliver superior value offerings through tailored customer solutions. Capabilities encompass the value chain of the firm and demonstrate the commitment of the firm to customers. *Organizational culture* shapes the focus of organizational processes and capabilities. In other words, the creation of enhanced customer solutions requires an organizational culture which acknowledges the customer as the focal point of strategic planning and execution. Figure 25 illustrates the three elements that influence the practice of marketing and the creation of solutions meeting changing customer requirements. It also illustrates the overarching effect of organizational culture on the deployment of processes and capabilities that engage the firm in the delivery of enhanced customer value.

This chapter focuses on the contribution of organizational processes and capabilities to the creation of customer solutions. Specifically, it draws insights from the *customer relationship management* (CRM) process and capabilities, and demonstrates

how these elements guide the strategies and practices of organizations towards the satisfaction of customer needs.

In the first part of the chapter, a framework of the CRM process in the organization is proposed and discussed. This framework includes four constructs integrally linked to CRM, i.e. the *strategic planning process*, the *information processes*, the *customer value process* and the *performance measurement process*. In the second part of the chapter, the framework is used as a basis for the identification and analysis of a set of CRM capabilities that may enhance CRM practice in the organization. The chapter concludes by summarizing the key points of the discussion.

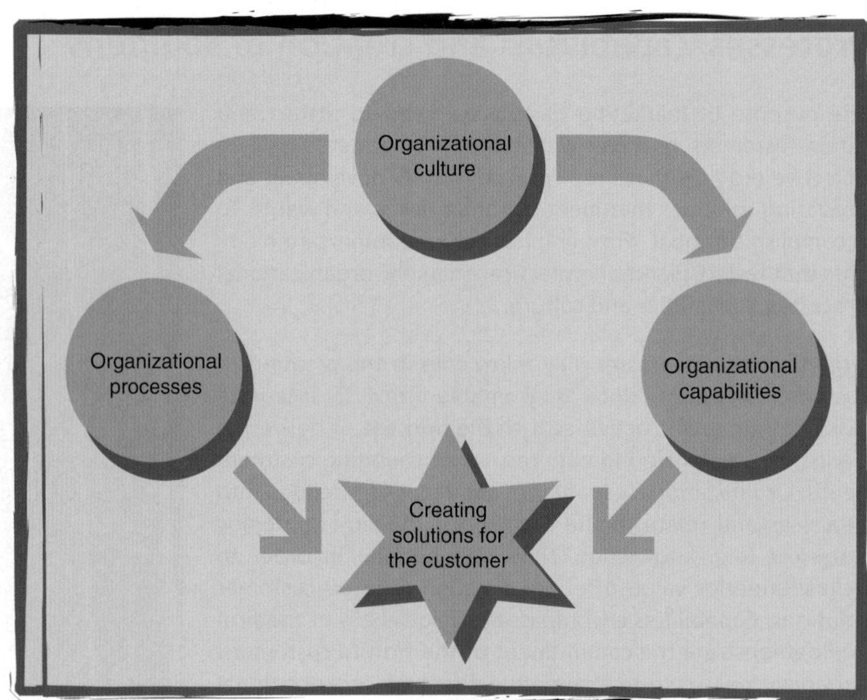

Figure 25 Organizational processes, capabilities and customer solutions

What is CRM?

Although CRM has gained some prominence in the marketing literature, there is still dissent among authors about its definition. Specialists' views of CRM appear to line up along a continuum, with one extreme referring to a view of CRM as an information technology (IT) solution for data collection and analysis, and the other viewing CRM as a marketing philosophy designed to achieve long-term business gains (Figure 26). In order to enhance our understanding of CRM, it is

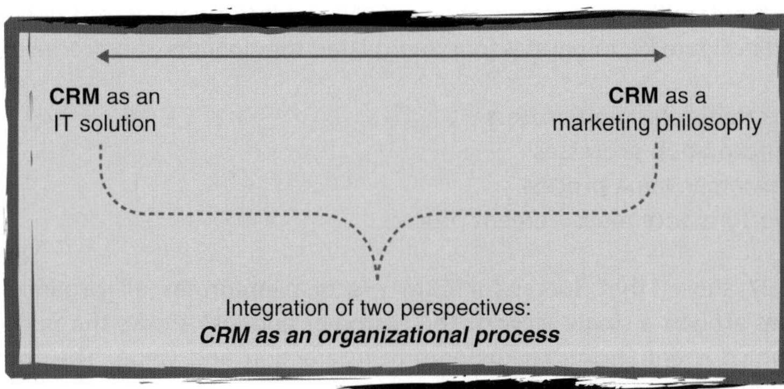

Figure 26 The CRM continuum

worthwhile combining these two perspectives so as to benefit from the synergies that the related ideas may generate.

From an information technology point of view, CRM changes the practice of marketing by enabling customer communication and dialogue. According to this perspective, technology is the key driver to profitability. From a marketing point of view, CRM addresses all aspects of developing interactions between the firm and customers, and shapes customers' perceptions of the organization and its products. It enables the creation and delivery of superior customer service and value. In that sense, the provision of customer value drives profitability and corporate success. This chapter approaches CRM as an *IT-enabled organizational process that places the customer at the heart of the firm's strategy and operations. CRM aims to provide enhanced customer value by establishing a creative dialogue between the firm and the customer*. This definition emphasizes the contribution of CRM to the creation of solutions that meet customer needs. It transcends the technological and marketing aspects of the notion in that it develops a view of CRM as an activity that extends to the entire organization. In other words, the practice of CRM is neither isolated purely in marketing tasks such as planning, development and execution of marketing campaigns, nor is it solely dependent on the launch of customer databases. Instead, it is linked to other practices such as human resource management and financial management, since these activities reflect on the value delivered to the customer. For example, human resource management practices such as reward initiatives aim at motivating employees to deliver the essence of CRM, namely customer value (see Marketing Contexts: Market value).

The CRM process

This subsection sets out a framework of the CRM process developed by adapting themes from the wider organization, management and relationship marketing literature (e.g. organizational learning, process theory, value creation and performance

measurement) to the conceptualization of CRM. The framework of the CRM process, depicted in Figure 27, integrates four interrelated components (sub-processes):

- The strategic planning process
- The information processes
- The customer value process
- The performance measurement process.

Figure 27 shows that successful CRM practice integrates all organizational processes around a single view of the customer and also shows the purpose of CRM, which is enhancing customer–firm interaction and value. The four sub-processes of CRM are briefly discussed below.

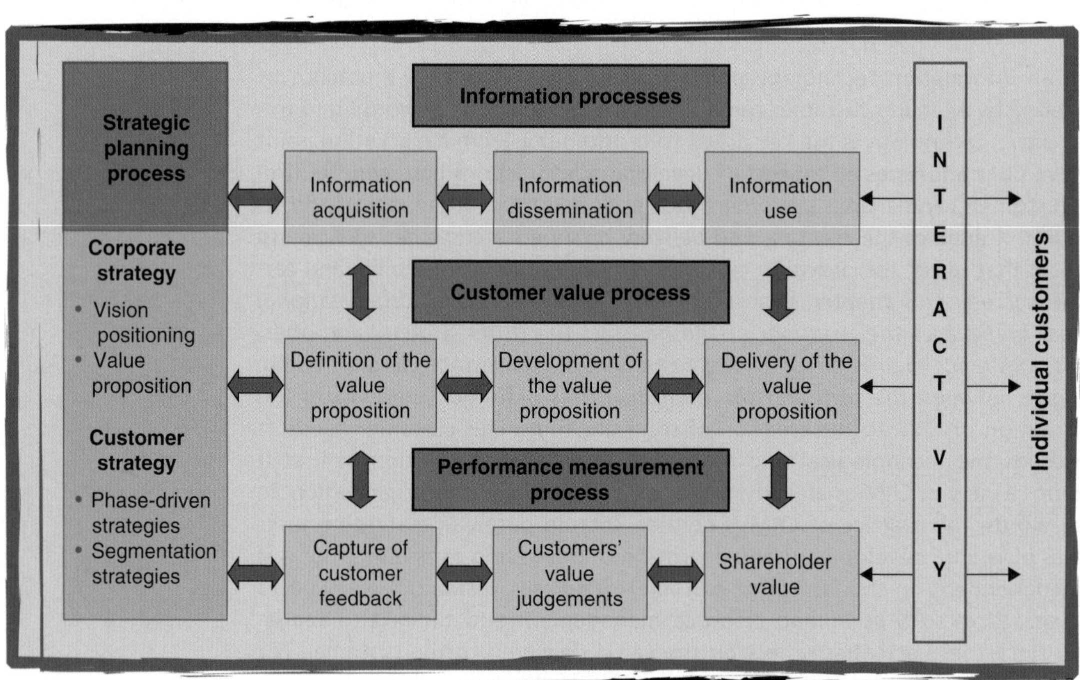

Figure 27 The CRM process

The strategic planning process

As demonstrated in Figure 27, the central stakeholders in CRM are the customers. However, the development of a continuous customer–firm interaction is the result of a long process that begins with strategic planning activities. In other

words, for CRM to thrive there is a need for an organizational strategy that aligns the competencies of the firm and the voice of the customer. The strategic planning process of CRM provides the direction for the development, implementation and control of customer-oriented action in the organization. However, the outcomes of strategic planning are apparent to customers when they experience the total value offering of the firm. The strategic planning process of CRM is comprised of two interrelated components: *corporate strategy* and *customer strategy*.

Corporate strategy involves the *vision*, *positioning* and *value proposition* of the business, and ensures that these components are integrated with the *customer strategy* of the firm. The *vision* provides an understanding of what the business wants to achieve in comparison with existing and potential competitors. It is an instrument of motivation for employees, since it provides the organization with a purpose and focuses the efforts of all organizational participants on the achievement of that purpose. But most seriously, organizational vision influences the perceptions of customers regarding the firm and its products and services. Specifically, it articulates the standards of customer–firm interaction and illustrates what the organization expects to contribute to its customers. The vision of an organization that implements CRM places the customer at the heart of the business and encompasses the concept of *customer value delivery* as the core of the firm's strategy and operations.

The *positioning* of the firm relates to the business vision and the development of a unique competitive advantage, sustainable over time. The positioning of the firm is manifested in the value proposition that customers experience and differentiates the firm (in relation to other market competitors) in the eyes of the customer.

The *value proposition* is central to consumers' interests, since it stems from customer criteria and aspirations of value that guide the selection of products/service in specific use situations. The value proposition is linked both to the internal and external environments of the organization. Internally, the value proposition determines the operations of the firm, as it is translated into value-generating processes and activities. Externally, the value proposition represents the firm in the eyes of the customer. In the context of CRM, the selection of the value proposition appears to be based on (1) the customer's needs and activities, and (2) the organization's existing and potential core capabilities.

In the context of CRM, two fundamental types of customer strategy can be identified. These are *phase-driven strategies* and *customer segmentation strategies* (Table 8). Phase-driven strategies are related to the relationship life cycle of the customer with the firm and may be classified into three groups – namely, customer acquisition strategy, customer retention strategy and customer recovery

Table 8 The strategic planning process of CRM

Vision	Positioning	Value proposition
Corporate strategy		
• What the business wants to achieve – purpose • Time horizon • Performance standards	• Relates to value proposition • Facilitates benchmarking with competitors • Enables identification of opportunities in the market	• Operationalized by means of processes and activities • Represents the organization in the eyes of the customer
Customer strategy		
Customer acquisition strategy: aims to attract new customers to establish a relationship with the firm	*Customer retention strategy:* aims to decrease the customer turnover of the firm	*Customer recovery strategy*: aims to regain lost customers
This is achieved by: 1 providing appropriate incentives that encourage customers to respond to the organization's initiatives (*stimulation strategy*); 2 reassuring customers that the supplier is able to satisfy their needs and desires (*persuasion strategy*)	This is achieved by: 1 providing psychological emotional benefits to customers, such as satisfaction and delight (*solidarity strategy*); 2 setting up barriers to switching providers (*dependence strategy*)	This is achieved by: 1 amending or improving problematic areas of customer–firm relationships that cause customer defections (*compensation and improvement strategy*)
Customer segmentation strategy: requires the identification of segmentation variables, the methods to form segments, and the appraisal and optimization of existing segmentations		
Non-differentiation of customers	Differentiation of customers	Customization (segment of one)

Source: adapted from Bruhn (2003).

strategy. Customer segmentation strategies allow firms to identify, profile, target and reach customer segments based on customer transactional data.

Although many organizations have developed in the market through differentiation and customization strategies, there are still firms that do not differentiate between customers. However, skilful management of customer relationships is usually linked to differentiation and customization strategies, since it requires an in-depth understanding of customer differences stemming from heterogeneous

preferences, lifestyles, demographics, psychographics and customer profitability variables.

The information processes

The framework illustrated in Figure 27 suggests that the generation of customer knowledge is based on a series of information processes – namely, *information acquisition*, *information dissemination* and *information use*. For instance, Barclays Bank, as a firm practising CRM, emphasizes information processes in order to manage multinational contacts and organization data, coordinate customer dialogue and manage key customer knowledge.

Acquisition is the process of gathering primary and secondary (customer) information from internal and external sources and bringing this data within the boundaries of the organization. Specifically, organizations may acquire customer information through customer survey activities and customer research (formal information acquisition), and communication and discussion with customers (informal information acquisition). In the context of CRM, information acquisition facilitates the customer–firm dialogue and provides the means to better understand the customer. The collected information is stored in the back-office infrastructure of the CRM system and utilized for customer segmentation and targeting purposes.

Dissemination relates to the degree that information is circulated among organizational participants. The dissemination of (customer) information may occur formally through organizational policies, training sessions, presentations of research, cross-departmental teams, company meetings and memoranda, and informally through interaction and conversation between organizational stakeholders. Information dissemination plays a crucial role in the CRM process, because it enhances the breadth of organizational and thus customer learning. In other words, when information is broadly distributed in the organization, more varied sources of information exist, making retrieval of information easier and learning more likely to occur. Additionally, dissemination of information contributes to the creation of new information by facilitating the synthesis of several bits of information previously acquired by different units in the organization.

Information *use* is probably the aspect of information processing more relevant to satisfying consumer needs, since it demonstrates the response of the firm to the customers based on the acquired information. The use of information may be either direct, referring to the application of information to decision-making purposes and the implementation of customer strategies; or indirect, pertaining to behaviours that organizations deploy in order to elaborate customer information for strategy-related actions.

Table 9 The information processes of CRM

Information processes	CRM
Information acquisition	• Emphasis on customer–firm dialogue • Emphasis on customer information
Information dissemination	• Dissemination of customer information enhances customer learning • Increased sophistication and intensity of information processes • Customer information tailors products, services and communication efforts • Information processes enable customers to reach the firm
Information use	• Relevant to the interests of the customers • Privacy concerns

Table 9 shows the information processes of CRM. A central theme illustrated in Table 9 is that CRM intensifies customer–firm dialogue as a means of acquiring information. Additionally, it increases the sophistication of information processes with the availability of new technologies. This is demonstrated in the development of customer databases that contain information regarding customer requirements, choices, contact background and unmet customer needs. The information processes of CRM enable organizations to tailor products and services according to the profile of customers. But most seriously, information processes help customers to communicate with the firm and express their opinions regarding the value offerings they receive. By processing customer information and linking it to customer behaviour patterns, organizations can generate information that can add value to customer–firm relationships. In the right hands, this information can increase the benefits offered to customers. But when used inappropriately, customers' interests are compromised. For example, mobile phone companies register their users to the network by acquiring personal details. Customers' personal data is used by the marketing team for promotional purposes (e.g. circulation of promotional text messages to the handsets of the customers). Such initiatives constitute bad practice in CRM and cause a number of privacy concerns, such as customer irritation and bad temper for getting unwanted promotional information and feelings of violation of the customer's personal space.

The customer value process

The second group of processes relevant to CRM are customer value activities. The central part of the customer value process is the *customers' resulting experiences* that occur when individuals engage in a personal way with the value offering of the organization. It is the customer's appreciation of the experience that determines the worth of the value offering and the survival of the organization. However, it should be noted that there appears to be a difference between the value offerings of the firm and how customers perceive these value offerings. The discussion below takes into consideration this distinction and focuses on customers' viewpoints of the value process The three value-generating activities – i.e. the *definition*, *development* and *delivery* of the value proposition – are considered, adopting the customer's frame of reference.

From a customer's point of view, the *definition of the value proposition* entails the benefits sought from the customer under particular circumstances, which are captured in the notion of *desired value*. Desired value can be a multidimensional concept, with each of these dimensions helping individuals to achieve certain goals. In other words, the definition of the value proposition articulates the customers' perceptions of what they want to experience in a specific situation with the help of a product or service offering in order to accomplish a desired purpose or goal. For example, customers might desire speed in the transaction with the firm because this attribute may deliver benefits such as allowing them to concentrate on other activities or be efficient in their professional lives. From a CRM perspective, organizations attempt to understand customers' perceptions of desired value by establishing a customer–firm dialogue capable of revealing the attributes of customer perceptions of value to the firm.

From a customer's perspective, the *development of the value proposition* includes decisions and formation of perceptions about products and services that address customer needs. In the context of CRM, what seems to be important at this stage of the value process is the incorporation of the voice of the customer into the design and production of new products and services, i.e. value co-production. This is because consumers' and firms' interests can be realized through cooperation and interdependence in the customer value process. In particular, the continuity of customer–firm interaction in the development of the value proposition may cultivate trust between the parties involved in the CRM process and offer additional benefits to the customer, such as superior service quality, tailoring of products and services according to the customer's characteristics, and preferences.

The involvement of the customer in the development of the value proposition is evident in the operations of IKEA and Volvo, who advance product and service solutions through experimentation and interaction with their customers. Other examples of firms that collaborate with and learn from their customers in order to create value offering are Toys 'R' Us, Home Depot, Wal-Mart and Fedex.

From a customer's point of view, the *delivery of the value proposition* helps individuals to experience the desired value, which takes on two aspects: value in use or possession value. Value in use pertains to the use of a product or service in a specific situation in order to achieve certain goals. Possession value reflects the inherent meaning of the product or service to the customer. The delivery of the value proposition is linked to the consumption process, which is in fact a value-producing activity in itself. Consumption is often a playful activity, which involves hedonism and communicates status and social position. During consumption, customers are autonomous and create value in their own arenas (by competition or collaboration) independent of the constraints that a firm's environment might impose. Consuming goods and services may be used as bases for individuals to compete against one another (e.g. conspicuous consumption) or join desirable groups that share the same aspirations, behaviours and lifestyles. Consequently, an in-depth understanding of the consumption process may enable organizations to appreciate customers' perceptions of value. Table 10 summarizes the characteristics of the customer value process in the context of CRM.

Table 10 The customer value process of CRM

Customer value process	CRM
Definition of the value proposition	• Desired value • Resulting customer experiences • Customer–firm dialogue reveals customers' perceptions of value
Development of the value proposition	• Customer–firm co-production • Provision of high-quality products and customer services • Continuity of customer–firm interactions cultivates trust and provides additional benefits to the customer
Delivery of the value proposition	• Possession value or value in use • Consumption

The performance measurement process

In order to assess the contribution of CRM to the firm, the outcomes of CRM practice are considered in relation to the objectives of CRM practice. Taking into consideration that the purpose of CRM is customer value creation and delivery, the performance appraisal of CRM initiatives involves the assessment of value that customers have received from the specific products/services of the firm. In other words, organizations need to assess the value judgements of their customer in order to evaluate whether the CRM has been successful or not. *Value judgements* include consumers' assessments of the value they receive given the trade-offs between all relevant benefits and sacrifices in a specific use situation. Consequently, organizations may enhance CRM performance by increasing the benefits (or decreasing the sacrifices) that customers experience in the use of products and services.

However, the performance measurement of CRM is considered in terms of the firm's responses not only to customer value expectations, but also to shareholder value maximization. For example, HSBC uses CRM in order to build up shareholder value through cross-selling activities, cost reduction, improved customer acquisition and retention. The linkage between the CRM process and shareholder value highlights the importance of CRM in the organization and provides a valid claim for capital investment in CRM initiatives.

The shareholder value (SHV) perspective involves the identification of four value drivers:

- Acceleration of cash flows; earlier cash flows are preferred because risk and the time adjustments reduce the value of later cash flows.
- Enhancement of cash flows by increasing revenues and reducing costs, working capital and fixed investments.
- Reduction in the risk associated with cash flows by decreasing both their volatility and, indirectly, the firm's cost capital.
- Augmentation of the long-term value of the business (at the end of the planning horizon) through investments in processes that result in both tangible and intangible assets.

Table 11 illustrates how the CRM process enhances the SHV of the firm. In particular, CRM initiatives contribute to *cash flow acceleration* by facilitating product entry, trial, acceptance and diffusion in the customer base. For instance, Levis Strauss builds

Table 11 The performance measurement process of CRM – the drivers of shareholder value

Shareholder value drivers	Contribution of CRM to shareholder value
Accelerating cash flows	• Reduces time for market acceptance (i.e. market penetration cycle time) • Minimizes customer solution development cycle time
Enhancing cash flows	• Supports high margins with branded products and superior service • Cross-selling of parts, consumables and complementary services • Up-selling of branded products and services • Maximizes customer value (and revenues) by combining customer solutions (including competitive products and services) • Acquires customers; grows existing customer base • Refines the quality of the customer base • Lowers product launch costs; lower sales and services costs
Reducing risk (vulnerability and volatility of cash flows)	• Enhances customer retention and loyalty • Increases customer switching costs • Retains excellence in the delivery of customer value and enhances customer experiences with the firm and its products/services • Cross-selling of parts, consumables and complementary services • Implementation of differential pricing and price concessions for long-term and profitable customers • Implementation of customer education and training programmes
Augmentation of the long-term value of the business	• Grows and refines customer base • Cross-selling/up-selling of products and services • Focuses on enhancing customer satisfaction and loyalty (involve customers in the development of the value proposition) • Aligns organizational capabilities to the delivery of customer value

Source: adapted from Srivastava *et al*. (1998).

upon customer relationships by using consumers' preferences to customize fit jeans for women. At the same time the company attempts to capitalize on its dialogue with the customers by sending them information regarding new products and sizes, lines and styles of jeans. Additionally, the execution of campaign management activities such as advertising and promotion play a central role in the development of brand awareness, motivate the product trail and minimize barriers to market.

The practice of CRM *enhances cash flows* through activities such as cross-selling, customer acquisition, and reduction of product, service and sales costs. For example, CRM enables Amazon, the online bookshop, to cross-sell its products and services by matching the profile of its customers with solutions of possible interest in order to generate repeat purchasing behaviour and increased cash flows.

Successful implementation of CRM initiatives contributes to *reduction of vulnerability and volatility of cash flows* by increasing customer switching costs, loyalty programmes, excellent customer value delivery and leveraging market-based assets. CRM contributes to the *augmentation of the long-term value of the business by cultivating customer loyalty and long-term customer relationships*, which minimize the risk associated with the cash flows, services costs and sales costs, and increase revenues. For example, Sainsbury's (the UK supermarket chain), Barclays Bank, BP and Debenhams department store are deploying a new CRM programme based on a loyalty scheme with the purpose of achieving financial and strategic growth and establishing a long-term competitive advantage in the market by personalizing offers to customers.

CRM capabilities

The success of cross-functional processes such as CRM is dependent on organizational capabilities that support the major goal of CRM practice, which is the creation and delivery of superior customer value. Taking into consideration that capabilities are embedded in processes (see Figure 27), we can identify five sets of capabilities deriving from the CRM process that enable CRM practice. These are (Figure 28):

- Learning and market orientation capabilities
- Integration capabilities
- Analytical capabilities
- Operational capabilities
- Direction capabilities.

These capabilities are interwoven in the culture of the organization, which has an important role in determining the degree to which employees demonstrate the capabilities that enable the success of CRM initiatives. Based on the discussion at the beginning of the chapter, it appears to be obvious that, for CRM to thrive, a cultural focus that places the customer at the heart of the business and encourages customer learning appears to be essential.

Learning and market orientation capabilities

Market orientation and learning are closely interrelated organizational capabilities deeply embedded in the CRM process. In particular, market orientation by focusing on creation and maintenance of superior customer value serves to facilitate the essence of CRM, which is maximization of customer value. The creation of customer value is achieved through the activities of the customer value processes of CRM (i.e. the definition, development and delivery of the value proposition) and is further

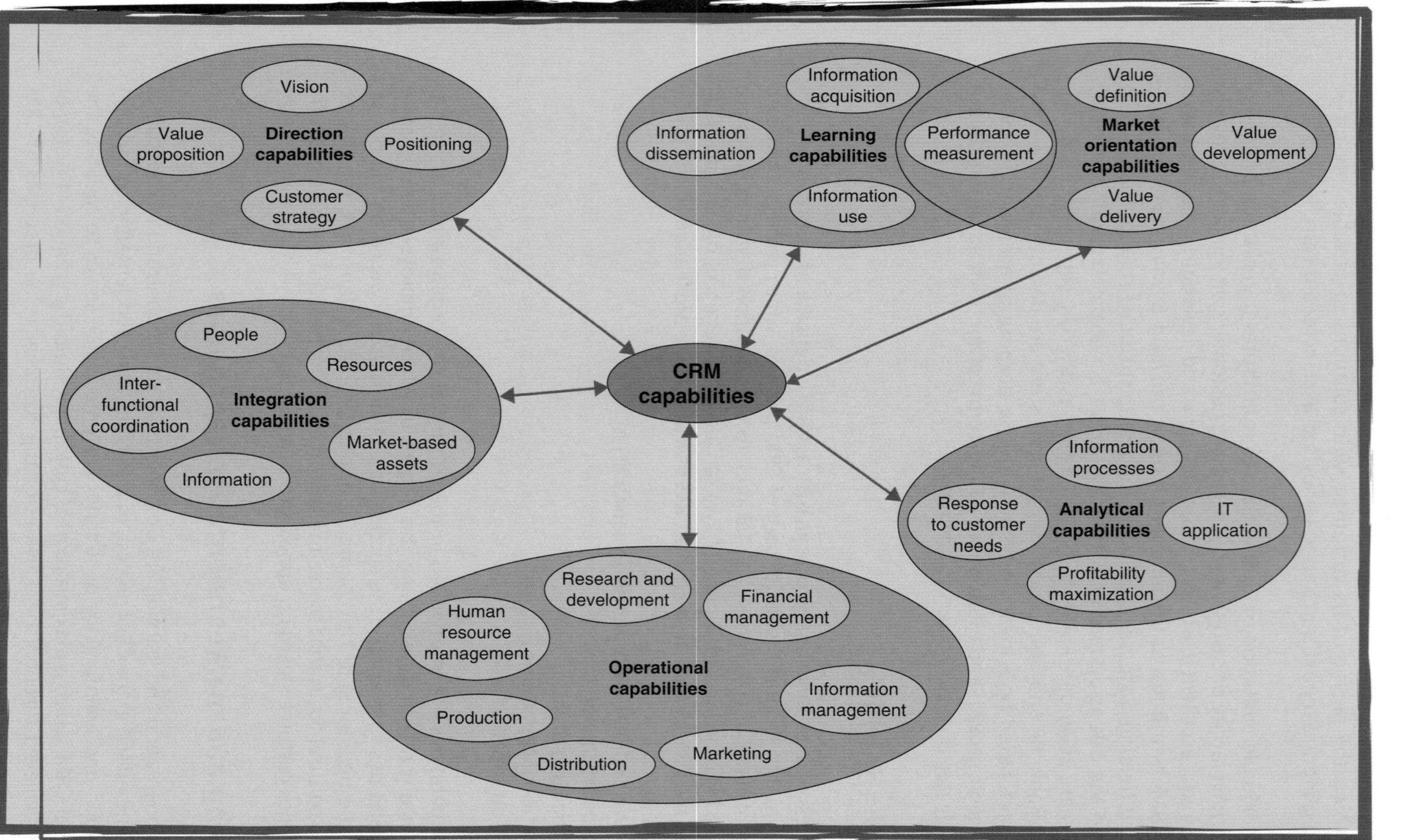

Figure 28 CRM capabilities

demonstrated in tasks such as customer service, innovative product development, cost-effective manufacturing and quality management. Market orientation directs the scope of learning towards the customer. In the context of CRM, learning capabilities are embedded in the (1) information processes, (2) customer value process and (3) performance measurement processes. First, customer insight generation occurs through learning and requires input of information, which is further used by members of the organization to respond to customer needs. Second, the customer value process of CRM is facilitated by learning capabilities that show the commitment of the organization to listen to customers' requirements and needs and the response to these needs through high-quality and innovative products and services. Third, the performance measurement process of CRM shows an inherent focus on learning, which is illustrated by the capabilities of the organization to measure and improve corporate performance based on customer feedback across all channels and points of interaction. Generally, it can be argued that companies that practise CRM successfully are *learning organizations* skilled at acquiring, disseminating and using (customer) information to respond to customer needs. Such organizations modify their behaviour in the market to reflect new knowledge and customer insights gained by means of learning and the CRM process.

Integration capabilities

The CRM process crosses all departmental boundaries with the purpose of maximizing the value delivered to the customers by establishing a creative customer–firm dialogue. This requires organizations to identify and develop integration capabilities that bring together individuals and organizational units/functions and create synergies that are most able to support successful CRM practice. The coordination of functions and people ensures that organizational actors serve the same goals and place the customer at the centre of the firm's strategy and operations. Furthermore, the alignment of functional areas promotes inter-departmental connections and use of shared resources. Integration capabilities facilitate information processing and align the operations of all business systems, extending from the back-office infrastructure to the front-line systems and channels of interaction.

Integration capabilities appear to reflect on the performance measurement of CRM. Specifically, the appreciation of market-based assets that CRM initiatives generate and their link to shareholder value lies in the integration of CRM measures in order to assess the contribution of the CRM process within the firm.

Analytical capabilities

Analytical capabilities are associated with the technological aspects of the CRM process and play an important role in the management of customer relationships for four reasons. First, they assist in the acquisition, dissemination and use of information which supports customer learning and development of clear market

segments. Second, analytical capabilities refer to the ability of organizations to deploy technological applications and scan for information regarding technological opportunities and threats that may advance CRM practice. Third, analytical capabilities enhance the ability of an organization to identify and respond to the changing needs of the customer base. Fourth, analytical capabilities enhance maximization of profitability from customer relationships, since they enable firms to link investments from customer relationships to the return these relationships generate for the firm.

Operational capabilities

Operational capabilities exploit and enhance resources. They are skills developed at functional and administrative levels that translate customer insights into value offerings. Operational capabilities cut across the CRM process and may be relevant in areas such as research and development, production, distribution, marketing (e.g. communication, customer serving), information management, financial management and human resource practices.

Direction capabilities

Direction capabilities are the compass for the course of the CRM process in the organization. They ensure not only that the organization has a clear and well-communicated corporate and customer strategy, but also that the components of these strategies are complementary. As far as *corporate strategy* is concerned, direction capabilities (1) facilitate the development and accomplishment of the corporate vision of CRM that places the customer at the centre of the organization's operations and philosophy; (2) define the positioning of the firm which addresses the development of competitive advantage in the marketplace; and (3) ensure that the value proposition focuses on customer experience, which truly differentiates the firm in the eyes of the customer.

With reference to *customer strategy*, direction capabilities enhance the organization's ability to focus its resources on its most valued customers. These capabilities have a significant impact on the development and implementation of strategies for customer acquisition, retention and recovery, as well as customer segmentation.

Summary

This chapter has described the organizational processes and capabilities that are necessary to manage customer relations so that solutions are created, managed and delivered competitively to the long-term advantage of the firm and its customers. The framework of the CRM process illustrated in Figure 27 attempts to provide a holistic understanding of the notion of an organizational process that cuts across business units and departments. The discussion on CRM, in the first part of the chapter, incorporated the customer's viewpoint of that process. The four sub-processes,

i.e. the *strategic planning process*, the *information processes*, the *customer value process* and the *performance measurement process* are relevant to customers' interests. Table 12 provides a summary of the CRM processes and activities discussed in the first part of the chapter. Furthermore, it puts forward key issues relevant to the practice of CRM and the customer.

The CRM processes outlined in Table 12 have been used as a basis for the identification of capabilities critical for the development and delivery of customer solutions. Specifically, the key organizational capabilities required are: *learning* and *market orientation capabilities*, *integration capabilities*, *analytical capabilities*, *operational capabilities* and *direction capabilities* (see Figure 28). It also follows that for CRM processes to deliver solutions for the firm and its customers, it is essential for the employees to be committed to these key organizational activities and capabilities. Additionally, management of the firm plays a key role in identifying and acquiring these capabilities, which requires devoting time and resources to organizational development and learning.

Table 12 The CRM process, its sub-processes and activities

CRM sub-processes	CRM activities	Key issues emerging from the findings
Strategic planning process (Table 8)	• Corporate strategy • Customer strategy	• Elements of strategy influence the perceptions of customers regarding the firm and its products and services
Information processes (Table 9)	• Information acquisition • Information dissemination • Information use	• Information processes enable customers to reach the firm • Privacy concerns linked to the analysis and use of customer information
CRM process		
Customer value process (Table 10)	• Definition of the value proposition • Development of the value proposition • Delivery of the value proposition	• Desired value • Customers' perceptions of value • Customer–firm co-production • Consumption as a value-generating activity
Performance measurement process (Table 11)	• Use of customer feedback and SHV measures to assess CRM performance	• Need for organizations to capture the value judgements of their customers

FURTHER READING

Customer relationship management

Bruhn, M. (2003) *Relationship Marketing: Management of Customer Relationships*. Prentice Hall, Financial Times: Harlow, UK.

Foss, B. & Stone, M. (2002) *CRM in Financial Services*. Kogan Page: London.

Payne, A. (2000) *Customer Relationship Management*. Retrieved from the World Wide Web at www.crm-forum.com.

Peppers, D. & Rogers, M. (2000) *The One-to-one Future – Building Business Relationships One Customer at a Time*, 3rd edn. Piatkus: London.

Sheth, J. & Parvatiyar, A. (1995) Relationship marketing in consumer markets: antecedents and consequences. *Journal of the Academy of Marketing Science*, **23** (4), 255–271.

Organizational processes and culture

Conduit, J. & Mavondo, F. T. (2001) How critical is internal customer orientation to market orientation? *Journal of Business Research*, **51**, 11–24.

Garvin, D. A. (1993) Building a learning organization. *Harvard Business Review*, July/August, 78–91.

Slater, S. F. & Narver, J. C. (1995) Market orientation and the learning organization. *Journal of Marketing*, **59** (3), 63–74.

Organizational strategy and capabilities

Day, G. S. (1994) The capabilities of market-driven organizations. *Journal of Marketing*, **584** (Oct/Dec), 37–53.

Fuchs, P. H., Mifflin, K. E., Miller, D. & Whitney, J. O. (2000) Strategic integration: competing in the age of capabilities. *California Management Review*, **42** (3), 118–147.

Plakoyiannaki, E. & Tzokas, N. (2002) Customer relationship management (CRM): a capability portfolio perspective. *Journal of Database Marketing*, **9** (3), 228–237.

Stalk, G., Evans, P. & Shulman, L. E. (1992) Competing on capabilities: the new rules of corporate strategy. *Harvard Business Review*, March/April, 57–69.

Walters, D. & Lancaster, G. (2000) Implementing value strategy through the value chain. *Management Decision*, **38** (3), 160–178.

Zwell, M. (2000) *Creating a Culture of Competence*. Wiley: Canada.

References

Aaker, D., Kumar, V. & Day, G. (2001) *Marketing Research*, 7th edition. Wiley: New York.

Ansoff, I. (1979) *Strategic Management*. Macmillan: London

Barnes, J. G. (1993) New technologies, new markets and changing marketing practice. *Irish Marketing Review*, 45–51.

Bloomfield, B., Coombs, R. & Owen, J. (1994) The social construction of information systems – the implications for management control. In: *Management of Information and Communication Technologies, Emerging Patterns of Control* (R. Mansell, ed.). Aslib: London.

Bock, T. & Uncles, M. (2002) A taxonomy of differences between consumers for market segmentation. *International Journal of Research in Marketing*, **19**, 215–224.

Booz, Allen & Hamilton (1982) *Management of New Products*. BAH Inc.

Brady, M., Saren, M. & Tzokas, N. (2002) Integrating information technology into marketing practice – the IT reality of contemporary marketing practice. *Journal of Marketing Management*, **18** (5/6, July), 555–578.

Braun, E. (1998) *Technology in Context, Technology Assessment for Managers*. Routledge: London.

Brown, R. (1999) Successful customer relationship management. *PM Network*, September, 27–28.

Bruce, M., Leverick, F., Littler, D. & Wilson, D. (1996) The changing scope and substance of marketing – the impact of IT. In: *European Academy of Marketing Conference – Marketing for an Expanding Europe*, Conference Proceedings, Vol. 1. Budapest University of Economic Science, pp. 185–204.

Bruhn, M. (2003) *Relationship Marketing: Management of Customer Relationships*. Prentice-Hall, Financial Times: Harlow, UK.

Conduit, J. & Mavondo, F. T. (2001) How critical is internal customer orientation to market orientation? *Journal of Business Research*, **51**, 11–24.

Davenport, T. H. (1994) Saving IT's soul: human-centred information management. *Harvard Business Review*, March/April, 119–131.

Davenport, T. H. (1997) *Information Ecology*. Oxford University Press: New York.

Davies, L. & Mitchell, G. (1994) The dual nature of the impact of IT on organisational transformation. In: *Transforming Organisation with IT* (R. Baskerville, S. Smithson, O. Ngwenyama and J. DeGross, eds), IFIP Transactions. Elsevier Science, Amsterdam, pp. 243–261.

Day, G. S. (1994) The capabilities of market-driven organizations. *Journal of Marketing*, (Oct/Dec), 37–53.

Demarest, M. (1997) Understanding knowledge management. *Long Range Planning*, **30** (3), 374–384.

Dobers, P. & Strannegard, L. (2001) Lovable networks – a story of affection, attraction and treachery. *Journal of Organisational Change*, **14** (1), 8–49.

Financial Times (2002) New twists for old tricks. *Financial Times*, 6 November, p. 4.

Flint, D. J., Woodruff, R. B. & Gardial, S. F. (1997) Customer value change in industrial marketing relations. *Industrial Marketing Management*, **26**, 163–175.

Ford, D. & Saren, M. (2001) *Marketing and Managing Technology*. International Thomson Business Press: London.

Fuchs, P. H., Mifflin, K. E., Miller, D. & Whitney, J. O. (2000) Strategic integration: competing in the age of capabilities. *California Management Review*, **42** (3), 118–147.

Foss, B. & Stone, M. (2002) *CRM in Financial Services*. Kogan Page: London.

Garvin, D. A. (1993) Building a learning organization. *Harvard Business Review*, July/August, 78–91.

Glazer, R. (1991) Marketing in an information intensive environment: strategic implications of knowledge as an asset. *Journal of Marketing*, **55**, 1–19.

Gordon, I. (1998) *Relationship Marketing*. Wiley: Canada.

Griffin, A. & Hauser (1995) The voice of the customer. In: *New Product Development: A Reader* (S. Hart, ed.). Dryden Press, Chap. 13.

Henry, P. (2000) Evaluating the implications for new media and IT. *Journal of Consumer Marketing*, **18** (2), 121–133.

Hitt, L. M. & Brynjolfsson, E. (1996) Productivity and business profitability, and consumer surplus: three different measures of information technology value. *MIS Quarterly*, **20** (2), 121–142.

Holtham, C. (1994) Current practice and future trends: an overview. In: *IT in Marketing* (J. Chapman & C. Holtham, eds). Alfred Waller in association with UNICOM, Henley on Thames, pp. 1–23.

Humby, C. (2004) *Scoring Points: How Tesco is winning customer loyalty*. Kogan Page: London.

Johne, A. & Storey, C. (1998) New service development: a review of the literature and annotated bibliography. *European Journal of Marketing*, March/April.

Kohli, A. K. & Jaworski, B. J. (1990) Market orientation – the construct, research propositions, and managerial implications. *Journal of Marketing*, **54** (2), 1–18.

Koppes, L., Trahan, W., Hartman, A., Perlman, B. & Nealon, D. (1991) Researching the impact of computer technology in the workplace: a psychological perspective. In: *Management Impacts of Information Technology – Perspectives on Organisation Change and Growth* (E. Szewczak, C. Snodgrass & R. Khosrowpour, eds). Idea Group: Pennsylvania.

Kotler, P. (1972) *Marketing Management: Analysis, Planning and Control*. Prentice-Hall: Englewood Cliffs, NJ.

Lanning, M. J. (1998) *Delivering Profitable Value: A Revolutionary Framework to Accelerate Growth, Generate Wealth, and Rediscover the Heart of Business*. Perseus Books: New York.

Leavitt, H. & Whisler, T. (1985) Management in the 80s. *Harvard Business Review*, **63** (1), 65–71.

Leverick, F., Littler D., Wilson, D. & Bruce, M. (1997) The role of IT in reshaping of marketing. *Journal of Marketing Practice: Applied Marketing Science*, **3** (2), 87–106.

Levitt, T. (1960) Marketing Myopia. *Harvard Business Review*, **38** (4), 45–56.

Li, T. & Calantone, R. J. (1998) The impact of market knowledge competence on new product advantage: conceptualization and empirical examination. *Journal of Marketing*, **62** (4), 13–29.

MacKenzie, D. & Wajcman, J. (1999) Introductory essay; the social shaping of technology. In: *The Social Shaping of Technology*, 2nd edn (D. MacKenzie & J. Wajcman, eds). Open University Press: Buckingham, pp. 3–27.

Mahoney, J. T. & Pandian, J. R. (1992) The resource-based view within the conversation of strategic management. *Strategic Management Journal*, **13**, 363–380.

Marchall, K. (1996) *Marketing Information Systems*. Thomson International: New York.

McKenna, R. (1991) *Relationship Marketing Successful Strategies for the Age of the Customer*. Addison-Wesley: Reading, MA.

McKenna, R. (1995) Real time marketing. *Harvard Business Review*, July/August, 87–95.

McKenna, R. (1998) Marketing in real time. *Executive Excellence*, **15** (4), 3–4.

McKenna, R. (1999) *Real Time Marketing*. Harvard Business School Press: Cambridge, MA.

McKeon, M. (1998) Telecom Eireann – taking Ireland into the information age. *Irish Call Centre New*, Jan/Feb, 12–13.

Meuter, M., Ostrom, A., Roundtree, R. & Bitner, M. (2000) Self service technologies: understanding customer satisfaction with technology based service encounters. *Journal of Marketing*, **64** (3), 50–64.

Moorman, C. (1995) Organizational market information processes: cultural antecedents and new product outcomes. *Journal of Marketing Research*, **32** (3), 318–336.

Narver, J. C. & Slater, S. F. (1990) The effect of market orientation on business profitability. *Journal of Marketing*, **54** (October), 20–35.

Parasuraman, A., Zeithaml, V. & Berry, L. (1985) A conceptual model of service quality and its implications for future research. *Journal of Marketing*.

Payne, A. (2000) *Customer Relationship Management*. Retrieved from the World Wide Web at www.crm-forum.com.

Peppard, J. (2000) Customer relationship management (CRM) in financial services. *European Management Journal*, **18** (3), 312–327.

Peppers, D. & Rogers, M. (2000) *The One-to-one Future – Building Business Relationships One Customer at a Time*, 3rd edn. Piatkus: London.

Plakoyiannaki, E. & Tzokas, N. (2002) Customer relationship management (CRM): a capability portfolio perspective. *Journal of Database Marketing*, **9** (3), 228–237.

Porter, M. (1985) *Competitive Advantage – Creating and Sustaining Superior Performance*. Free Press: New York.

Porter, M. J. & Millar, V. E. (1985) How information technology gives you competitive advantage. *Harvard Business Review*, July/August, 149–160.

Power, C. (2002) Laundry payment scheme has tech companies in a spin. *The Irish Times*, 18 October, p. 9.

Prahalad, C. & Krishnan, M. (1999) The new meaning of quality in the information age. *Harvard Business Review*, **77** (5, Sept/Oct), 109–139.

Prahalad, C., Ramaswamy, V. & Krishnan, M. (2000) Consumer centricity. *Information Week*, 4th Oct, **781**, 67–72.

Rappaport, A. (1986) *Creating Shareholder Value*. Free Press: New York.

Ravald, A. & Grönroos, C. (1996) The value concept and relationship marketing. *European Journal of Marketing*, **30** (2), 19–30.

Reichheld, F. & Schefter, P. (2000) E-Loyalty – your secret weapon on the web. *Harvard Business Review*, 105–113.

Rogers, E. (1962) *Diffusion of Innovations*. Free Press: New York.

Rogers, E. M. (1983) *The Diffusion of Innovations*, 3rd edn. Free Press: New York.

Saren, M. & Tzokas, N. (1998) The nature of the product in market relationships. *Journal of Marketing Management*, **14**, 445–464.

Scarbrough, H. (1998), Linking strategy and IT-base innovation: the importance of the 'management of expertise'. In: *Information Technology and Organisation Transformation, Innovations for the 21st Century* (B. Galliers & W. Baets, eds). Wiley Series in Information Systems, Chichester, pp. 19–36.

Schroeder, J. (2002) *Visual Consumption*. Routledge: London.

Sherry, J. (2000) Place, technology and representation. *Journal of Consumer Research*, **27** (2), 273–278.

Sheth, J. & Parvatiyar, A. (1995) Relationship marketing in consumer markets: antecedents and consequences. *Journal of the Academy of Marketing Science*, **23** (4), 255–271.

Slater, S. F. & Narver, J. C. (1995) Market orientation and the learning organization. *Journal of Marketing*, **59** (3), 63–74.

Srivastava, R. K., Shrevani, T. A. & Fahey, L. (1998) Market-based assets and shareholder value: a framework for analysis. *Journal of Marketing*, **62** (January), 2–18.

Stalk, G., Evans, P. & Shulman, L. E. (1992) Competing on capabilities: the new rules of corporate strategy. *Harvard Business Review*, March/April, 57–69.

Trott, P. (2005) *Innovation Management and New Product Development*, 3rd edn. Financial Times/Pitman: London.

Tzokas, N. & Saren, M. (2004) Competitive advantage, knowledge and relationship marketing. *Journal of Business and Industrial Marketing*, **19** (2), 124–135.

Venkatraman, N. & Henderson, J. C. (1998) Real strategies for virtual organising. *Sloan Management Review*, **40** (1), 33–48.

von Hippel, E. (1978) Users as innovators. *Technology Review*, **80** (3), 30–34.

Walsham, G. (1993) *Interpreting Information Systems in Organisations*. Wiley Series in Information Systems: London.

Walters, D. & Lancaster, G. (2000) Implementing value strategy through the value chain. *Management Decision*, **38** (3), 160–178.

Ward, J., Taylor, P. & Bond, P. (1996) Evaluation and realisation of IS/IT benefits: an empirical study of current practice. *European Journal of Information Systems*, **4**, 214–225.

Webster, F. E. (1997) The role of marketing in the organization. In:, *Reflections on the Futures of Marketing* (D. R. Lehmann & K. E. Jocz, eds). Marketing Science Institute: Cambridge, MA.

Wikström, S. (1996) The customer as a co-producer. *European Journal of Marketing*, **30** (4), 6–19.

Willcocks, L. (1996) Introduction: beyond the IT productivity paradox. In: *Investing in Information Systems – Evaluation and Management* (L. Willcocks, ed.). Chapman & Hall: London, pp. 1–12.

Wilson, D. T. & Jantrania, S. (1994) Understanding the value of a relationship. *Asia–Australia Marketing Journal*, **2** (1), 55–66.

Wind, Y. & Mahajan, V. (1997) Issues and opportunities in new product development. *Journal of Marketing Research*, **34** (1), 1–12.

Winer, R. S. (2001) A framework for customer relationship management. *Sloan Management Review*, **43** (4), 89–105.

Woodruff, R. B. (1997) Customer value: the next source of competitive advantage. *Journal of the Academy of Marketing Science*, **25** (2), 139–153.

Zwell, M. (2000) *Creating a Culture of Competence*. Wiley: Canada.

Brand Selection

The more our world is dominated by mass media, mass production, mass markets, the greater need for producers to identify their products and services to distinguish them from others and grab our attention. This is the original role of 'branding', which, although far from being a new phenomenon, has evolved to such an extent that the word itself has become ubiquitous – you see it everywhere – consumer brands, high street brands, virtual brands, corporate brands, personal brands, celebrity brands, household brands, sub-brands . . . . These are just a few of the various different categories of branding. This section reviews these and discuss the various roles that branding plays particularly for corporate image and 'fast fashion'.

The role of branding

In modern society human beings instinctively want to be unique and identified as individuals. The more our world is dominated by mass media, mass production, mass markets, the greater the desire for individuality. The conventional identification for a person is their 'given' name and surname. Individuality requires making one's own choice, however, and therefore we ascribe other labels of identification on others and ourselves in addition to our formal 'names'. So much so that labels such as nicknames, coats of arms, tattoos, furnishing, language, our living spaces, entertainment haunts and the clothes we wear make more statements about who we are than our names and initials do (see Consuming Experience).

In a business world of first impressions, you're only as good as your last impression.

In the same way, marketers seek to identify their products and services to distinguish them from others and grab our attention. This is the original role of what marketers traditionally call 'branding'. The logic is apparently a simple behavioural one: if the name is catchy, you like it and remember it; if you think the logo is cool, the product looks good and makes you feel great; if it is available in your favourite outlets and is within your price range, you buy it.

The use of branding is far from being a new phenomenon. It originated in branding of animals, cattle, sheep, in order to identify who owned them. Nowadays the subject of branding has evolved to such an extent that the word itself has become ubiquitous – you see it everywhere. In the marketing literature you can read about consumer brands, high street brands, virtual brands, corporate brands, personal brands, celebrity brands, household brands, sub-brands, brand extensions, fashion brands, luxury brand 'fever', brand communities, own-label brands, diffusion brands, brand stretching and lifestyle brands. In everyday use the term is applied to political parties, movies, TV programmes, footballers, nations, pop stars, military regiments, science, works of art, artists, cartoons, fictional characters and literary icons.

Making your mark – brand categories, types and roles

The implication of Baudrillard's observation (below) for branding is that if a label can be applied to almost anything, it becomes meaningless as a distinguishing feature. The paradox is that this is exactly what has happened to the use of the concept of branding itself.

> *As Baudrillard (1990) starkly illustrates, once a concept gains totality and becomes appropriate to everything and anything, it also becomes appropriate to nothing. An absolute definition is also meaningless.*

Nevertheless, there are various different categories of branding. The accompanying parts of Brand Selection review these and discuss the various roles that branding plays, particularly for corporate image and 'fast fashion'.

High street brands

These are the successful high street brands that consumers are quick to recognize by their distinct taste, style, packaging, service, technology, innovation, performance or premium pricing. Unlike luxury brands, their prices are not prohibitive and so are consumed by a larger share of the market. They are the likes of Coca-Cola, Häagen Dazs, Diesel Jeans, Nokia, Hewlett Packard and Vodafone.

Household brands

Similar to high street brands, but most often used as 'household' products. This is largely subjective, of course. The term was used in the 1950s and 1960s in the advertising of food items, detergents and other cleaning materials, what would today be called 'FMCG' brands (fast-moving consumer goods). This category would now include some consumer durables (so-called 'white goods' labels), e.g. Hoover, Bosch, Indesit, Sony.

Sub-brands

These are the results of a strategy known as 'brand stretching'. Aaker (1997) defined a sub-brand as a brand with its own name that uses the name of its parent brand in some capacity to bolster its reputation. A well-known brand from the UK, Richard Branson's Virgin, is now branding over 30 different products and services – from planes, trains, finance, soft drinks, music, mobile phones, holidays, cars, wines, publishing to bridal wear! (www.virgin.com). However, sub-brands do not necessarily include the name of the parent company (i.e. corporate brand). In the luxury goods industry, any such connection is usually undesirable. Thus, in the case of Rolex, its less expensive sub-brand trades under the name 'Tudor'. The idea is both to maintain the parent's credibility and prestige regardless of how the sub-brand performs and to protect the original brand from 'cannibalization', a phenomenon where the cheaper brand takes sales away from its more expensive 'parent'.

Luxury brands

These are usually high-profile brands with a history well rooted in fashion, design, superior quality, exclusivity, performance and that are able to command a price premium to the equivalent consumer brands which offer the same functionality. For example, whilst the recording time function for a Swatch watch and a Bulgari is the same, the price tag is quite different because of the prestige, quality and image of the label. Other examples of luxury brands are Chanel, Louis Vuitton, Tiffany & Co., Manolo Blahnik, Porsche, Frette (see also Fast fashion branding chapter).

Brand stretching

This refers to the extension of an established brand name, identified with one product in one market, to another type of product in other markets. The similar words 'extension' and 'diffusion' are also used both as adjectives to describe the dynamics that exist within the process of stretching and also as nouns to describe the strategy itself (see Fast fashion branding). A number of luxury brands, including Givenchy, Pierre Cardin, YSL and Gucci, adopted this strategy in the 1980s. Their logos and brand names were printed across a wide range of trivial, inexpensive and poor-quality items, such as pens, tie-pins, baseball caps, socks and key rings – there was even a Gucci toilet roll holder. Since then, faced also with the problem of counterfeiting, luxury brand companies have much more carefully limited their product portfolios in an effort to protect their investments in brand building. Most luxury brands now adopt a more discreet approach – small logos, labels and tags, and monograms.

Supermarkets are not only offering a larger range of products but also, through what is known as 'category management', a number of different brands for any one product.

Own-label brands

With increased 'share of spend', turnovers and volumes, the big supermarket chains have themselves become significant 'brand owners', chipping away at consumer brand volumes by competing with their own-label brands. Own-label brands are invariably positioned as being a cheaper option to the equivalent consumer brands, e.g. Wal-Mart/Asda's Smart Price range of foodstuffs and paper products or Tesco's 'Value' brand range. Advertising of own-label products is limited, mostly to in-store promotion and prominent shelf or stand-alone display. Unlike manufacturer brands, there is little emphasis on product origins. We do not see pineapples growing in the Del Monte plantations in South America or Irish farmers milking healthy-looking cows with green, rolling hills in the background as in the Kerrygold advertising. Own labels are more likely simply to state, for instance, that 'these dates are the product of more than one country' (what, all in one pack?).

Celebrity brands

These are brands where celebrities endorse the label as the one they use, the best, or simply impress the audience by wearing the branded sunglasses or dress. Manufacturers pay the music, movie or media star to use their name and image on or with the brand. Pop music tours are sponsored by Pepsi or Coke; famous actors advocate brands in advertisements, sometimes with their signature at the end; there are multimillion dollar sponsorship deals with sports champions in order to associate the brand with the sport/the champion/with winning. Celebrity branding goes much further than paid endorsement. There are many cases now where the celebrity's agents initiate the celebrity brand. They hire the manufacturer to develop and supply the product, and then brand it with the celebrity and launch it onto the market themselves as their own perfume, lingerie collections, clothing, accessory ranges, cooking sauces etc. (see 'Brand it like Beckham' subsection).

Branding in movies and TV

Branding can take the more subtle form of 'product placement' within the scenes of cinema and TV programmes. Notable examples are Omega, BMW and Vodafone in James Bond movies; Apple Mac in *Jurassic Park* and *You've Got Mail*.

The media can make an unknown brand famous. Manolo Blahnik shoes were incorporated in the TV series *Sex and the City* by the actor Sarah Jessica Parker, also the producer of the series, because they 'fitted' the character of Carrie whom she plays. Manolo Blahnik, a brand previously known only by a few, gained prominence and exposure. In one storyline, Carrie is mugged in a New York alley. After the robber took her wallet and jewellery, the next thing he demanded was her Blahnik high-heeled shoes.

Internet branding

The Internet has given a new dimension to branding and more involvement for consumers with brands. Consumers are now only one click away from finding out more about brands and products, whether for further information about the company which produces them, shop location, looking for job vacancies or even asking for samples. Likewise, companies have direct access to consumers or potential ones, a mine of information which companies can tap into to find out more about the people who buy their brands (see Moving Space). The Internet has given a new form of life to the 'total brand experience' that marketers aspire to achieve.

For example, Ferrero (www.ferrero.it) has created a total immersion experience for children with its flagship product Kinder Surprise. In addition to the plastic figurine enclosed in the chocolate egg, children can also find a Magicode, which gives them access to a unique, interactive game on the Internet (www.magickinder.com). The games import characters from the collection series in season at the time. The site is heavily branded with the Kinder Surprise logo and pack shots. Children enter the Kinder world to play with Kinder characters whilst they munch through the Kinder Surprise chocolate egg, and when all is over they can play with their own Kinder figurine they animated on the Internet.

www.opodo.com – the case of a virtual brand

Unlike Kinder Surprise, which also has a physical entity, a number of totally virtual brands exist on the Internet. We cannot drink them, eat them, visit their headquarters or offices to buy or make a booking – their existence depends entirely on the Internet. An example is Opodo (www.opodo.com), a pan-European travel portal founded in the summer of 2001 by nine of Europe's leading airlines. The brand was developed by the brand consultants, Wolff Olins (www.wolff-olins.com), whilst the online marketing was developed and created by Planetactive, Germany (www.planetactive.com).

The original plan was for Opodo to support the launch of the portal with an aggressive offline advertising campaign, including TV, billboard and print advertising in Germany, scheduled for November 2001. Instead, they cancelled their offline advertising to minimize the risk of their investment and stuck to online marketing instead. The objectives of the online campaign were:

1 To launch the Opodo brand as an online travel portal
2 To increase the online ticket sales
3 To capture respondents' email addresses.

The campaign included banner advertising, microsites created especially for the campaign and online promotions, including a quiz, which had an hourly prize of a flight offered by one of the nine airlines. Participants in the quiz had the chance to increase their chances of winning by communicating the site to a friend. This viral marketing effect generated some 650 000 participants in the quiz in just eight weeks and around half of them registered for the Opodo newsletter, which again enabled more distribution of information. Within three months and a budget of significantly less than 1 million euros, Opodo became the second most visited travel portal in Germany behind the national train company's official website, www.bahn.de. After the online launch and once a stable travel market post-9/11 was restored, Opodo launched an offline campaign.

The Internet provides means for potential and actual customers to get involved in the branding of products, which we consume. This Opodo online quiz is the epitome of this involvement.

Brand it like Beckham: the case of celebrity as brand

WARNING: This section is not about David Beckham, nor is it about Posh. It is about the phenomenon of celebrity as brand that the Beckham name represents.

Right from the beginning, I said I wanted to be more famous than Persil Automatic.
Beckham, V., quoted in Beckham, D., 2003

The American pop singer, Jennifer Lopez, recently re-branded herself as J.Lo – undoubtedly a catchier version. J.Lo is now branding her own clothing collections for toddlers, girls and teens: J.Lo Toddlers, J.Lo Girls and J.Lo Lovelies, which are available for sale on her website, www.shopJLo.com. Glow by J.Lo is also a new fragrance, which she describes as being very simple. On her website she uses three words to sum up the fragrance: 'fresh, sexy, clean . . . and it describes what I want for myself'. When asked how does the fragrance represent her, she says:

> It's very much about me, because it represents everything I've loved ever since I was very young – fresh, clean, simple, sensual things. Things like fresh air, the breeze coming in through the window, the ocean, summer sunshine. People might have expected a Jennifer Lopez fragrance to be more musky, more overtly sexy, but Glow is much more the real me, rather than the two-dimensional image you see on screen or in a magazine.
>
> *www.jenniferlopez.com*

So, according to her own story, Jennifer Lopez has interpreted herself in this fragrance. We have a product with a soul and not an endorsement. She likes the perfume because she created it herself and it carries her very own name – she is the brand.

Formula 1 World Champion Michael Schumacher (MS) has branded his very own carting track in Kerpen, Germany, as the Michael Schumacher Kart Center, which also houses the MS Sports Bar. He also brands a range of casual clothing and accessories (www.michael-schumacher.com).

Kylie Minogue, the Australian pop singer, launched her own lingerie collection under the brand Love Kylie (www.kylieshop.com) in 2003. Holeproof, the manufacturer, claims on its corporate website that the items, personally designed by Kylie, are 'a reflection of that distinctive Kylie style – pert and provocative but still stylish and sophisticated. We are constantly amazed at how our busy Kylie finds the time to dedicate to the creation of the Love Kylie ranges. She is absolutely involved in every aspect.' As with J.Lo's fragrance, we now have lingerie with attitude – created, modelled and initialled by Kylie herself.

The Love Kylie brand is not simply or even primarily about panties and bras, but more an association with the glamour surrounding the image of the singer/celebrity; it is *an extension of the brand that 'Kylie' already is herself* within the music industry.

Celebrity branded products are not all about perfume and lingerie. The 77-year-old American actor, Paul Newman, launched his 'Newman's Own' brand of salad dressings and spaghetti sauces in 1982. Newman's Own claims on its website (www.newmansown.com) to reflect Mr. Newman's goal to create nutritious, all-natural versions of his favourite foods. Starting

with 'Newman's famous Oil & Vinegar Salad Dressing', the brand has now expanded to a line of salad dressings, pasta sauces, salsas, popcorn, steak sauce and lemonade.

Celebrities are brands. They are defined by what people think about them, they have competitive positioning relative to other celebrities. Unlike the people behind them, celebrities exist in the minds of their audience precisely the same way that corporate or FMCG brands do.
Grannell & Jayarwardena, 2004

What these examples show is that famous people, as celebrities, have themselves become brands, extending their name to commodities of various and often of unrelated kinds. Their name adds brand recognition, image and glamour to the otherwise indistinguishable commodities (Agrawal & Kamakura, 1995; McCracken, 1989).

Although many celebrities are 'famous for being famous', celebrity is not the same as fame, however. It is still possible to be famous in a localized way, such as in a village or a professional community. Evans and Wilson (1999) link the rise of the celebrity with the decline of 'real' heroes and the ascendancy of the media industry which spawns and sustains them:

> What is remarkable about the whole 20th century is the substitution of fantasy for reality. The real heroes of history are played by actors in the movie industry. Media reality substitutes for actual reality, fiction substitutes for fact, or interrelates with it as 'infotainment'. Our present-day versions of celebrity are media ones; at least two-thirds of those we consider famous are actors, musicians, presenters and entertainers in the media world.

Celebrities' brands are graded, like other commodities, by quality and price. They are ranked by hierarchy (A, B, C, D list) and share values (www.celebdaq.com), the difference to other businesses being the celebrity industry's invisibility, with no tangible products or services in the traditional sense, its manufacturing operations unclear, its backroom personnel anonymous, and its distributors in PR and the media remaining in the background; only the brand itself is relentlessly drenched in the oxygen of publicity (Harbison, 2004).

FURTHER READING

Brand building

Aaker, D. (1996) *Building Strong Brands*. Free Press: New York.

Berthon, P., Hulbert, J. & Pitt, F. (1999) Brand management prognostications. *Sloan Management Review*, **40** (2), 53–65.

de Chernatony, L. & McDonald, M. (1993) *Creating Powerful Brands*. Butterworth-Heinemann: Oxford.

Keller, K.L. (2002) Branding and brand equity. In: *Handbook of Marketing* (B. Weitz & R. Wensley, eds). Sage: London, pp. 151–178.

Murray, W. (2000) *Brand Storm*. Prentice-Hall/Financial Times: London.

Celebrity branding

Evans, A. & Wilson, G. (1999) *Fame: The Psychology of Stardom*. Bath Press: Bath.

Grannell, C. & Jayarwardena, R. (2004) Celebrity branding: not as glamorous as it looks. 19 January 2004, www.brandchannel.com.

McCracken, G. (1989) Who is the celebrity endorser? Cultural foundations of the endorsement process. *Journal of Consumer Research*, **16**, 310–320.

corporate branding: image and identity

Claudia Simoes

> *. . . whatever else it may be, identity is connected with the fateful appraisals made of oneself – by oneself and by others. Everyone presents himself to the others and to himself, and sees himself in the mirrors of their judgement.*
> *Strauss, 1969*

Companies develop their image and identity in order to present themselves and enhance their reputation with customers, employees, governments, the public and other organizations. A basic question may be asked at the outset: what is meant by corporate identity and how does it work in the marketplace? This chapter seeks to provide an answer by presenting an understanding of the realm of corporate identity. In particular, it will explain the definitions and purposes of key elements in building corporate identity. Then there is a brief analysis of the concept of *corporate identity* and the related notions of *corporate brand* and *corporate image*. Finally, there is an overview of the relevance of corporate identity for consumers and its role in dealing with environmental forces.

Why build corporate identity?

Companies are always looking for new sources of competitive advantage to address their audiences or stakeholders (e.g. customers, publics, media, suppliers, financial companies). One approach is to develop strategies that are based at the overall corporate level, as opposed to the individual products or brands. Indeed, organizations generally last longer than products, and the market perceptions of the business are usually more difficult for competitors to imitate than perceptions of a brand. It is, for example, hard to emulate companies that are perceived as having the highest quality and best-qualified personnel or the most clearly defined and relevant mission. Managing the perceptions of an organization may, thus, provide an important basis for a more sustainable, long-term advantage (Aaker, 1996). Creating a strong *corporate identity* (CI) is one possible route for companies to encourage positive attitudes towards their business and establish a positive corporate image among audiences.

Generally, CI is what distinguishes one company from another. For example, since identity is shaped according to what the company stands for, it articulates the business philosophy through the company's mission and values. Additionally, corporate

identity facilitates the establishment of a close relationship with stakeholders, encouraging identification. As a result, customer loyalty and goodwill among relevant stakeholders is more likely to occur. Ultimately, corporate identity underpins differentiation and may help improve its reputation and relationships.

What is corporate identity?

The term *identity* has been referred to in various contexts. Expressions such as group identity, social identity, national identity, individual identity, and more recently corporate identity, are frequently used in both scientific and non-scientific settings. To understand the notion of identity, try to answer the following questions. How do I define myself? What distinguishes me from other human beings? How do I want others to perceive me? Your answer to these questions would be founded on a wide variety of dimensions such as personality and character traits, personal history, cultural background, physical appearance, etc. The outcome would be the portrait of a unique human being. Nobody else would exactly fit that description. Your identity is what makes you distinct and different from others. The Oxford Advanced Learner's Dictionary defines identity as '*the characteristics, feelings or beliefs that distinguish people from others*'. Thus, this term embraces traits that allow one person or object to be distinguished from another.

Corporate identity is what helps an organization, or part of it, feel that it truly exists and that it is a coherent and unique being, with a history and a place of its own, different from others.
Kapeferer, 1996

If we transpose the concept of identity to organizations, we can say that identity may be seen as an abstract idea, suggesting that every organization has its own personality, uniqueness and individuality. Corporate identity is '*what the organization "is", e.g. its innate character*' (Balmer, 1995, p. 25). It has, in this sense, an internal perspective in that it represents what is reflected by the company. Identity '*comprises the ways that a company aims to identify itself or position its product*' (Kotler, 1997, p. 292). Nike, the sports footwear, apparel and equipment producer, partly grounds its identity on the company's 30 years of experience in the sports and fitness business and its evolution as a global company. As a worldwide known company, Nike shapes its identity based on the core purpose and mission '*to bring inspiration and innovation to every athlete* in the world. *If you have a body, you are an athlete*'. This purpose is linked to Nike co-founder, Bill Bowerman's, vision about the business (http://www.nike.com). The asterisk emphasises the company's interest in reaching each individual in the marketplace. Throughout its history Nike went through ups and downs in the public opinion arena; building a strong identity has been a powerful instrument to handle adverse times and create a unique position in the market.

The notion of corporate identity is grounded in various subject domains. Insights from four core disciplines have contributed to the evolution and study of CI: the *graphic design*, *marketing*, *organizational studies* and *interdisciplinary* approaches. The *graphic design* perspective encompasses all forms of visual presentation of the company, such as the management of corporate symbols (e.g. logos and signage) (Riel & Balmer, 1997; Olins, 1991). The *marketing* approach builds on brand management and integrated communications research (e.g. De Chernatony, 1999; Duncan & Everett, 1993). The *organizational studies* perspective analyses the concept of organizational identity and is mainly concerned with members' feelings towards their organization (Dutton *et al.*, 1994). Finally, a holistic perspective in *interdisciplinary* studies acknowledges the overlap in areas of knowledge and advocates an eclectic view of corporate identity (Riel & Balmer, 1997).

Perspectives on corporate identity

Centres on the management of corporate symbols that transmit the strategic, visual dimensions of corporate identity to internal and external audiences (Riel & Balmer, 1997; Hatch & Schultz, 1997). It is concerned with all forms of visual presentation of the company that stakeholders come into contact with. Accordingly, a firm's identity is expressed through name, symbols, logos, colours and rites of passage, premises, packaging, stationary, vehicles (Henrion & Parkin, 1967; Olins, 1991).

Initial work on corporate identity emanates from the creation and management of visual identity systems. This perspective is strongly linked to practitioners' work on visual design systems. Although the field has evolved to a wider approach to the subject, there are specialized consulting companies addressing corporate identity by embracing visual identity dimensions (e.g. logo design, business cards, visual identity manuals, package design, etc.). Check the following websites: www.global-reach.com; http://logopurchase.com/corporate-identity-package_2a.html; www.circle-design.co.uk.

Builds on work relating to brand management *(see subsection on corporate brands) and* integrated communications.

The integrated communications *approach advocates that it is critical to develop and manage the impressions that customers and other stakeholders hold of the organization. The desire for consistency in corporate communications has fuelled interest in* integrated marketing communications *(Riel & Balmer, 1997). Duncan and Everett (1993) define integrated marketing communications as* 'the strategic coordination of all messages and media used by an organization to influence its perceived brand value'. *Integrating communication strategies creates synergies among different forms of communication (e.g. advertising, public relations) and encourages a consistent approach throughout the organization (Gould* et al., *1999).*

There are agencies that devote part of their work to the development of integrated communication programmes in companies. Have a look at EURO RSCG's work on www.euroscg.com. It is also worthwhile taking a tour of the Strata-G Communications website (www.strata-g.com). Get an idea about the type of work that they develop and check samples of their outputs.

Analyses the concept of organizational identity and is mainly concerned with internal aspects of identity, emphasizing the feelings of members towards their organization (Albert et al., *2000; Hatch & Schultz, 1997;* Dutton et al., *1994). In creating identity, businesses internalize a cognitive structure of what the organization stands for and where it intends to go. A frequently used definition of* organizational identity *suggests it is what is central, enduring and distinctive about an organization (Albert & Whetten, 1985). Employees' views/perceptions of the organization's identity and external image affect how they behave towards it. In general, organizational identification occurs when the images they receive are favourable, distinct and enduring (Dutton* et al., *1994). Companies permanently try to enhance their employees' identification with the company and their sense of belonging. For example, McDonald's, the fast-food company, created a corporate people promise and vision stating the company's commitment to every employee:* 'we value your growth and your contributions'. *The company's values also stress their internal audience and the aspired relationship (http://www.mcdonalds.com).*

Bringing it all together: interdisciplinary perspective

Supports a holistic perspective based in interdisciplinary *studies that acknowledge an overlap in various areas of knowledge and advocates a more eclectic view of corporate identity (Riel & Balmer, 1997).*

Current approaches to corporate identity and its management tend to look for input from several backgrounds – e.g. design, brand management, strategy, organizational culture and communications. This is confirmed by a study conducted in several European countries, which revealed that managers tend to view corporate identity as embracing a wide range of dimensions, such as public image/external projection, visual presentation, expression of culture/values philosophy, internal projection/staff behaviour, product brand support and advertising/ communication support (Schmidt, 1995).

This interdisciplinary view is visible in firms assisting companies in the development of their corporate identity. For example, Wolff Olins, a major corporate brand consultancy, undertake a comprehensive approach to corporate identity.

From the firm's website you can download interesting case histories based on work developed on very diverse companies (http://www.wolff-olins.com). You may also check identity consultants Henrion, Ludlow, Schmidt's website (http://www.henrion.com). This company proposes *holistic solutions* that take into account dimensions such as design, communications and behaviour.

The corporate brand

[The corporate brand is] more than just the outward manifestation of an organization, its name, logo, visual presentation. Rather it is the core of values that define it. The communication of those values is of course an important part of what an organization is.
Ind, 1997

The linkages between brand and corporate identity are revealed when the branding concept is applied at the corporate level. If brands are regarded as hierarchical, then according to Keller (2002), the corporate (or company) brand represents the highest level in the ranking. Aaker (1996, p. 68) defines brand identity as '*a unique set of brand associations that the brand strategist aspires to create or maintain*'. The core component of this identity is the so-called '*essence*' of the brand – the values and beliefs underpinning it, with which it is associated. Identity also has a number of dimensions that complete and give texture to the brand, such as symbols, logos and brand design. Employees have an important role to play in this process, because their behaviour affects external perceptions. The way in which the brand is communicated and explained inside the corporation, as well as outside it, is therefore of the utmost importance (de Chernatony & Harris, 2000). When fully embodied in the organization in this manner, de Chernatony (1999) argued that corporate branding becomes the *strategic direction* for the organization's activities, providing consistency through the connection between positioning, communication and staff working style or behaviour.

Confusingly, the concept of corporate brand identity is very similar to the notion of corporate identity. In many cases the terms are used synonymously, involving identical activities. This is particularly so in the case of service companies (Schmitt & Pan, 1994), where the company is the primary brand, encompassing specific service offerings. Thus, TAP AirPortugal, Barclays Bank and Real Madrid Football Club have each developed their identity around the corporate brand.

The corporate image

Corporate identity is exhibited in the image that a company presents to its audiences (e.g. customers, competitors, communities). Academic research supports the idea that strong corporate identity assists image formulation. For example,

LeBlanc & Nguyen (1996) detected that CI significantly influences customers' perceptions of the image projected by a particular financial institution. Corporate identity is filtered by audiences and becomes the image that they perceive of the company (i.e. company image). Whereas the notion of identity embodies the self-awareness of the subject (the company), the concept of *image* is centred on the reception by the audience (Hatch & Schultz, 1997; Kotler, 1997).

Companies cultivate distinct images in order to be taken as unique by their markets and other stakeholders. Benetton, the Italian clothing producer and retailer, created a global brand image based on the overall idea of overcoming cultural and racial barriers. Benetton's sometimes controversial advertising campaigns depicted people and accessories, such as national flags, allusive to different racial, national, cultural and political backgrounds. This image was translated in the caption 'United Colours of Benetton' (Mantle, 1999). Nowadays Benetton's outlets are spread all over the world and the company was ranked by Interbrand in 2001 among the world's 100 most valuable brands (www.interbrand.com). Log onto www.benetton.com and you will find examples of previous campaigns.

The influence of corporate identity on consumers

[Corporate image is] the associations that consumers have in their memory to the company or corporation making the product or providing the service as a whole.
Keller, 2002

Corporate identity clearly influences markets because corporate image affects consumers' attitudes and behaviour. However, there is more than meets the eye to the connection between identity, markets and consumption. During the last decades consumption culture and values have changed. Companies find various ways to adjust their market approaches and overall business attitude, taking into account new market dynamics. Corporate identity directly or indirectly influences consumers. In fact, CI assists buyers on basic functions such as reducing search costs, i.e. the time and effort consumers spend finding out about an array of alternative products to meet a particular function. In addition, because consumption is increasingly grounded on (the sharing of) a symbolic identification (see Consuming Experience), corporate identity may entail a more complex aura such as instilling identification with the company and establishing commitment and loyalty. Figure 29 introduces the main topics addressing the link between CI and markets.

Basic functions

In general, brands allow product identification, reduce search costs and, consequently, the perceived risk (monetary, social and safety) (Berry, 2000; Berthon *et al.*, 1999). Consumers want to simplify their decision process and brands aid that endeavour. However, sometimes confusion occurs as products and services are similar and individual brand names abundant. Increasingly organizations link their

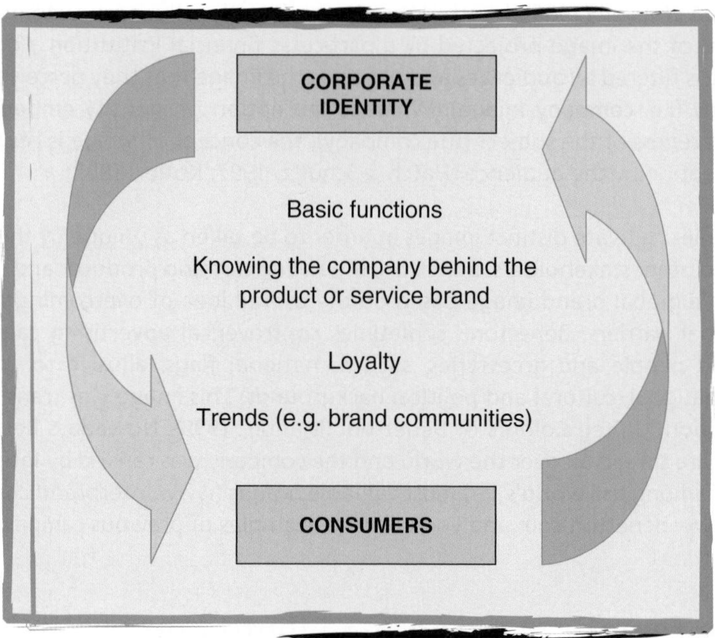

Figure 29 When corporate identity bridges with consumers

corporate brand name to individual products and/or make the company's name visible. For example, Kellogg, the breakfast cereals manufacturer, noted how it was becoming harder for consumers to differentiate among competing brands. In 2000, Kellogg launched an overall new design on its packages. You may find that Kellogg's products' packages either have the company 'K' logo highlighted and/or the company name incorporated. Consumers can easily see that Kellogg is the company behind the individual brands. As the company's identity statement affirms: '*we build gr-r-reat brands and make the world a little happier by bringing our best to you*' (*The Times* 100, Edition 6, 2000; www.kelloggs.com).

The corporate brand conveys values and features that are consistent across the company's products. Moreover, 'branding assures buyers of uniform service quality and can provide service marketers with a greater degree of pricing freedom, if the brand image is properly created and promoted' (Onkvisit & Shaw, 1989). A strong corporate brand simplifies the consumer buying decision process as it differentiates and creates confidence in consumers' minds. For example, Boots, the manufacturer and retailer of consumer healthcare products, conveys an image of a reliable company with heritage but modern. Consumers frequently buy the company's brand products relying on the trust they have in the company (for further details on the company and its identity background check the website, www.boots-plc.com).

Indeed, if buyers cannot evaluate the product or service prior to consumption they will rely on the company's brand image and reputation. Bharadwaj and Menon (1993) found that, in these circumstances, an image or reputation can become a key cue in the evaluation of products and services by consumers, and therefore corporate identity, through the image formation process, is a relevant input for consumers' buying decisions.

Knowing the company behind the product or service brand

Customers are increasingly interested in knowing who is behind the brand that they buy. Indeed, research demonstrates that new product evaluations are affected by customers' perceptions of the organizations (Brown & Dacin, 1997). For instance, in Japan and other Asian countries, television commercials for consumer products from large companies usually display the company logo at the end. It would appear that the respectability of a company's image influences product brand success. Company identity is a major feature in marketing products in Asia, as company image affects market responses (Schmitt & Pan, 1994).

Moreover, consumers want to identify with product or service providers. They want to view a company as an entire entity and make sure that they identify with the companies' values and that they trust their overall business approach and attitude. For example, buyers are increasingly concerned with environmental issues, and corporations respond to this concern by creating an environmentally friendly brand or corporate image (Menon & Menon, 1997). Symbols are also frequently used by corporations in order to entice a higher level of identification between publics and company. For example, national symbols such as the thistle were used by Scottish broadcasting companies in their visual identities (Meech, 1996).

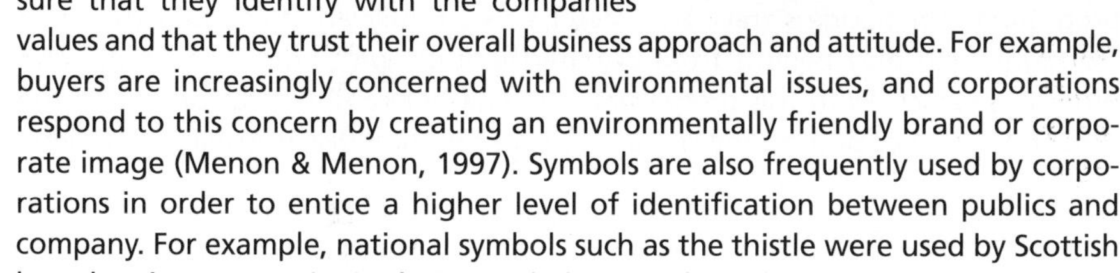

In the marketplace, there are numerous opportunities for consumers to make connections between organizations and particular products. Body Shop, the cosmetic and retail company, founds its reason for being on its mission statement, which implies protecting the environment and balancing stakeholders' interests. The following five values entail the company's identity: against animal testing, support community trade, activate self-esteem, defend human rights and protect our planet. You can learn more about how the company articulates the link between company values and market at www.thebodyshop.com.

Loyalty

Recent marketing literature emphasizes the construction of relationships between customers and the company. Relationship marketing, as it is known, suggests that businesses should be retaining customers and building loyalty (see Building Relations). It is consistent with this line of thought that attention has focused on the notion of brand loyalty. Oliver (1997, p. 392) defines brand loyalty as 'a deeply held commitment to re-buy or re-patronize a preferred product or service consistently in the future, despite situational influences and marketing efforts having the potential to cause switching behaviour'.

Identity and image are relevant variables in the relationship between consumers and companies. Research supports this connection. Findings suggest that for both airline and hotel industries, consumers' identification with company's values and self-images are important determinants of the strength of their commitment to a particular brand. As Pritchard *et al.* (1999) noted, '*the more strongly consumers identified with the values and images embodied by a particular brand, the greater their sense of resistance to change that preference would become*'. Similarly, Zins (2001) found a strong relationship between image and future loyalty for consumers in the commercial airline industry.

Eventually, customer brand responses lead to loyalty as the customer builds 'emotional' links with the company (brand) and thus tends to be more loyal towards it. You may find numerous examples of companies developing consumer loyalty programmes or schemes. Normally, these schemes establish a link between the corporate brand/company and customers. This leads to mutually beneficial and continuous relationships. For example, the airline company British Airways' aim is to provide '*a full service experience*'. The company developed the executive club programme for business travellers. Members earn miles that can be exchanged for flights and may benefit from BA's partnerships with hotels, car rental and other businesses. With this programme the link between the customer and the organization goes beyond the company's core service (www.britishairways.com).

Trends

Currently, there is general agreement in the marketing literature that the brand is more than a name given to a product; it embodies a whole set of physical and socio-psychological attributes and beliefs (see Creating Solutions). Consumption may entail symbolic idiosyncratic or shared meanings. Consumers may buy organic food because it symbolizes that they 'care for the environment and animal rights'. Indeed, in order to build and maintain their identity, consumers may recur to the symbolic meanings of consumer goods and brands. Brands may, therefore, play a role in the construction of consumer identity (see Consuming Experience).

This idea may be widened by the concept of brand communities notion. Muniz and O'Guinn (2001, p. 412) define brand community as a *'specialized, non-geographically bound community, based on a structured set of social relationships among admirers of a brand'*. Relationships in brand communities have been extended beyond the customer–brand–customer triad. McAlexander *et al.* (2002) considered relevant to consumers the relationships between the customer and their branded possessions, marketing agents, brand organization manager and owner. Figure 30 depicts these relationships in the customer-centric model of brand community.

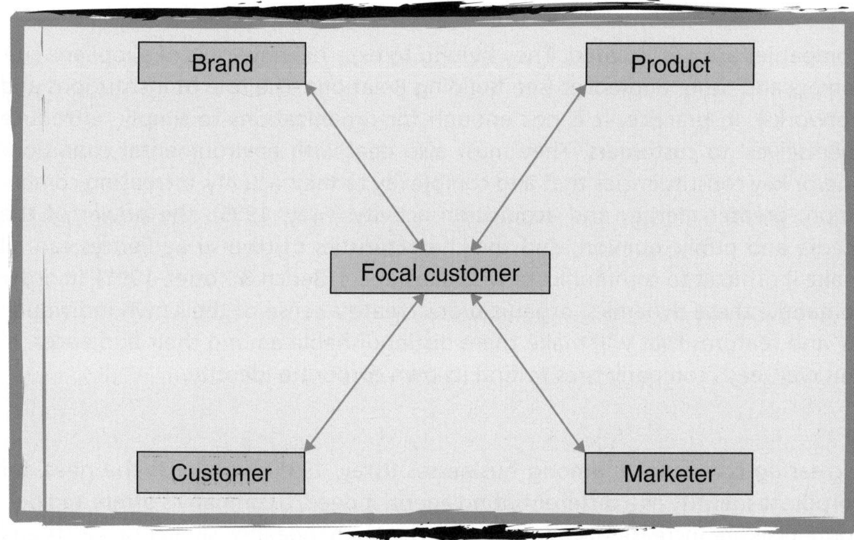

Figure 30 Customer-centric model of brand community. *Source:* McAlexander *et al.* (2002)

Companies have acknowledged the benefits of such communities. For example, they impact on the brand's equity as they affect, for instance, consumers' loyalty. The stronger the corporate identity the most likely these communities will emerge. Indeed, as you may find Rolling Stones' fan clubs all over the world, you may see a similar phenomenon related to a brand and/or their experience. Lego, the toy company, is an example. Before the official Lego site on the Internet was created in 1995, the company detected sites all over the world, where consumers expressed their opinions and values towards Lego usage (Lindstrom, 2002). The company realized the potential of such phenomena and currently manages the Lego Club (check www.lego.com). Similarly, Harley Davidson, the motorcycle company, developed a strong identity based on the company's charisma and overall style. Harley Davidson is a legend. If you log onto Harley Davidson's website you will find a link to Harley Owners Group (HOG). The invitation is clear: *'Love to ride? We know how you feel. Join HOG and become a part of hundreds of thousands who feel the same way*.' Here you can get information about all Harley Davidson's communities around the world, events and social gatherings, etc. This group's mission is: '*to ride and have fun*'; to join HOG '*may not provide you with the meaning of life, but it's a pretty good feeling*' (www.harley-davidson.com).

Corporate identity: responding to environmental forces

Companies are not isolated. They belong to external networks of suppliers, customers and other audiences (see Building Relations: The role of institutions and networks). In practice, it is not enough for organizations to simply 'introduce themselves' to customers. They must also deal with environmental conditions and/or key constituencies that add complexity to their activity. Increasing competition, greater merger and acquisition activity (Gray, 1995), the power of the media and public opinion, and the characteristics of diverse audiences can all make it difficult to communicate with consumers (Barich & Kotler, 1991). In order to handle these dynamics, organizations create a sense of their own individuality and features that will make them distinguishable among their audiences. In this way, each company tries to find its own corporate identity.

Increasing competition among businesses (Gray, 1995) highlights the need for corporate identity as a differentiating agent. Indeed, a company's offers and performances are increasingly analogous and interchangeable; similar products and services need to be differentiated in some way. Corporate identity is a key tool that enables organizations to differentiate themselves in their markets through, for instance, service features, symbols and corporate communications (Schmidt, 1995). This means that it is especially important that each company finds its own corporate identity. Coca-Cola company and Pepsi Cola try to differentiate their offer by establishing distinct identity features in their markets. As an exercise you may try to specify the main vectors that distinguish these two corporate brands (find more information on www.pepsico.com and www.coca-cola.com).

The growing *internationalization* of companies and rising number of *mergers and acquisitions* compromise the unity of organizations (Gray, 1995). For example, the services literature debates the ability of international companies to maintain global brands with consistent quality levels (Piercy, 1998). This phenomenon requires that each organization has a strong corporate identity in order to create a unified image. Overseas suppliers and the wide range of geographically dispersed and culturally diverse audiences with which companies deal have brought the development and management of corporate image to the fore. In such an international environment, corporate identity may stimulate local (national) acceptance for the company and/or work as an integrative force and driver (Schmidt, 1995). For example, in the late 1980s, Kodak restructured its activities to expand beyond the provision of camera film products. The company created business synergies in five different groups: photographic products, commercial and information systems, diversified technologies, Eastman chemicals, and life sciences. Communication was used as a strategic tool to adapt Kodak to a new and uniform image and attach the corporate name to diverse products. Kodak tried to position itself as an organization with broad business capabilities. By coordinating communication strategies, Kodak informed customers about the non-consumer products it was involved with and created a worldwide brand identity. Currently, Kodak keeps its promise of being a global state-of-the-art company devoted to marketing a wide range of products and services to its consumer and business markets (Strong, 1987; www.uk. kodak.com).

Other environmental aspects that determine the relevance of corporate identity can be noted. These include the *challenges and opportunities of the European Union* (EU); the *globalization, deregulation and privatization of markets* and the *wide range of audiences* and public opinion with which companies must deal (e.g. mass media, local communities) (Dowling, 1986; Barich & Kotler, 1991; Schmidt, 1995). For example, during the 1990s, the Portuguese telecom company's – Portugal Telecom – environment underwent a profound change. The government decided to gradually deregulate the market, opening it up to competition, and privatize the company. In order to handle these dynamics the company needed to reshape its identity. It created a new vision and business attitude: it was no longer a telephone company but a company able to provide all the communications solutions that the market needed. This meant creating a whole new concept to the company's internal and external attitude. A new imagery, business approach and identity mirroring this idea was then developed. The company has now a renewed image among constituencies and is regarded in the market as a modern organization in tune with its environment (www.wolff-olins.com/files/PTPortugal TelecomCaseStudyWeb.pdf; www.portugaltelecom.pt).

Key points

- *Corporate identity enables organizations to build the reputation of their company and make a positive impression on customers, employees and other publics.*
- *Corporate identity emerges from a company's capacity to understand and manage internal and external reality, its history and decisions, and its overall business attitude.*
- *Identity must be based on solid foundations that contain an overall message.*
- *The expression of an identity is a dynamic process and that identity itself may evolve over time.*

FURTHER READING

The corporate identity concept

Balmer, J. (1999) Corporate identity. In: *Encyclopaedia of Marketing* (M. Baker, ed.). Thomson Learning: London, pp. 732–746.

European Journal of Marketing (1997) Special edition on Corporate Identity, **31** (5/6).

Hatch, M. & Schultz, M. (2000) Scaling the tower of Babel: relational differences between identity, image and culture in organisations. In: *The Expressive Organisation* (M. Schultz, ed). Oxford University Press: Oxford, pp. 11–35.

Schmidt, K. (1995) *The Quest for Identity – Corporate Identity, Strategies, Methods and Examples*. Cassel: London.

www.corporate-id.com. This site merges information from practitioners and academics into corporate identity and related topics.

www.reputationinstitute.com. The Reputation Institute's website presents useful information and resources about research in reputation and related topics, conferences, publications, and links to companies, professional associations, discussion forums, etc.

More on corporate image

Andreassen, T. & Lindestad, B. (1998) The effect of corporate image in the formation of customer loyalty. *Journal of Service Research*, **1** (1), 82–92.

Barich, H. & Kotler, P. (1991) A framework for marketing image management. *Sloan Management Review*, **32** (2), 94–104.

Gray, E. (1995) Corporate image. In: *Encyclopaedia of Business* (J. G. Maurer, J. M. Shulman, M. L. Ruwe & R. C. Becherer, eds). Gale Research: Detroit, MI.

Corporate branding

Berry, L. (2000) Cultivating service brand equity. *Journal of the Academy of Marketing Science*, **28** (1), 128–137.

European Journal of Marketing (2003) Vol. 37.

Lindstrom, M. (2002) Give your brand away, Part 1. *The Enterprise IT Conference & Expo*; www.clickz.com/brand/brand_makt/print.php/1557431.

Rubinstein, H. (1996) Brand first. *Journal of Marketing Management*, **12** (4), 269–280.

More on brand communities

McAlexander, J., Schouten, J. & Koenig, H. (2002) Building brand community. *Journal of Marketing*, **66** (January), 38–54.

Muniz, A. & O'Guinn, T. (2001) Brand community. *Journal of Consumer Research*, **27** (March), 412–432.

(See also Consuming Experience.)

fast fashion branding

~ from Prada to EatMyHandbagBitch

Christopher Moore

When, in December 2001, the luxury Italian fashion brand Prada opened a new store on the site of a former Guggenheim museum on Broadway in New York, the stakes for fashion marketing were raised to a new level. Various press reports suggested that this store cost between $30 and $140 million dollars. None of these figures have been verified, but it is safe to assume that this store did not come cheap. With the blend of the very latest in technology, the use of luxury materials and the creation of computer-managed changing rooms, the brand's owners were making a statement to the world about what Prada stood for and what Prada's customers believed in. The merchandise is presented on hanging cages that glide on ceiling tracks. At the flick of a switch, the products can be transported away and the area can then be used as a performance, exhibition or meeting space.

It is an interesting juxtaposition that the new store of one of the world's leading brands should be a former Guggenheim museum. For just as the former use of the space was based upon experience and engagement, the architect for the Prada Guggenheim, Rem Koolhass, explained that Prada's use of the space is likewise to deliver an experience; this time, an experience of luxury that is derived from the products and their presentation, the staff, the store environment. Consequently, the Prada Guggenheim is a new take on the museum experience – only this time, if you have the dollars, you can take the artefacts home with you.

To discover more about Rem Koolhass and the ideas surrounding the Prada Guggenheim in New York, read Harvard Design School Guide to Shopping *by Chung* et al. *(2001).*

The notion of fashion experience is now a defining feature of fashion branding. For many companies, creating the correct atmosphere, the right feeling in the store, matters as much as the products themselves. More on *fashion experiences* later in this chapter.

Prada is one of the world's most successful fashion brands. Brands are important to fashion marketers – it is what they create, manage, nurture, love, protect and make huge amounts of money. The importance of the brand to fashion marketing was brought home to me whenever I was commissioned to undertake research for a Japanese luxury fashion brand. When talking to young men, having the right brand was crucial to them, since they believed it radically improved their chance of having sex with the person of their choice. Also, even for children, brands are enormously important. Having the right brand means that you can be part of the group, you are accepted – indeed, having the wrong brand is worse than having no brand at all. In the boardroom, for company directors, having the right brand matters too, because it serves as a sign of success. Given the importance of fashion brands to the whole fashion marketing effort, further consideration will also be given to the *process of creating a fashion brand* – with a little help from an interview with two fashion marketing gurus.

According to the eminent fashion historian Colin McDowell, Ralph Lauren is the very master of fashion marketing and after a visit to his flagship store[1], the Rhinelander Building on Madison Avenue in New York, it is easy to see why Lauren is deserving of this title. The store does not have the feel of a store. With the clever

Believe it or not, 'EatMyHandbagBitch' is the name of a new and very successful British fashion brand. Reference is made to the company for three reasons. The first is that the name is just genius. The second is that it is a prime example of a fashion brand that has successfully built a business around a very specific target market segment (i.e. twenty/thirtysomething, fashion-aware, fairly affluent, sassy career women). And thirdly, this is a brand that through the power of positive word-of-mouth recommendation and favourable media recognition and coverage has become something of a cult fashion brand without having spent huge amounts of money on advertising. This is fashion marketing with a small 'f' and 'm' – but with, nevertheless, a huge impact.

[1] A flagship store is a major outlet, normally located in a capital city, which retails a fashion brand's full merchandise range. These stores typically enjoy significant financial investment in areas such as store design and fixtures and fittings.

use of furniture, paintings and other artefacts, it has the feel of an English baronial mansion. The success of the Ralph Lauren store on Madison Avenue is evidenced by McDowell (2003), who noted that in its first year, the store attracted an average of 15 000 visitors each day and exceeded first year forecasts with sales of more than $30 million.

For more details of the Ralph Lauren marketing phenomenon, read Colin McDowell's (2003) account of Lauren the man, the vision and the style. See References for details.

However, what is especially interesting about Lauren's store in Madison Avenue is that it sells more than just fashion. The Polo Ralph Lauren label now extends to underwear, perfumes and cosmetics, candles and home fragrance, cutlery and crockery, bed linen, and even wallpaper and paint. It would seem that there is no product category that is not eligible for the Ralph Lauren treatment. As such, Ralph Lauren could arguably be described as the one of the world's most successful fashion lifestyle brands. Given the importance of *lifestyle brand extension* to fashion marketing, this area will also be considered later in this chapter.

These three dimensions of fashion experience, fashion branding and lifestyle brand extension are arguably the defining features of fashion marketing. There is also one other dimension that serves to define fashion marketing and that relates to the *speed* of fashion marketing.

Fast fashion is a term that is now commonly used to describe fashion marketing. Fast fashion refers to the time scale that exists between the emergence of a new fashion trend and the time it takes for a company to respond to that trend by having the product available in the market for sale. Fashion retailers, such as Top Shop and Zara, have invested heavily in manufacturing, information technology and distribution systems, which enable them to respond to new fashion trends within a seven- to ten-day period. A commitment to fast fashion puts considerable strain on an organization. It requires that they are totally up to date with consumer trends and developments as these emerge and that they be fully prepared to respond to these developments with new product ranges in advance of their competition. As a result of the shift towards fast fashion, the product life cycle of fashion products has declined considerably. Within the UK, the average life cycle for a product range is approximately eight weeks, while for those leaders of fast fashion, such as Top Shop and Zara, the life cycle span has decreased to around three weeks.

It is the sheer speed of change within the fashion sector that distinguishes fashion marketing from the marketing of products and services in other sectors. It is difficult to imagine any other situation where as many as 500 products are launched onto the market at any one time, only to be superseded by 500 others within a period of less than two months.

Product life cycle (PLC) refers to the time period from when a product is initially introduced into the market to when it is withdrawn because of a lack of customer demand (see Creating Solutions). Fast fashion shrinks the time that elapses between the launch of a product and its withdrawal from the market. In other words, the faster the 'time to market', the shorter the PLC.

The difference between clothing and fashion

As a preliminary to any review of the nature of fashion marketing, it is important to first distinguish between fashion and clothing.

Clothing is, by its essential nature, functional. Clothing is boring and dull because clothing is about utility. It is the generic term for those garments that provide us with warmth, modesty and tedium. Clothing is above all about function, performance and visits to the laundry.

Fashion is about something else; it is something other and something greater. Fashion is about escape – an escape from who we really are to who we aspire to be. Fashion is transient. The least fashionable thing in the world today was the most fashionable thing in the world yesterday. Fashion is about meaning and symbol, it deals with representation and also sensation. Clothing is of the mind; fashion is of the heart. OK – that distinction is clear. Clothing is rational, while fashion is emotional.

So if clothing is concerned with function, then fashion is concerned with symbols and belonging and self-esteem. This distinction has important implications for

Psychologists tell us that our 'need' for fashion arises from a primary desire to construct, augment and communicate our self-image. We use fashion as a language to invent a personal image. Different fashion identities afford us the opportunity to possess a portfolio of many self-identities, each of which is relevant to the context that we find ourselves. Sociologists also recognize the importance of fashion within society. Fashion acts as a form of 'social glue'. It communicates group identity and membership; it contributes to group cohesion. In addition to defining group membership, fashion simultaneously denotes social group distance, distinctions and difference (see Consuming Experience).

See Horn & Gurel (1981) for a seminal review of the meaning and function of fashion in society.

the marketing of fashion, since it must by necessity be concerned above all with generating images, signs and meanings (see Consuming Experience).

The brand serves as the mechanism that transforms clothing into fashion. The next subsection will consider how fashion brands are created. The process of brand creation is discussed in the form of a light-hearted interview with two Paris-based fashion marketing aficionados, Lulu and Fabian.

Interview transcript: creating the fashion brand

Interviewer: Lulu – I love the brand Fendi. Can you tell me what makes Fendi Fendi?

Lulu: It is a recipe. It is a formula. Each brand is different and it requires a different set of ingredients. But the process is the same every time. It begins the same way. You think of a way of living, a lifestyle, a view of the world that you want your brand to represent. Define the features of that world view – whether it is Burberry, which is essentially English, or The Gap, which is the American Dream. Define the values of the lifestyle and isolate these. You make a list. You now have the values that your brand will represent.

Fabian: Fashion brands that fail are the ones that do not mean anything. You say the name and nothing happens, nothing springs to mind, nothing falls out from it. That is a brand failure; a brand in need of therapy.

Lulu: With my list of brand values, I now think of how I can get a link between my brand and these values. I have to make sure that when people see my brand they automatically think about certain attitudes; a certain way of life; a certain view of the world. They think of these values.

Fabian: He is right you know. I start off by insisting that the garments represent the values of the brand. It cannot be that the brand image is about luxury and the collection is not about luxury fabrics, good design, wonderful craftsmanship. Gorgeous. Gorgeous. Gorgeous.

Lulu: Next, we must communicate. *Advertising* is important for fashion. People are lazy sometimes. They need to be shown that this brand means these things. An advertisement for Hermes will be constructed differently from one for PUMA. Hermes will have references to luxury, serenity, elegance, tradition, craftsmanship, France. PUMA's references will be urban, the mood will be modern, technical, energetic. Not only will the advertisements differ, but where these appear will also differ. So I would expect to see Hermes in *Vogue*, but perhaps to see PUMA in *GQ* – because it is essentially still a male brand.

Fabian: Advertisements are not the only communication method. Fashion brands also get their message across through *public relations and media management*. It is as important for a brand to be mentioned in the editorial of the fashion and lifestyle magazines and to get press coverage in the right newspapers. If I can get the Editor of *Vogue* or *Tatler* to even mention us, then we see the benefit immediately. Expert endorsement is very important and it is something that the most successful fashion brands court. In fact, there is a growing consensus of opinion that editorial coverage is more effective than advertisements, particularly among younger people. They are sceptical when it comes to advertising. They do not always believe the message or subscribe to the hype. Instead, they value the views of their experts. If one of these magazines says the brand is cool that is much more effective than any number of advertisements. Who would accept our advertisements if we declared that we were cool. No brand is born cool. Coolness is thrust upon it.

Media management *involves the development of relationships between the brand and those individuals from the world of television, magazines and newspapers who are felt to influence public opinion.*

Lulu: For those brands with money to spend, then *events sponsorship*, like tennis matches or awards ceremonies, is a powerful way of creating an association between the brand and a particular lifestyle. Brands are built upon connections and associations. Sponsoring the right event puts the brand in view of the customer. Many fashion marketers believe that people are more likely to remember a brand's sponsorship of an event that they are interested in than they would an advertisement. The problem with an advertisement is that it often comes at the wrong time. The person's mind may be on something else. They may be in a bad mood; they may be sleepy. They do not notice your great advertisement that cost millions to think up.

But, if you are associated with an event that was enjoyable and memorable, then there is the chance that the person will remember the brand's association with the event. Better still, the positive feelings that they had about the event may transfer to the brand.

Event sponsorship *typically involves the provision of some form of financial support or gifts in kind (such as champagne at a reception) in exchange for publicity that recognizes the company's sponsorship of the event. Event sponsorship is used when a brand seeks to establish in the minds of consumers a relationship between a particular activity or event and their product. For example, leading sportswear brands compete to be able to sponsor important events such as the World Cup.*

Fabian: There is no better example of connection building than the whole process of *celebrity endorsement*. When Givenchy dressed Audrey Hepburn he was associating himself with someone famous, glamorous and beautiful. He made Audrey Hepburn even more beautiful and she made him known throughout the world.

For more on the role of celebrities, see the subsection on celebrity branding in The role of branding.

Lulu: Whether it is Elizabeth Hurley and the Versace dress, Victoria Beckham wearing Gucci or Madonna wearing Camper shoes, the process is the same. By wearing the brand, the celebrity becomes the face of the brand. They become the personification of the values, attitudes and the lifestyle associations of the brand. The celebrity can bring glamour to the brand and sometimes the brand can bring benefits to the celebrity. We all know that the Versace safety-pin dress gave Elizabeth Hurley more media coverage than her acting success had up to that point.

Fabian: Yes, yes that is all true. But equally as important to the fashion brand is *location, location, location*. The great fashion houses of the world make sure that they are represented in all of the great world centres: London, Tokyo, New York, Milan and, of course, Paris. And not only do they locate in these important locations, they also locate in the most prestigious shopping districts: Bond Street in London or Fifth Avenue in New York. These locations all add to the allure, the prestige, the overall standing of the brand both locally and globally.

The 'New York, London, Paris syndrome' was coined by Hollander (1970), who recognized that a retail presence within these world centres was a crucial ingredient in the development of a prestigious, luxury brand identity.

Distribution decisions have a huge impact upon how a brand is perceived by consumers. For example, if I want to generate and maintain an allure of exclusivity for a brand, I must limit its distribution. I must make sure that it is not overexposed, make it difficult to find. I make sure that the retailers who stock our brand have similar values to us and attract a similar target customer segment. They must enjoy a positive reputation in the market. If the stockists are wrong, then they will undermine the integrity and standing of the brand. It is for this reason that the owners of prestigious fashion brands carefully manage and control their distribution channels.

You know, one of the greatest threats to fashion brands is not so much the actions of the competition, but the dangers of the grey market and parallel distribution.

The grey market and parallel distribution refer to the unauthorized distribution of fashion brands to unauthorized dealers. The stock is made available as a result of unauthorized over-production by manufacturers; the availability of excess stock as a result of poor sales performance or as a result of the actions of unscrupulous but authorized agents, distributors or stockists, who sell the stock on to unauthorized dealers.

Our French fashion brands are masters of brand control. How often do you see Chanel in your local discount store or market? Never. We French realize that in order to protect the brand you must protect who gets their hands on the brand. The American brands are the worst for it. The Americans source their ranges from every corner of the globe. They manufacture under complex licensing agreements. None of them actually make anything for themselves. This makes it impossible for the American brands to control where their brand ends up. When it ends up in the local discount store, it does not do much for the standing of the brand. From a customer's perspective, why risk buying a brand at full price when everyone will think that you were smart and paid a third of the price in the local discounter.

Lulu: Yes, I agree that location and distribution management are important. But I say this to you – *experience, experience, experience*. Fashion is about sensation, memories, feeling better about yourself, feeling better about the world. Branding in fashion is as much about branding the experience as it is branding the product. Branding the experience is when the experience of acquiring the brand is managed so that it matches and reflects the values of the brand. The experience of the brand is where all of the attributes of the brand are brought together and are brought to life. It is about living the brand and experiencing the brand.

The capital investment that many fashion brands make in their stores is significant. This investment underlines the importance of the experiential dimension of fashion branding. In some cases, the experience matters almost as much as the

product. It is the added value element. It is the factor that justifies the price premium that successful fashion brands can generate.

Interviewer: What are the signs of a successful fashion brand, then?

Fabian: One that has consistent demand, that can consistently attract a premium price. One that celebrities want to wear and the fashion press want to write about. It does not have to continually reinvent, re-define itself. It knows what it stands for and remains true to its values. Of course, it updates itself with new images, new products and new ideas. But it is also sufficiently different from its competition. It is not a me-too, look-alike brand.

Lulu: Yes, it is all of these elements. But a successful fashion brand is one that can credibly be extended into new product areas – but without, at any time, undermining the integrity of the brand and its values. It moves into new product areas but without the customer thinking: 'This is stupid. This is exploitation.' Yes, a strong brand is one that can be extended into other product areas.

Fabian: The brand is really what fashion marketing is all about. But we must go now and lie in a darkened room. We are exhausted with all this explaining, explaining. You are too cruel to us, you know.

End of interview

Creating a fashion brand experience

It has been noted that only one company can be the cheapest in the market. Therefore, all the others must find some method of differentiating themselves. As has been identified above, many fashion companies have generated brands as the vehicle that makes them stand out from the competition and generate customer loyalty. As was noted in the interview with Lulu and Fabian, a crucial dimension of the process of building a powerful fashion brand is through the creation of a brand experience in store that both augments and enhances the core values of the brand.

The recognition of the contribution of positive brand environments to competitive advantages is not confined to luxury fashion brands. In the early 1980s George Davies, the founder of the British fashion chain Next, developed a store brand formula which he replicated in all of the Next stores. The Next brand experience sought to generate an up-market boutique feel within the British high street through the use of expensive, bright and attractive store fittings. Next invested in state-of-the-art lighting and their changing rooms were larger and more comfortable than those of their competitors.

A number of studies have shown how the design of a store can enhance the mood of the consumer and alter their perception of a brand.

Peter McGoldrick's chapter on 'the selling environment' in Retail Marketing *(see Further reading) provides some interesting insights into how brand atmospherics can influence customer behaviour in store.*

There are a variety of ways in which a brand experience can be generated. The store branding process begins before the customer even comes into the store. The very street, the part of town in which the store is located, says something about the brand and what it stands for in the market.

Take the example of the Comme des Garcons shop in Paris, which is shown in Figure 31. The store, while located in a very prestigious shopping district, is positioned off-centre and is quite difficult to find. The store exterior is discreet and, to the uninitiated, it does not initially look like a fashion store. These features are the very characteristics of the Comme des Garcons positioning. It is brand that it subtle, that in fashion terms is likewise positioned off-centre. Only those in the 'fashion know' would recognize the brand from these very discreet cues. It is for the discerning consumer. The placement and the entrance into the store clearly evoke and define these core brand values.

Figure 31 Entrance to the Comme des Garcons store, Paris

Even the signage for the store is discreetly positioned on a side wall. This is not a brand that wants to scream about itself. Everything is carefully managed, carefully executed, even down to the colour of the signage, which is in the classic red and white signature colours of the Comme des Garcons brand.

Not all stores adopt the understatement of the Comme des Garcons store in Paris. For their flagship store in New York's Soho district, the Italian fashion brand Max Mara has adopted a radical store exterior that is architecturally stimulating and which draws the attention of the passer-by to the brand. Through the mixed use of traditional materials, such as solid wood, with the latest in window and lighting technology, the new store serves as a potent emblem of the defining elements of the Max Mara brand.

Figure 32 Fashion store window design

The store windows also serve as an important device for communicating the values of the brand to prospective customers. The primary purpose of a fashion retailer's store windows is to generate brand awareness and interest. High street fashion retailers, such as USC, adopt large scale graphics for their store window presentations and integrate these with products in order to communicate the latest fashion trends to passing consumers. It is interesting to note that male consumers, in particular, use window displays for guidance when they select their fashion products. Often, the sales of particular styles rise dramatically as a result of their inclusion within a window display.

The use of large-scale graphics within the store serves as an immediate and highly effective means of creating a mood and fashion attitude within the store, as is evident in the example shown in Figure 33.

Figure 33 Large-scale graphic in-store

The development of an in-store brand identity is dependent upon the integration of visual images, fixtures and fittings, and the careful arrangement of merchandise. These elements serve as visual cues that communicate the attitudes and values of the brand to prospective customers. The findings of many empirical research studies indicate that these visual dimensions can serve to change the mood of the customer and may even alter how they engage with the brand. The presentation of the Miss Sixty brand (Figure 34), through the use of vibrant colours, stark images

Figure 34 Miss Sixty display

and modern merchandising materials, readily communicates to prospective customers that Miss Sixty is a modern, confident, sexy and feminine brand.

In contrast, the presentation of men's jeanswear labels, such as Diesel (Figure 35), relies on more masculine colours and the merchandise is presented in a more straightforward manner in order not to confuse or confound men who may be reluctant shoppers!

Figure 35 Diesel display

Alternatively, some brands deliberately upturn traditional approaches to merchandising and display as a means of communicating their idiosyncratic brand identity. For example, the cult Spanish footwear brand, Camper of Spain, defy the age-old superstition of not putting new shoes on a table by doing just that as a method of merchandise presentation (see Figure 36).

Within their store in London, the shoes are attached with Velcro to the wall. Customers pull down their choice of shoe from the walls to try on and return them to the wall once they have made their mind up.

All these various activities of fashion marketers attempt to generate and develop a distinctive identity for their brands. These various activities invariably require significant capital investment and this expenditure is justified on the basis that it serves to enrich and enhance the brand-purchasing experience. The development of a credible and attractive brand image may also allow the company to charge a premium price for their products. The creation of an interesting brand shopping experience contributes significantly to the development of a premium brand image.

Figure 36 Camper display

Lifestyle brand extension

As was indicated in the introduction to this chapter, brands such as Ralph Lauren have evolved to become more than just a label on a set of garments. Instead, they now operate as lifestyle brands. A lifestyle brand is typically associated with a particular way of life. For example, the Ralph Lauren lifestyle is ostensibly an American interpretation of the life of an English aristocrat. The images that are used in Ralph Lauren advertisements and the merchandising props that are used in his flagship stores all evoke the lifestyle of the English gentleman. Ralph Lauren's association with this very specific lifestyle was a shrewd marketing move, for it provided a platform for the company to extend its participation into other product sectors that are also associated with the lifestyle. As such, given that Ralph Lauren-branded products now extend into areas such as soft furnishings, crockery, wallpapers and paints, and bathroom accessories, it appears to satisfy almost every product need for this particular lifestyle. Ralph Lauren helps their customers live their dream. That is what makes Ralph Lauren a lifestyle brand.

All of the products that Ralph Lauren offers as part of its branded lifestyle are manufactured under licence agreements by specialist suppliers. This strategy has

enabled Ralph Lauren to rapidly extend the breadth of their product range without the risk and costs associated with producing products outside their area of immediate expertise.

A licence agreement *is when a brand owner delegates the responsibility for designing, manufacturing and distributing a branded product range to a specialist supplier. The third party must pay an initial fee in order to obtain the brand licence, as well as an annual fee and a percentage of sales as a royalty. In return, they enjoy the benefits of selling a range that is supported by a brand with international appeal.*

It should be noted, however, that licence agreements do not always provide fashion retailers with a range of positive benefits. While it may be difficult to believe now that the ultra-hip Gucci brand was ever associated with anything other than equally ultra-hip products, in the 1970s and 1980s the company entered into a number of licence agreements that saw the Gucci name emblazoned on mass-market products, such as disposable cigarette lighters. This strategy undermined the luxury brand positioning of Gucci and contributed to their fall from grace in the early 1990s. A key element of the turnaround strategy masterminded by Tom Ford, Gucci's Design Director, was to cancel scores of these inappropriate licence agreements. Ford, while recognizing that licence agreements are an important source of revenue, also recognized that these extensions can tarnish the brand's reputation and therefore must be tightly controlled. A brand can never be viewed as a luxury brand when it is available on a cigarette lighter in every tobacconist shop in sight.

Not only do fashion companies extend the breath of products that they market under their brand name, many extend the number of brands that they operate. This activity is usually called brand diffusion (see The role of branding).

Brand diffusion *is when a company develops other brands in order to target specific customer groups. These brands are typically targeted towards younger customers and they are generally less expensive than the main brand.*

Successful brand diffusion is built upon the strength of the reputation of the original brand. For example, the reputation enjoyed by the Giorgio Armani brand served as the basis for the development of a range of Armani diffusion brands.

Armani diffusion brands

- Emporio Armani – *an upper mid-priced, ready-to-wear range of tailoring and casualwear targeted towards men and women aged between 18 and 45 years. Sold in Emporio Armani stand-alone stores across the world.*
- Armani Exchange – *a lower mid-priced range of casualwear. Targeted towards a younger customer group. Sold in stand-alone stores, principally in the Far East.*
- Armani Jeans – *a premium-priced jeanswear and casualwear brand. Sold in stand-alone stores, department stores and independent stores.*
- Armani Perfumes – *fragrance manufactured under licence and sold in perfumeries and department stores the world over.*

Diffusion brands provide for brand democracy in that they allow a wider range of customers to access the brand. Brand diffusion is a lucrative strategy for many fashion firms and for most firms these diffusion brands provide the highest profit contribution by virtue of the fact that these tend to generate higher net margins and higher sales levels. As a word of caution, it is important to note that brand diffusion can undermine the standing of the brand by virtue of its over-availability. Some American fashion brands have been criticized for over-extending their brand diffusion strategies. This has often meant that the availability of the brand has exceeded supply. As a result, much of the stock for these diffusion brands has ended up being reduced and sold in discount stores.

Summary

While fashion may appear to some people to be frivolous, the marketing that supports the fashion system is, in reality, very sophisticated. This chapter has examined some of the key dimensions of fashion marketing activity. In particular, consideration was given to the processes that support fashion brand development and the dimensions that contribute to the creation of a fashion brand experience. The democratization of luxury fashion brands has been a defining point of the past generation and this has been achieved through the development of lifestyle marketing and the creation of diffusion fashion brands.

FURTHER READING

Chung, C. J., Inaba, J. & Koolhass, R. (2001) *Harvard Design School Guide to Shopping*. Taschen: New York.

Fernie, J., Hallsworth, A., Moore, C. & Lawrie, A. (1997) The place of high fashion retailing. *Journal of Product and Brand Management*, **6** (3), 151–163.

Hines, T. & Bruce, M. (2001) *Fashion Marketing: Contemporary Issues*. Butterworth-Heinemann: Oxford.

McDowell, C. (2003) *Ralph Lauren: The Man, The Vision, The Style*. Cassell Illustrated: London.

McGoldrick, P. (2002) *Retail Marketing*, 2nd edn. McGraw-Hill: London.

Moore, C. M. (1998) L'internationalisation du Pret a Porter: the case of Kookai & Morgan's entry into the UK fashion market. *Journal of Fashion Marketing and Management*, **2** (2), 153–159.

Moore, C., Fernie, J. & Burt, S. (2000) Brands without boundaries: the internationalisation of the designer retailer's brand. *European Journal of Marketing*, **34** (8), 919–938.

References

Aaker, D. (1996) *Building Strong Brands*. Free Press: New York.

Aaker, D. (1997) Should you take your brand to where the action is? *Harvard Business Review*, **75** (5, Sept/Oct), 135–139.

Agrawal, J. & Kamakura, W. (1995) The economic worth of celebrity endorsers. *Journal of Marketing*, **59**, 56–68.

Albert, S. & Whetten, D. (1985) Organisational Identity. In: *Research in Organisational Behaviour* (C. Cummings and B. Straw, eds). JAI Press: Greenwich CT, pp. 263–295.

Albert, S., Ashforth, B. & Dutton, J. (2000) Organisational identity and identification: charting new waters and building new bridges. *Academy of Management Review*, **25** (1), 13–17.

Andreassen, T. & Lervik, L. (1999) Perceived relative attractiveness today and tomorrow as predictors of future repurchase intention. *Journal of Service Research*, **2** (2), 164–172.

Andreassen, T. & Lindestad, B. (1998) The effect of corporate image in the formation of customer loyalty. *Journal of Service Research*, **1** (1), 82–92.

Balmer, J. (1995) Corporate branding and connoisseurship. *Journal of General Management*, **21** (1), 24–46.

Balmer, J. (1999) Corporate identity. In: *Encyclopaedia of Marketing* (M. Baker, ed.). Thomson Learning: London, pp. 732–746.

Barich, H. & Kotler, P. (1991) A framework for marketing image management. *Sloan Management Review*, **32** (2), 94–104.

Baudrillard, J. (1990) *Fatal Strategies*. Semiotext(e): New York.

Beckham, D. (2003) *My Side*. Collins Willow: London.

Belt, J. & Paolillo, J. (1982) The influence of corporate image and specificity of candidate qualifications on response to recruitment advertisements. *Journal of Management*, **8**, 105–112.

Berry, L. (2000) Cultivating service brand equity. *Journal of the Academy of Marketing Science*, **28** (1), 128–137.

Berthon, P., Hulbert, J. & Pitt, F. (1999) Brand management prognostications. *Sloan Management Review*, **40** (2), 53–65.

Bharadwaj, S. & Menon, A. (1993) Determinants of success in service industries. *Journal of Services Marketing*, **7** (4), 19–44.

Brown, T. & Dacin, P. (1997) The company and the product: corporate associations and consumer product responses. *Journal of Marketing*, **61** (January), 68–84.

Chung, C. J., Inaba, J. & Koolhass, R. (2001a) *Harvard Design School Guide to Shopping*. Taschen: New York.

Chung, C. J., Inaba, J. & Koolhass, R. (2001b) *Great Leap Forward*. Taschen: New York.

Cowley, D. (1991) *Understanding Brands*. Kogan Page: London.

de Chernatony, L. (1999) Brand management through narrowing the gap between brand identity and brand reputation. *Journal of Marketing Management*, **15** (1–3), 157–179.

de Chernatony, L. & Harris, F. (2000) Developing corporate brands through considering internal and external stakeholders. *Corporate Reputation Review*, **3** (3), 268–274.

de Chernatony, L. & McDonald, M. (1993) *Creating Powerful Brands*. Butterworth-Heinemann: Oxford.

Dowling, G. (1986) Managing your corporate images. *Industrial Marketing Management*, **15**, 109–115.

Duncan, T. & Everett, S. (1993) Client perceptions of integrated marketing communications. *Journal of Advertising Research*, May/June, 30–39.

Dutton, J., Dukerich, J. & Harquail, C. (1994) Organisational images and member identification. *Administrative Science Quarterly*, **39**, 239–263.

Elliot, R. & Wattanasuwan, K. (1998) Brands as symbolic resources for the construction of identity. *International Journal of Advertising*, **17** (2), 131–144.

Evans, A. & Wilson, G. (1999) *Fame: The Psychology of Stardom*. Bath Press: Bath.

Gould, S., Lerman, D. & Grein, A. (1999) Agency perceptions and practices on global IMC. *Journal of Advertising Research*, Jan/Feb, 7–20.

Grannell, C. & Jayarwardena, R. (2004) Celebrity branding: not as glamorous as it looks. 19 January 20004, www.brandchannel.com.

Gray, E. (1995) Corporate image. In: *Encyclopaedia of Business* (J. G. Maurer, J. M. Shulman, M. L. Ruwe & R. C. Becherer, eds). Gale Research: Detroit, MI.

Gray, E. & Smeltzer, L. (1987) Planning a face-lift: implementing a corporate image program. *Journal of Business Strategy*, **8** (1), 4–10.

Fernie, J., Hallsworth, A., Moore, C. & Lawrie, A. (1997) The place of high fashion retailing. *Journal of Product and Brand Management*, **6** (3), 151–163.

Fernie, J., Moore, C. & Lawrie, A. (1998) A tale of two cities: an examination of fashion designer retailing within London and New York. *Journal of Product and Brand Management*, **6** (3), 151–163.

Harbison, A. (2004) Brand it like Beckham: an investigation into the cult of $ellebrity branding. Unpublished BA marketing dissertation, University of Strathclyde, Glasgow.

Hatch, M. & Schultz, M. (1997) Relations between organisational culture, identity and image. *European Journal of Marketing*, **31** (5/6), 356–365.

Hatch, M. & Schultz, M. (2000) Scaling the tower of Babel: relational differences between identity, image and culture in organisations. In: *The Expressive Organisation* (M. Schultz, M. Hatch and Larsen, eds). Oxford University Press: Oxford, pp. 11–35.

Henrion, F. & Parkin, A. (1967) *Design Co-ordination and Corporate Image*. Reinhold: London.

Hollander, S. (1970) *Multinational Retailing*. Michigan State University: East Lancing, MI.

Horn, M. & Gurel, L. (1981) *The Second Skin*. Houghton: Boston.

Ind, N. (1997) *The Corporate Brand*. Macmillan Press: London.

Kapeferer, J. (1996) *Strategic Brand Management*. Kogan: London.

Keller, K. (2002) Branding and brand equity. In: *Handbook of Marketing* (B. Weitz and R. Wensley, eds). Sage: London, pp. 151–178.

Kotler, P. (1997) *Marketing Management: Analysis, Planning, Implementation and Control*, 9th edn. Prentice-Hall International: London.

LeBlanc, G. & Nguyen, N. (1996) Cues used by customers evaluating corporate image in service firms. *International Journal of Service Industry Management*, **7** (2), 44–56.

Lindstrom, M. (2002) Give your brand away, Part 1. *The Enterprise IT Conference & Expo*. www.clickz.com/brand/brand_makt/print.php/1557431.

Mantle, J. (1999) *Benetton – the Family, the Business and the Brand*. Little, Brown: London.

McAlexander, J., Schouten, J. & Koenig, H. (2002) Building brand community. *Journal of Marketing*, **66** (January), 38–54.

McCracken, G. (1989) Who is the celebrity endorser? Cultural foundations of the endorsement process. *Journal of Consumer Research*, **16**, 310–320.

McDowell, C. (2003) *Ralph Lauren: The Man, The Vision, The Style*. Cassell Illustrated: London.

McGoldrick, P. (2002) *Retail Marketing*, 2nd edn. McGraw-Hill: London.

Meech, P. (1996) The lion, the thistle and the saltire: national symbols and corporate identity in Scottish broadcasting. *Screen*, **37** (1), 68–81.

Menon, A. & Menon, A. (1997) Enviropreneurial marketing strategy: the emergence of corporate environmentalism as market strategy. *Journal of Marketing*, **61** (January), 51–67.

Moore, C. M. (1997) La mode sans frontiers: the internationalisation of fashion retailing. *Journal of Fashion Marketing and Management*, **1** (4), 345–356.

Moore, C. M. (1998) L'internationalisation du Pret a Porter: the case of Kookai & Morgan's entry into the UK fashion market. *Journal of Fashion Marketing and Management*, **2** (2), 153–159.

Moore, C., Fernie, J. & Burt, S. (2000) Brands without boundaries: the internationalisation of the designer retailer's brand. *European Journal of Marketing*, **34** (8), 919–938.

Muniz, A. & O'Guinn, T. (2001) Brand community. *Journal of Consumer Research*, **27** (March), 412–432.

Murray, W. (2000) *Brand Storm*. Prentice-Hall/Financial Times: London.

Olins, W. (1991) *Corporate Identity*. Thames & Hudson: Toledo.

Oliver, R. (1997) *Satisfaction: A Behavioural Perspective on the Consumer*. McGraw-Hill: New York.

Onkvisit, S. & Shaw, J. (1989) Service marketing: image, branding, and competition. *Business Horizons*, Jan/Feb, 13–18.

Pepall, L. & Richards, D. (1999) *The Simple Economics of Brand Stretching*. Department of Economics, Tufts University.

Piercy, N. (1998) Marketing implementation: the implications of marketing paradigm weakness for the strategy execution process. *Journal of the Academy of Marketing Science*, **26** (3), 222–236.

Piercy, N. & Cravens, D. (1995) The network paradigm and the marketing organisation. *European Journal of Marketing*, **29** (3), 7–34.

Pritchard, M., Havitz, M. & Howard, D. (1999) Analysing the commitment–loyalty link in service contexts. *Journal of the Academy of Marketing Science*, **27** (3), 333–348.

Riel, C. & Balmer, J. (1997) Corporate identity: the concept, its measurement and management. *European Journal of Marketing*, **31** (5/6), 340–355.

Rubinstein, H. (1996) Brand first. *Journal of Marketing Management*, **12** (4), 269–280.

Schmidt, K. (1995) *The Quest for Identity – Corporate Identity, Strategies, Methods and Examples*. Cassel: London.

Schmitt, B. & Pan, Y. (1994) Managing corporate and brand identities in the Asia-Pacific Region. *California Management Review*, **36** (4), 32–48.

Stobart, P. (ed.) *Brand Power*. Palgrave.

Strauss, A. (1969) *Mirrors and Masks*. Sociology Press: San Francisco.

Strong, F. (1987) A company study – Kodak: beyond 1990. *Journal of Business and Industrial Marketing*, **2** (4), 29–36.

Varley, R. (2001) *Retail Product Management – Buying and Merchandising*, 1st edn. Routledge: London.

Zins, A. (2001) Relative attitudes and commitment in customer loyalty models. *International Journal of Service Industry Management*, **12** (3), 269–274.

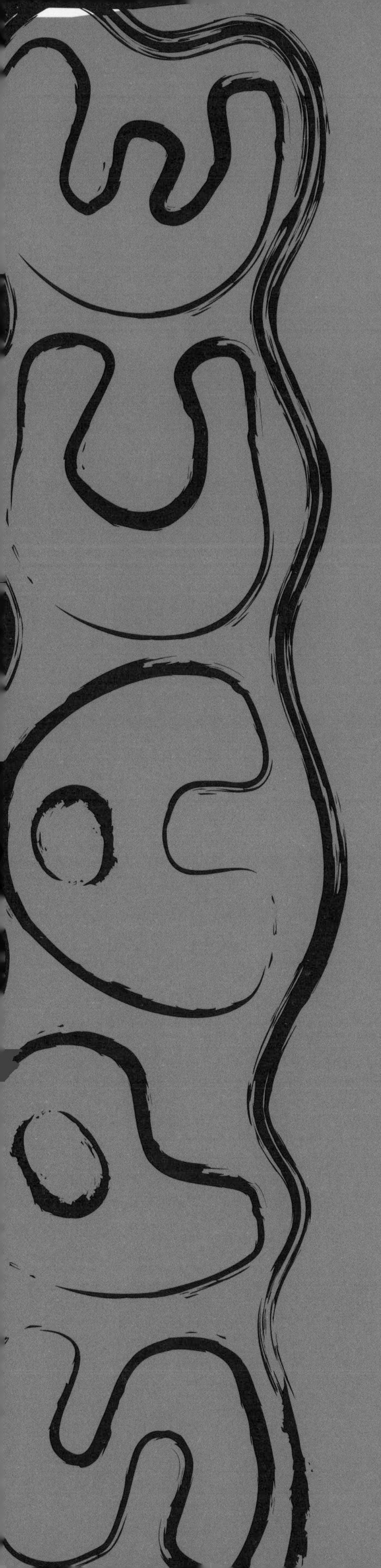

Moving Space

Marketing involves the transfer of something from one person to another, from one place to another, bringing it to the marketplace. It enables goods to be brought to consumers, not the other way round. This section looks at the role of logistics and distribution and goes further to show how the exchanges in markets nowadays are much more than just a process of delivery, moving things from place to place. It also matters where things come from (location, location, location) and where they are purchased. We see how shopping is essentially a spatial practice, and how its activities alter spaces through the architecture of retailing – the mall, the window displays, the arcades. This section also illustrates the effect of IT and the Internet making market 'space' virtual.

How markets move space

Marketing involves exchange between sellers and buyers (see Marketing Contexts). It involves a transfer of something from one person to another, from one place to another, bringing it *to the marketplace.* It enables goods to be brought to consumers, not the other way round, with consumers travelling to sources of supply. Without a market distribution system consumers would have to travel to Kent or Somerset to buy their apples, to France to get wine. Place is very important for marketing of course (location, location, location), but the exchanges that occur in the marketing system nowadays are much more than just a process of delivery, distribution or logistics, moving things from place to place. Marketing now is 'moving space'.

And it matters where things come from. The 'country of origin' label provides a firm quality assurance for customers which applies to manufacturers but is particularly influential for agricultural produce. Indeed, the geographical source of farm and mineral products is part of the brand (see Brand Selection), with the labels being the name of the region of origin, e.g. cheeses, milk, bottled water, wine. French wine is defined and controlled by its regional source – the '*appellation d'origine controlée*' (AOC) labelling system protects the famous wine growing area boundaries, such as Bordeaux, Macon, Alsace, Burgundy and Beaujolais. The AOC is the legal expression of *terroir*, a concept of geographical source of the grape that goes way beyond territorial origin,

Baudrillardians never make it past the shopping mall.
Massumi, 1992

Traditional marketing models describe the exchange and distribution process in terms of movement through supply chains, distribution channels, logistics organization, transportation networks, inventories, retail outlets, delivery systems, intermediaries and agents for assortment, conveyancing, consignment and shipment. Indeed, this is where marketing as an academic discipline began (see Marketing Contexts: Marketing values).

The spaces in which exchanges take place in marketing are all these things and more.

Shopping is expanding into every program imaginable: airports, churches, train stations, libraries, schools, universities, hospitals. Airports and malls are starting to look indistinguishable. The experience of the mall is becoming increasingly seamless with that of the department store. Even the city is being configured according to the mall.
Koolhaas, in Chung et al., *2001*

embodying the soil, climate, history, folklore, savoir-faire and emotional attachment of the region in which it is grown.

Giddens (1990) explains this ability of markets to move space as a consequence of the institution of money, which permits exchange to occur across large time–space distances. On the contrary, barter, exchange without money, is limited in distance by the requirement for the concurrent transfer of commodities between parties. The institution of money as a medium of exchange is a key feature of 'modernity', he argues, which enables socio-economic activity to be transformed beyond the particular circumstances of local places and practices.

The most obvious illustration of this is the effect that the Internet has had on consumer buying and market delivery. When shopping, looking or buying through company websites, the interaction between the buyer and seller does not just move things from place to place; the space in which it occurs is changed. The retailing aspects regarding physical space, architecture, layout, design, store atmospherics, colour schemes, displays, etc. (see Brand Selection: Fast fashion branding) that have been found to affect customer responses are all changed by Internet shopping. Of course, here the 'space' is virtual, the customer can be anywhere and the 'shop' can be nowhere. Internet marketing has altered the space in which exchange takes place. Clarke and Purvis (1994) argue that the advent of this 'hyperspace' with its simulations and 'hyperreality' (Baudrillard, 1983) will have radical effects on the retailing system.

Many marketers would accept that the Internet changes space, but they would also point out that 90% of the products and services that are still exchanged in terrestrial markets must be moved from place to place, perhaps by new and faster means, nevertheless by the same essential processes. This is true; however, these marketing processes are themselves changing the use of spaces – turning more of them into retail outlets. Retailing and shopping space is turning cities into gigantic shopping malls, according to Rem Koolhaas, who designed the new Prada store in New York, which has taken over the site of the Soho Guggenheim art gallery (see Brand Selection: Fast fashion branding). In the *Harvard Design School Guide to Shopping*, he paints an apocalyptic picture of the spread of what he calls this 'junkspace', the shoppingization of urban

life, in which cities of the future are consumed by the mass of their own buildings and road signs and advertising hoardings (Koolhaas, in Chung *et al*., 2001).

The continued accumulation of commodities and the physical speed of marketplaces can be expected to produce more 'junkspace' of this kind. Indeed, it may be that such spatial entropy in the city, in the marketplace and everywhere else *is inevitable*.

Spatial and territorial affiliations are powerful social influences on consumers, as they are for society generally. The role of proximity in creating tactile and affectual affiliations is well documented. For example, Mafessoli (1996) suggests that spatial 'proxemics' reinforce feelings of belonging to group or a 'tribe' and 'co-presence' is central to the customers, ethics and aesthetics of society. So too in marketing activities, the 'sites of consumption' bring into spatial presence consumers with other consumers, sellers, commodities and a network supporting artefacts (see Consuming experience).

'Terrestrial' shopping is essentially a spatial practice, and its activities alter spaces. The shopping mall, the window displays, the arcades and the galleries all utilize glass constructions enabling shoppers to be in and see through both the public street and the shopping space simultaneously. This is what Benjamin (1955) described as the 'porosity' of the nineteenth century arcades of Paris and Naples – the transparency between boundaries of the public and private domains – apparently open spaces that are 'harnessed' to the needs of the market.

The capacity of porosity in city spaces is illustrated nowadays by the activity/sport of 'freerunning', where athletes/artists utilize the architecture and spaces of the built environment in cities to create athletic runs, jumps and moves. Their elite exponents have been recruited for several advertisements and marketing events worldwide to create a visual spectacle of movement and space, such as for the Toyota new 'Aygo' car launch at the motor shows in Barcelona and Geneva in February 2005 (for more on freerunning, see www.urbanfreeflow.com).

FURTHER READING

Moving shopping space

Chung, C. J., Inaba, J. & Koolhass, R. (2001) *Harvard Design School Guide to Shopping*. Taschen: New York.

Clarke, D. & Purvis, M. (1994) Dialectics, difference and the geographies of consumption. *Environment and Planning A*, **26**, 1091–1109.

Virtual spaces

Arefi, M. (1999) Non-place and placelessness as narratives of loss: rethinking the notion of place. *Journal of Urban Design*, **4** (2), 179–193.

Lefebre, H. (1991) *The Production of Space* (D. Nicholson-Smith, trans.). Verso: London.

Morley, D. & Robbins, K. (1995) *Spaces of Identity: Global Media, Electronic Landscapes and Cultural Boundaries*. Routledge: London.

Moving information – the role of IT

Mairead Brady

Information is the key to moving space in marketing. The organization and operation of supplying customers – distribution, chains, logistics, material flows, order processes, retailing outlets, etc. – have become more complex with the need for more and faster information to manage these processes across boundaries, national, international and organizational. In the global economy few firms do it all themselves, from source to delivery, but they have to be able to manage a complex network of processes, often across great distances. Information technology (IT) provides the capability to speed up information collection and processing, enabling marketers to improve their understanding and responses to customer needs (see Creating Solutions), and to manage their supply processes, to move space, better and faster.

Information does more than support transactions, however; it is an object of exchange in its own right. Boisot (1995) elegantly showed how information is compressed, codified and diffused through his concept of 'information space'. The more that information is broken up into bit-sized chunks, as it were, the more easily people can understand it, thus the greater its potential diffusion and use. The more it is broken up into discrete units for use, however, the greater the need for an integration function to coordinate all the elements and 'rebuild' a complete picture. IT can also assist firms to better manage these central functions associated with information space.

The second law of thermodynamics holds that the amount of disorder in the world can never decrease. A display of stacked boxes in a supermarket is always in danger of falling down, but once fallen it is never in danger of righting itself. It takes fewer bits of data [i.e. amount of information] to specify the positions of the boxes if they are stacked up in a pyramid than if they are littering the floor. Information always grows with disorder.
Minkel, 2002

Collation of information

- *How do marketers gather information?*
- *Why do marketers gather so much information?*
- *What do marketers use this information for?*

This chapter discusses what sort of information marketers need, how it is packaged and exchanged/moved through space, and how IT helps them collect and analyse it.

Information – why is it crucial and where do marketers get IT?

Before we look at how marketers gather, move and analyse information, we need to consider what they use this information for. What marketers are always

looking for is knowledge about consumers. They make all internal marketing decisions in order to satisfy customers and also consistent with meeting company objectives. Perceived uncertainty in decision-making is reduced by the collection and use of information. For managers to have knowledge of customers (or anything else) requires not only information, but also the ability to integrate and frame the information within the context of their experience, expertise and judgement (see Creating Solutions: Information technology and innovation). Managers utilize a mixture of intuition (suppressed expertise which resides in the subconscious), skills in classifying and reducing incoming information and holistic analysis, in order to sort out and evaluate information in the decision-making process. Modern developments in IT now enable the fusion of data and instinct with computer models.

What do consumers look like to marketers? Marketing data and analyses rarely deal with individuals; what marketers deal with are groups of people whom they call *target markets.* Target markets are groups of people who have similar needs or/and characteristics. Marketers divide consumers into groups by using segmentation variables (see Creating Solutions). This is the marketing term for saying that consumers are all different but not that different. So rather than mass marketing or using the same techniques for all consumers, what marketers do is take information from a variety of sources and analyse groups of consumers. They use variables like:

- Demographics
- Socio-economics
- Lifestyle
- Purchase-related usage and behaviour.

Q. Why is it that all too often business decisions are made by using gut instinct, based on limited information, when most companies are data rich?
A. *Because there are major challenges in collecting, analysing, interpreting and utilizing information.*

When they have grouped these consumers into segments, they decide on useful segments to target. They then design a marketing plan to satisfy these consumers. So in order to employ a segmentation methodology, a core information requirement is information about consumers' characteristics of the above types.

Information collection – a continuous challenge

Creating a picture of the customer is not a one-off task. The consumer cannot be considered as a static entity; consumers keep changing. The values and lifestyles, profiles and influences of consumers change over time. So marketers must keep researching consumers, gathering, analysing and interpreting information from a variety of sources – as in the Disney example.

Marketers thrive on information and the most crucial pieces of information are about consumers' actual behaviour, as opposed to a common set of characteristics such as their age, income and location, which at best can only provide a rough, general guide to their purchase behaviour. Indeed, there is some evidence that as society has become more individualistic the emphasis on creating customer categories based on similarities between them rather than differences is much less appropriate (Dibb, 1998). Traditional customer segments based on traditional economic and demographic characteristics are now an even less accurate guide to commonalties of purchases amongst members of each group (van Raaj, 1993). Yet marketers still want to, and need to, know what drives consumers to buy, what they purchase, how they purchase, when they purchase, whom they purchase for and where they purchase?

Inner space – the theatre of the mind

Marketers operate in what has been called the 'theatre of the mind' (Ingram, 2005). They wish to get inside consumers' heads. If you think of a movie like *Minority Report* with Tom Cruise, you can get some idea of how far developments in this area could go. By scanning the retina and working out his desires, the billboards change as Cruise walks down the street, thus 'narrowcasting' his personalized advertising. The technology for this future is not so far away.

The mind is a wonderful information processor. Consider the range of choices and decisions that one person must go through just to carry out one shopping trip. In any supermarket visit a consumer may encounter up to 30 000 product lines within a 40-minute trip. Think of the agony of indecision if consumers could not process this mass of information and make decisions quickly. Marketers need to know how consumers make these decisions and what they can do to help making these decisions easier for consumers.

Once marketers have information about the drivers of consumer decisions they try to design products and messages that speak to them on the subconscious level. For example, the 'L'Oreal – because you're worth it' *advertising campaign.*

Customer information at Disney World

The Walt Disney World team works hard at 'guestology', the study of the guests, who they are and what they want . . . A Research and Statistics Department conducts over 200 external surveys a year . . . Disney is constantly keeping track of guest information such as the following: demographics, evaluation of current marketing attraction evaluations, payment preferences, price sensitivity and the economy . . . To close the information loop and provide invaluable feedback to operations, guest comments reports, which condense the essence of all guest comments, are generated and distributed weekly to management. An Industrial Engineering Department continues the guestology process by constantly evaluating the resort's operating systems with daily inspections, show quality monitoring, wait-time studies,

maintenance punch-lists and utilization studies . . . With the potential to generate so much data concerning its guests, Disney has learned to focus on what matters most. *The company quantifies data and includes it in pro formas for future projects. Through the process of guestology, it is fair to say that guests are helping to design the future Walt Disney World.*
Johnson, 1991

Information collection – market research

Gathering information about the consumer is known as market research by marketers. Sometimes consumers will share this information with companies. In other instances consumers are very protective of their information and preferences, and companies have to struggle to gather this information. In many cases consumers want companies to know what is going on in their minds. They want companies to greet them, understand them, remember them and value them. Regardless of the orientation or desire of the consumer, companies must research consumers if they want the companies to be able to react to their needs. Capturing information is a major challenge for marketers. Their credibility and power within the company is, in many ways, connected to their knowledge of the consumer, yet they have great difficulties in capturing the information available. In a recent study, Brady *et al.* (2002) highlighted that marketers encountered the difficulties outlined below in attempting to receive data or information. Once companies collect information they will store this information for analysis.

Information technology – a core requirement for market research, analysis and planning

The techniques by which companies store, manage, analyse and interpret information rely heavily on information technology. Table 6 (in Creating Solutions: Information technology and innovation) shows the extent to which marketing practice has a dominant IT dimension (see Brady *et al.*, 2002). Here we will concentrate on exploring the ITs focused on information and decision-making, those under the headings 'Analysis and planning', 'Databases' and 'Research' in Table 6.

Database management

Most information collected by marketers nowadays resides in some form of database. The database is the main IT in the marketing function (Coviello *et al.*, 2001; Domegan & Doyle, 2000; Desai *et al.*, 1998). The usage of databases can still be considered to be in its infancy and there is a lack of sophisticated usage as marketers struggle to embrace this technology. Holding consumer information in databases can be quite a contentious issue between the consumer and the company. Many consumers are aware that collecting database information is a critical operation for companies, but are anxious to avoid any repercussions from the provision of this information. Companies require centralized databases so that disparate elements of data can be collated to provide a very useful picture of customers and by extension a very useful picture of segments and markets. Every contact point and source of information between the company and the consumer needs to be tapped. The reality is that companies have 'islands of data'. It must be noted, as Desai *et al.* (1998) also confirmed, that there were major challenges to database usage within marketing, highlighting the lack of sophisticated use of systems. Every time an item is scanned at a checkout we assume that this information is being fed into a giant database and utilized for some marketing purpose. The reality is quite different.

Data warehouse

The major task in database management is to generate *usable* information as the crucial ingredient in databases. A data warehouse simply holds the information. A data warehouse is '*An enterprise-level data repository that draws its contents from all critical operational systems and selected external data sources.*'

Two useful websites:
www.bmrb.co.uk/newsdesk/index.cfm
www.databaseamerica.com/html/gspecial1.htm

Data mining

Once the information is collected, the marketer must look at ways of using this information. A database only collects data in a centralized location – marketers must *do something* with this data. What is needed is a search in the data for gems, for useful pieces of information, for links, connections, interesting observations – this is called data mining.

When Wal-Mart utilized data mining on their extensive database of consumer purchases they found some interesting links. They noted a group of consumers who only brought two items – nappies and beer. Can you guess the connection and the gender of the purchasers? What can Wal-Mart do with this information? They can look at a store plan and move the items further away to stimulate impulse purchase as the consumer walks between the two items. Or they can bring the items closer together to speed the purchase process and trigger connections between the two items.

So the IT can supply the statistical analysis but gut instinct, education and knowledge are needed to analyse the findings.

Data mining *is 'the automated discovery of "interesting" non-obvious patterns hidden in a database that have a potential for contribution to the bottom line . . . it also encompasses the confirmation or testing or relationships through the discovery process' (Peacock, 1998).*

Q. What does data mining do?
A*. Once data has been acquired from internal and external sources, it allows marketers to do the following:*

- *Translate, clean and format the data.*
- *Analyse, validate and attach meaning to the data.*
- *Score the database.*
- *Build and implement decision support tools and systems to make data mining results available to decision makers and other staff.*
- *Place filters on the data. The critical decision though is which filter.*

For a demonstration of the technology available within databases and how to utilize data-mining techniques within a database, you can take the tour on the following website: http://bayesware.com/products/discoverer/tour_files/frame.htm. This site shows you how to utilize database information for marketing purposes, demonstrating how the software produces correlations and connections between disparate pieces of information.

Customer relationship marketing software

More and more companies are becoming consumer orientated. There are many buzzwords for this phenomenon. Some call it relationship marketing, others call it customer focused, others bringing the voice of the consumer inside the company, one-to-one marketing and so on. Whatever title it is given, what companies are saying is that they want to know more about consumers in order to serve them better and more profitably. That the more they know about consumer needs and wants, the more they can satisfy them.

What does consumer-orientated or relationship marketing mean from a consumer and IT perspective? What relationship marketing means to a company is that they endeavour to retain consumers instead of always focusing on new consumers. How they do that is by tracking consumers in some way and learning from defecting consumers what went wrong; they utilize creative customer relationship strategies (Reichheld & Schefter, 2000). From the limited academic studies that exist, we know that companies struggle to embrace relationship marketing (Peppers & Rogers, 2000).

For practical applications of relationship marketing practices and more information, log on to The Peppers and Rogers Group. They are a business and management consulting firm that specializes in maximizing the value of customer relationships through one-to-one marketing – http://www.1to1.com/Building/CustomerRelationships/home.jsp.

IT is a core requirement of relationship marketing and many companies would find it very difficult to follow a relationship marketing strategy without IT (Li *et al.*, 1993; Brady *et al.*, 2002). The ability to '*"individualize" mass markets, due to modern information, communications and production technology, is an important reason for this development*' (Mattsen, 2000). What does this consumer focus with an IT perspective look like from within the company and where are you the customer in this? This focus is known as customer relationship management or CRM (see Creating Solutions: Organizational processes and capabilities).

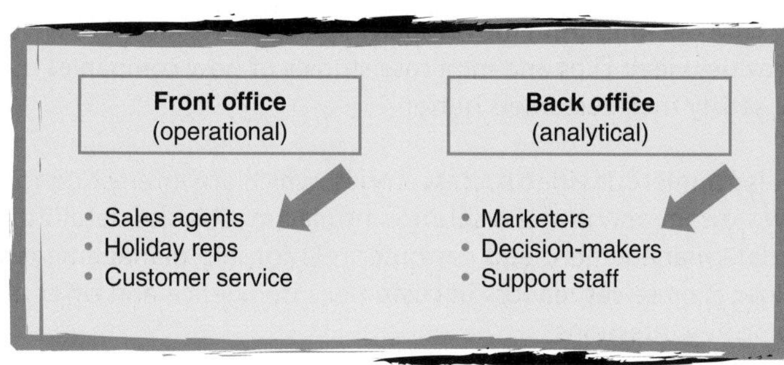

Figure 37 CRM Software

Although the picture in Figure 37 looks quite user friendly, an actual CRM system looks like the screen shot shown in Figure 38.

This type of static information as provided by the software must be turned into usable information and creative strategies in order to work.

The main point is that currently the failure rates of these CRM systems are high (Dempsey, 2000). Marketers are struggling to collect usable and useful information and to assimilate these ITs in practice (Brady *et al.*, 2002).

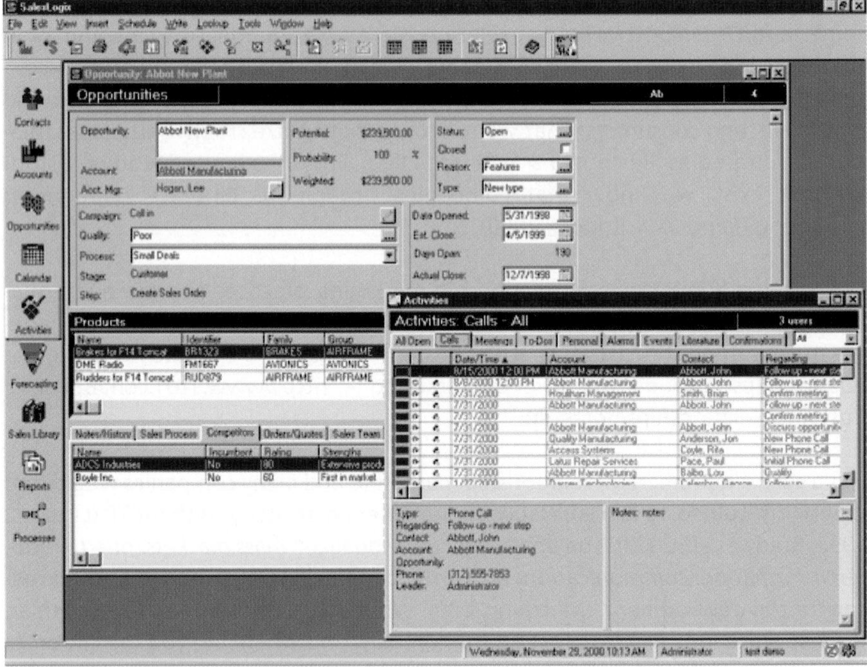

Figure 38 Screen shot of a CRM system

To see how CRM operates from the company's perspective, log on to www.sas.com. This site provides video clips and mini case studies of how companies use marketing data to satisfy their customers better.

There are also numerous video success stories, which are interesting to watch, at http://www.sas.com/news/success/solution.html#crm. This site details the successful use of data management and customer relationship management software. They consider themselves leaders in customer intelligence and offer answers to the following key questions:

- How do you understand and anticipate customer behaviour?
- How do you build more profitable customer relationships?
- How to leverage a customer's lifetime value.

From traditional surveys to scanning, monitoring and tracking

A core task of marketing is information gathering. In general, marketers will gather two types of data – qualitative and quantitative (see Creating Solutions: Researching markets).

1 *Qualitative data* – information which focuses on quality, emotions, feelings, perceptions and attitudes.
2 *Quantitative data* – large quantities of descriptive data, analysed using statistical techniques.

Qualitative techniques

- *Observation*
- *Experimental research*
- *Eye cameras*
- *Mystery shopping*
- *Diaries*
- *Omnibus surveys*
- *Personal interviews/focus groups*
- *Online/video links:*
  - *Projective techniques*
  - *Critical incident analysis*
  - *Cognitive mapping*

Quantitative techniques

- Personal interviews – *one human to another either individually (personal) or in a group (focus group).*
- Telephone interviews – *usually just when you are sitting down to dinner the phone will ring with a telemarketer on the other end with a very important survey.*
- Postal/fax/email interview – *if you get enough of these you could consider them junk mail. If you are interested in the topic or have little or nothing to do you may fill it in – if not, you will throw it in the bin. Average return rates are 4%.*

For further information, see Malholtra (1996).

Most of these traditional methods involve some level of collaboration and awareness between the consumer and the company. Some of these processes have been automated so that they can be carried out with the aid of IT applications. For example:

- Video conferencing *allows for focus group discussions to take place independent of location.*
- Web surveys *allow for online completion of surveys.*

Tracking, scanning, surveillance – are you being watched?

Marketers often observe consumers without consumers being aware that they are being monitored, but now more than ever marketers are tracking consumers' behaviour through IT observation-based techniques. Marketers monitor, scan and track consumers on a regular basis.

Hidden cameras are not that unusual. We are all being watched in shopping areas by ATM cameras for security purposes. Marketers can make valuable use of security footage of consumers. In the retail trade, companies have placed tracking devices on shopping trolleys to monitor the store traffic. Web tracking has become very sophisticated, with more and more software applications available to track consumers' every move on the Internet. Companies can now tell what site the consumer was on prior to their site and what site they go to on leaving their site. Scanning techniques are now widespread. Every time a product is blipped through a checkout there is an information database entry. Marketers can then use this information to plan marketing campaigns (see Humby, 2004).

Information technology – is this IT?

As discussed earlier, IT is central to marketing practice. The use of information technology provides the marketers with something that they have always wanted – information. And not just information, real-time, up-to-date information, readily accessible. All marketers' dreams come true, or is it? Information technology can supply marketers with loads of information, a proliferation of information, a magnitude of information. Information, information everywhere, but the reality is that many companies are drowning in a sea of useless data. In a *Harvard Business Review* article, Fisher *et al.* (2000) suggested that rocket science retailing is arriving, but they were unsure if markets are ready for it:

> Contrary to popular perception most retailers have considerable difficulty capturing and maintaining sales data that are accurate and accessible to their employees.

Technology – the information provider

If we look at technology we can observe that technology is a wonderful automated application. It can repeat the same task over and over again without complaint and

almost flawlessly. It is when much more is asked of technology that the problems start. 'The wisdom of its use is in the wisdom of the user' (Glazer, 1991). Technology on its own is a useless morass of boxes and cables which need the intelligence of the human to operate it.

There are a variety of systems (see Figure 39) that are utilized for information provision purposes. This subsection briefly introduces some of them. Many of these systems are looking at ways of capturing the information that flows around, into and out of companies. There needs to be a two-way information flow of materials, money and information all along the value chain, from the supplier right through to the final consumer.

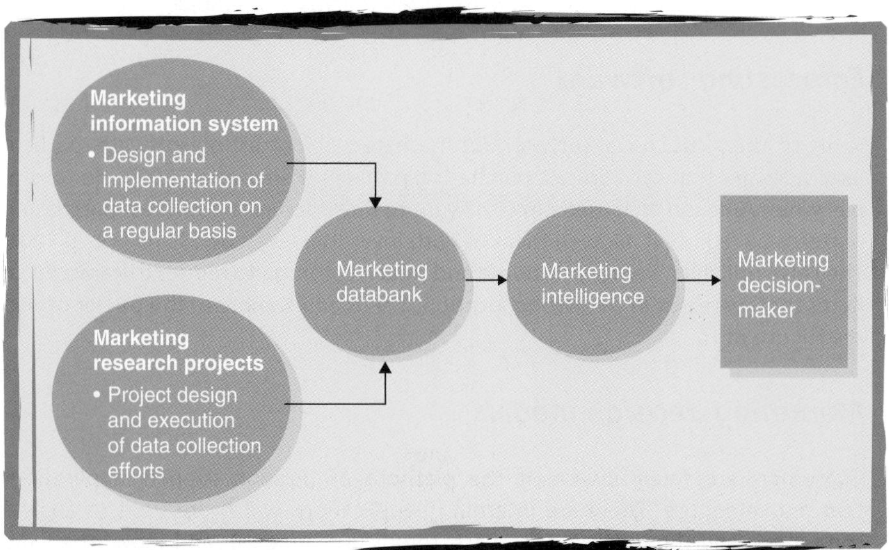

Figure 39 Systems used for provision of information. *Source*: Kotler (2001)

Marketing information system

A marketing information system (MKIS) is '*a computer-based system that works in conjunction with other functional information systems to support the firm's management in solving problems that relate to marketing the firm's products*' (Li *et al.*, 1993). Marketing information systems (MIS) include three subsystems – the accounting information system, marketing research and marketing intelligence. The marketer must manage the information flows (see Figure 39) to aid in the decision-making process.

Geographical information systems (GIS)

We are intuitively aware that people in different parts of the world behave differently. We know that populations are not necessarily homogeneous and that cultural and regional preferences exist and that there are large product-specific patterns within regions. Research can confirm or refute our instincts, with some geographic information running contrary to what would be expected. For example, research has shown that Californians drink less coke than Hungarians. GIS are systems that can provide marketers with information from household figures upwards and are very useful for companies. An example of one is the Mappoint2000 from Microsoft. The result is a geographic map overlaid with digital data about customers in a particular area. Developments in this area allow more detailed geographic information to exist. Most western countries now have highly developed demographic information, with some countries being able to pinpoint actual households.

Forecasting software

> *The art of prophecy is very difficult especially with respect to the future.*
> *Mark Twain, 1835–1910*

Some of the most crucial software for marketers is forecasting software, particularly software that can forecast purchasing patterns (Fisher *et al.*, 2000). For example, when Amazon.com used new software to more accurately forecast purchasing patterns by region, it allowed them to slash inventory levels by $31 million in 2001. They also utilized inventory software and smarter storage to reduce the amount of items that were put in the wrong location. This is an example of the power of successful use of IT.

Marketing decision models

Consumers are rarely aware of the plethora of decision support applications that marketers use. These are internal IT applications which are used to analyse consumers and how they will react (predictive models) and how they did react (descriptive models) to certain marketing techniques. For more information on decision support systems, log on to www.dssresources.com/history/dsshistory.html.

> ***Q***. For example, the shelf displays in supermarkets. Do they occur naturally?
> ***A***. *No! Marketers now use sophisticated shelf space maximization software products in order to optimize the use and effectiveness of shelf space.*

There are a variety of software packages and customized software to aid the manufacture and the retailer in maximum utilization of shelf space. One brand name is Shelf Logic and they supply Planagram software (http://www.shelflogic.com/).

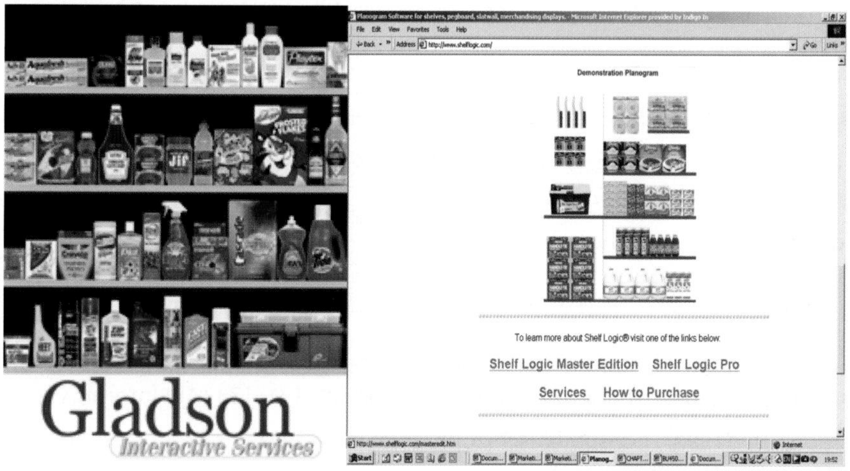

Figure 40

Information technology – the challenges

If we analyse the two words 'information technology' we can assume that this technology provides us with information. We can also assume that if IT provides managers with information they will use it. It must be remembered that information is a source of power and as such people will not want to share it (Davenport, 1994). Also, in many ways we are in the era of information overload.

> *The next retail innovator will be the one that best combines access to consumer transaction data with the ability to turn that information into action.*
> *Fisher* et al., *2000*

Advances in IT research techniques

There have been many advances in information-gathering and research techniques. The major challenge is to make computers more human. One of the major traits that humans have that technology does not is the ability to make a decision with limited knowledge. The data flood unleashed by advances in IT has only just begun.

FURTHER READING

Uses and assimilation of IT

Brady, M., Saren, M. & Tzokas, N. (2002) Integrating information technology into marketing practice – the IT reality of contemporary marketing practice. *Journal of Marketing Management*, **18** (5/6, July), 555–578.

Coviello, N., Milley, R. & Marcolin, B. (2001) Understanding IT-enabled interactivity in contemporary marketing. *Journal of Interactive Marketing*, **15** (4), 18–33.

Zuboff, S. (1988) *In the Age of the Smart Machine*. Heinemann Professional: Oxford.

Data collection and interpretation for retailing and logistics

Fisher, M., Raman, A. & McClelland, A. (2000) Rocket science retailing is almost here – are you ready? *Harvard Business Review*, July/August, 115–124.

See also www.datamining.com.

Consumers and IT

Henry, P. (2000) Evaluating the implication for new media and information technology. *Journal of Consumer Marketing*, **18** (2), 121–133 (ABI Inform).

Kardon, B. (1992) Consumer schizophrenia: extremism in the marketplace. *Planning Review*, **20** (4), 18–22.

Moving materials

This chapter explores moving *materials* from the following perspectives:

1 The *definition* of materials has changed.
2 Consumers now consider the *environment* that surrounds the materials that make up the goods and services they are buying.
3 Marketers *bundle* materials.
4 Materials must be *available and ubiquitous*; customers demand delivery immediately.
5 The definition and role of logistics.
6 Technology advances and logistics.

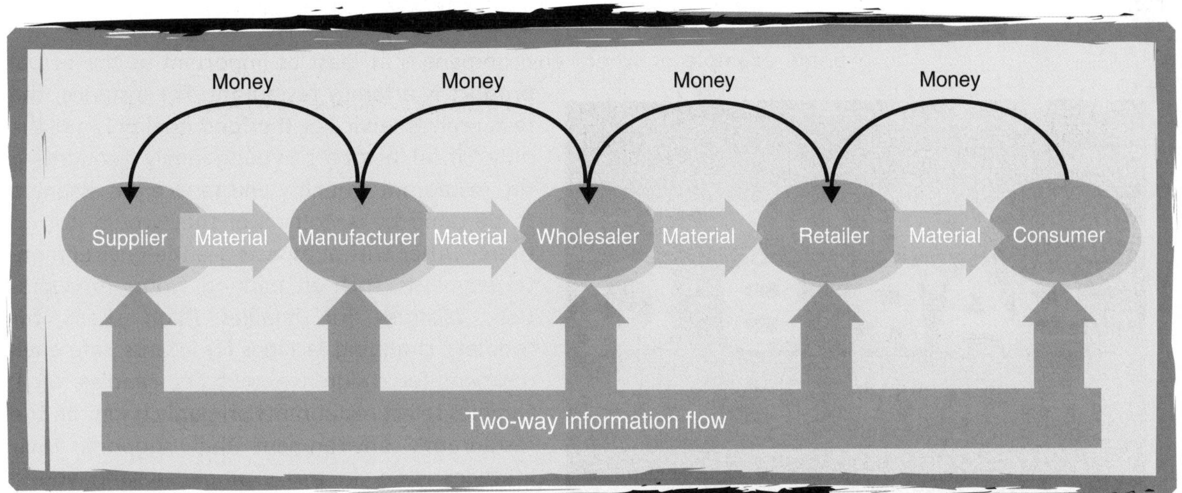

Figure 41 Material, money and information flow

The definition of materials has changed

Materials are tangible assets – furniture, bottle of wine, a letter, a chair. Today we must add *intangible* materials to the list – in the past, putting these two words together would have been an oxymoron, but not now. An e-ticket for air travel, an email message, data that travels via the Internet are examples of intangible materials. As marketers we have to rethink our definition of 'materials' to include intangibles.

Not only is our environment made up of materials – houses, shops, trees, etc. – today it is the materials that are determining the environment. In the past the goal of marketing was to provide the right material items at the right time in the right space – finding the market niche and delivering the product to the place where the

customer wants. This process does not necessarily apply like this today, as this chapter will show.

Environmental influences on buying 'materials'

The idea of providing the right environment to enhance your product or service goes beyond that traditional marketing principle of *promotion*. Companies still need to advertise and deliver products but marketers must also understand the environment and context in which they will be used (see Consuming Experience). If the environment is not conducive to its use, then it is the marketers' role to improve the environment so their product will be more attractive. In services marketing this is referred to not as the landscape, but the 'servicescape'.

A prime example of where environment is at least as important as the actual product is a family restaurant. For instance, the restaurant's service or the food quality is not the only critical factor for a young family frequenting the restaurant – quality and service are assumed to be good by customers or they would not go there. Other critical aspects are the environmental elements, such as: parking, hours of operation, facilities for families (high chairs for toddlers, changing facilities for infants, safe environment for children – no stairs, candles, etc.). Families select restaurants primarily based on the restaurant's environment that supports their lifestyles – i.e. in this example, having young children.

A comparable situation can be found in the airline business. What differentiates one airline from another? Many travellers will say 'service'. However, we have accepted the fact that there are many low-cost, 'no-frills' local and national flights, which don't provide much service at all – just the seat. What is happening is that the airlines are now competing to provide the right environment and the right materials. In the low-cost airline market, such materials include:

- Parking
- Choice of airport arrivals and departures
- Frequency of flights
- Number of destinations
- Ground transportation
- Ease of purchasing a ticket (e-ticketing).

With international travel in addition to all of the above materials, the in-flight services will be more important due to the length of the journey. The airline must think of materials that make up the environment to win customers. Providing a cheap seat is not enough, as competitive prices can be researched on the Internet in minutes. For travellers, their purchasing decision includes all the related materials; therefore, marketers must consider *all* the materials that make up the environment that will enhance and promote their offering.

Such 'holistic' considerations have led marketers to offer 'bundles' of materials to consumers. Indeed, bundling was traditionally regarded as one of the functions

Example of bundling

Consider how the menu is displayed in fast-food restaurants today. Often, the menu listing single items is difficult to locate – it's posted on the side wall *in smaller print without any pictures or illumination. Behind the staff member taking your order is the glossy, well-lit picture menu of the* bundled *options. This is because customers have come to expect bundled services and products. By providing 'bundled meals', fast-food restaurants are no longer competing on price. The products are being bundled and fast-food connoisseurs no longer know the price of each food item.*

of the distributor or retailer, who combines several items from different sources into convenient packages. This saves customers time and effort in putting these items together themselves and even saves them thinking about what combinations are possible because the options are presented for them .

Availability – materials must be ubiquitous

The two trends of '*being available any time and almost anywhere*' have now become norms within many consumer and business markets. This demonstrates how, over the last two decades, the requirements for supplying materials has changed and constant availability is expected. In order to explore why this has occurred, consider the example of the building materials 'DIY' store described below. It is a real store but the name is disguised here.

Home Depot is a US-based multinational company that has expanded their retail opening to 24 hours, seven days a week. These stores sell building materials, hardware items, seasonal products, tools, houseplants, paint, doors, windows, etc. They service residential customers, large and small contractors, and commercial tradesmen.

Unless you are an insomniac homeowner, you may ask yourself 'Who would ever want to buy planks of wood at 3.00 a.m. on a Tuesday morning?' However, the pilot project of being open all hours was so successful that Home Depot extended it to all of their North American stores in 2001. Contractors and delivery couriers have enthusiastically embraced the concept. They have discovered there are numerous cost savings of purchasing their materials at night. Firstly, they avoid the traffic congestion during the day. Secondly, there is no downtime at the job site since the materials are available immediately in the morning when the tradesmen arrive. Thirdly, if any subsequent items are required they can be picked up by mid-morning delivery without impacting the production schedule. For Home Depot they are maximizing their sales and serving these larger and more dependable buyers. It is a 'win–win' outcome for both the seller (Home Depot) and the buyers (mainly contractors).

The example above illustrates how availability of materials has changed the operating and purchasing practices of the construction business. It also reflects how marketing has shifted the way materials are bought and sold, with the customers' needs coming first. This illustrates the way in which marketing practices have moved materials, spaces and time in the marketplace.

Moving materials – logistics

This subsection will discuss how logistics contributes to the 'moving' operations for marketing. Logistics includes the transportation and tracing of materials as they flow between the manufacturer and their customers. Logistics also includes the services of recording necessary production and shipping information that is beneficial to learning more about customers' needs. Logistics is also concerned with the steps involved in producing and moving materials. It is the role of logistics to document the processes involved in marketing. These processes include: production scheduling, determining the best method of delivering the materials, collecting customer feedback, managing the company's website.

The store known as La Chaussee d'Antin had recently announced its new inventory of yard goods. Over 2 million metres of barege, over 5 million of grenadine and poplin and over 3 million of other fabrics – altogether about 11 million metres of textiles. Le Tintamarre now remarked, after recommending La Chaussee d'Antin to its female readers as the 'foremost house of fashion in the world' and also the 'most dependable': 'The entire French railway system comprises barely ten thousand kilometres of tracks – that is only ten million metres. This one store, therefore, with its stock of textiles, could virtually stretch a tent over all the railway tracks of France. Three or four other establishments publish similar figures. How are stores supposed to find room to stock this gigantic quantity of goods? The answer is very simple and very logical: each firm is always larger than the others.' Ebeling, 1863, (Quoted in Benjamin, 1955/2004)

Definition

Logistics is the series of events required to move materials in a timely and cost-effective manner. It also includes the events or necessary steps in completing a project.

Key logistics activities

- *Land transportation*
- *Airfreight forwarding*
- *Sea freight forwarding*
- *Customs clearance*
- *Raw materials and finished goods warehousing*
- *Time-critical air transport*
- *Inventory management*
- *Cross-docking*
- *Transportation management*
- *Product assembly/configuration*
- *Quality inspection and testing*
- *Packaging*
- *Product marking/labelling.*

Past	Present
• On-time delivery • Limited offices, limited reach • Specialized in local or national delivery areas • Move space the fastest means between points	• Many offices, many partnerships 'interlink' • Virtual tracking using GPS for the items; detailed costing and efficiency reports • Providing a service vs simply moving space • Globalized service • Hub + spoke network

Figure 42 Developments in the logistics function

The nineteenth century story of La Chaussee d'Antin shows, on a grand scale, why logistics has always been a critical operation in order to ensure the delivery of goods to customers in a timely and cost-effective manner. Nowadays logistics deals with more than the 'moving of materials', encompassing the organization, tracking and tracing of the shipments and movements involved, and the entire flow of materials into and out of the company. In the global economy, with multiple transportation modes and millions of such movements every day, logistics is a complex coordination and control function. It requires managing across national and company boundaries and balancing internal and external objectives. The former can include short lead times, small batch production, low inventories and external objectives, and cover speed and reliability of delivery and immediate availability of many products.

Recently, many businesses have added logistical services to complement the products or services they provide their customers.

An example of this is the services a travel agent provides. The travel agent not only sells airplane tickets, but also provides a wide assortment of related travel services. These services may include car rental, hotel booking, sightseeing packages, etc. But, in addition to these services, the travel agent offers logistical services. Some of the logistical services travel agents now offer are listed in Table 13.

These logistical services are considered essential for today's travelling customer, and therefore they are now regarded as core competencies of a good travel agent. By providing these logistical services, the travel agent is providing greater

Table 13 Logistical services provided by travel agents
• Insurance • Calculate the best flight connections • Provide advice of which airline's service meets the travellers' expectations • 'Watchdogs' for price savings and reducing travel costs • Advise when the best time to travel • May have partner hotels, hence giving their customers better accommodation value

value to their customers, saving them time and money. In other words, the travel agent can become the customer's buying agent for the entire trip.

During the past decade, however, major airlines have lowered the commissions paid to travel agents and they have also persuaded the traveller to book online with various reward schemes. Indeed, more travellers are conducting these search and booking services for themselves on the Internet. Where does this leave the travel agents: how can they survive? One solution could be for travel agents to expand their logistics services and shift their core business actions of booking travel tickets and hotels to become *travel logistics consultants*.

Another industry that has changed drastically over the past 20 years is the overnight courier and the freight companies.

Years ago, the customer was happy to receive the package/freight on time and in good condition. Today that is not good enough. Customers are demanding that their courier/freight company provide the following logistics:

- Instantaneous tracking of their package/freight
- Confirm receipt of the package by the recipient within minutes of it being delivered
- Guaranteed delivery
- Guaranteeing the package will not be damaged
- Proper handling equipment.

This industry has spent millions of dollars to improve its fleet to be equipped to handle highly specialized containers and temperature controls.

Also, many companies have now installed temperature-controlled holding areas on their premises to ensure goods are kept fresh (e.g. meats, flowers, fruits, chemicals).

In the past 20 years there has been a dramatic shift in the type of goods the customer is shipping. In the past the majority of the items were overnight envelopes or small boxes. The freight being moved now is heavier, bulkier, going further distances and is much more time sensitive. Today's courier/trucking firms have become the customer's warehouse, shipper and logistics manager.

Simply moving the materials around the block or across the globe is no longer considered sufficient. To remain competitive the freight company (freight is used here to include courier and trucking) must also provide the logistical services that are required by the customer. Such logistical services are similar to the services listed above, including the following:

- *Daily* detailed *electronic* billing
- Trucks displaying/advertising the *customer's* products
- Compensation to the customer for any lost revenues due to delayed or damaged packages/freight
- Detailed inventory records of incoming and outgoing shipments
- Custom brokerage
- Foreign currency exchange
- Storage if needed
- Able to handle seasonal demands
- Advice for shipping items in the most efficient way.

The customer is no longer expecting the basic service from their freight company – that is a given. It is the added logistical services they have come to expect that will differentiate the leading companies in this industry. Again, providing the service (in this case the conveyance of the packages) is no longer the accepted norm by the customer. It is the added logistical services the customer is looking for. The customer's own business success is now dependent on the reliability, effectiveness and speed of the courier. And how is the customer's trust gained? By providing all of the logistical services. Freight companies are no longer being paid simply to move materials. They're being rewarded by their customers for 'peace of mind', knowing that the logistics and movement of goods is now being safely handled by specialists. The customer can strengthen their core competencies and contract out the delivery, pick-up, warehousing, custom brokerage, etc. to their freight company. The courier is now providing 'the complete door-to-door shipping solution for each of their individual customers'.

The role of technology in logistics

As explained above, logistics also means 'the ability to track and trace' the movement of materials. When a customer urgently needs to send a parcel to a foreign country as quickly as possible, they will likely choose an 'overnight courier'. The most critical factors for the courier in getting the parcel to its final destination are likely to include: cost; timelines and on-route tracking capabilities. The last factor, 'tracking', has become an essential component of the courier/freight industry.

Technology provides the equipment to enable companies to perform their logistical services much better. The logistical equipment for moving materials includes: computers, Internet connections, product code scanners, specialized material handling equipment. By providing the logistics, a company can add value to the core services they provide.

Take a simple example. A bicycle shop in London wants to start exporting bicycles to Morocco. The shop's expertise is selling bicycles, not shipping and exporting. By using an international courier, the bicycle shop will have the courier company handle all of the logistics, such as packaging, customs, shipping, foreign exchange and local delivery services. In fact, the bicycle shop will contract out the logistical activities, since they are not part of their core competencies. The bicycle shop will remain focused on their core competencies, selling bicycles.

The advances in information technology since the 1990s have enabled companies to use computers and related software programs to track and trace materials as they travel from the senders to their final destinations (see Moving information – the role of IT). Since then, the IT infrastructure and the Internet have provided the framework to monitor the movement of materials instantaneously from anywhere in the world, and that allows the interwoven activities of logistics to occur. Without these technological changes in the application and innovations of specialized electronics and communication systems, the effectiveness and speed of logistics would be greatly reduced.

The role of logistics in marketing

Logistics has become an integral part of marketing. Marketers can even use logistics to help determine the appropriate price for various products by calculating and recording production schedules, shipping details and determining the most cost-efficient way of transporting the goods.

Logistics are also used in marketing to collect and analyse consumer information (see Moving information – the role of IT). Logistics can gather marketing data such as how many materials are being produced, who is buying and where the customers are located. Logistics can also be helpful in recording historical marketing information that will assist in studying consumer decisions. Such information could include the data that was collected when a customer survey was conducted.

Other logistical data could be sourced from a company's website and from the customers who log onto the company's website. Company websites are excellent marketing tools and can provide a variety of marketing information (see Table 14 for examples of such information). It is the logistics of networking and sorting all of this data that enables the marketer to understand and manage the complexity of moving materials.

Table 14 The company website used as a logistical marketing tool

Subject areas	Benefits to the company
Determine where the customers are located	Websites are able to track where customers log in from; that is, able to determine geographical location
Determine how many customers are interested in which products	Logistics can calculate the number of people who view each component of the web page and how long the customer views each page
Promotional tool; list and detail the company's materials available for sale; FAQ (frequently asked questions)	Allows the company to effectively promote and price their materials; feedback for customers
Convey logistical information, such as: production schedules, delivery timetables, product specifications; guarantees; accepted methods of payment	Customer is well informed, making the buying decision easier
Sales tool to accept orders, directly over the Internet; 'e-tailing' (electronic sales)	Website will process the sales order; ensure all necessary information is obtained to complete the sale – logistically inform the sales department of the sale and begin the process of preparing the sales order

FURTHER READING

Ballou, R. (1992) *Business Logistics Management*. Prentice-Hall: Englewood Cliffs, NJ.

Coyle, J., Bardl, E. & Lawley, C. (2003) *The Management of Business Logistics, a Supply Chain Perspective*, 7th edition. Thomson Learning/South-Western: Pennsylvania.

Shapiro, B., Rangan, V. & Sviokla, J. (1992) Staple yourself to an order. *Harvard Business Review*, July/August, 113–122.

A virtual firm in moving space

~ Newmedia Marketing Solutions (NMS), www.nmsglobal.com

Alexea Grech

Background

Technology is driving major change to all business on a large scale and it is important that companies are proactive. The foundations and structure of sound traditional marketing theories that were visionary at the time need to be readdressed. Owing to digital technology, the old rules are no longer valid. Technology makes the movement of information in the networked economy possible; therefore, industries in which the product or service is information, such as retailing, recruitment, financial services, travel and entertainment, are involved in major shifts.

One such shift in thinking is to replace the 'supply chain' with the 'demand chain'. Demand chain thinking starts with the customers and moves backwards. The Internet is a critical part of the demand chain because it has transformed

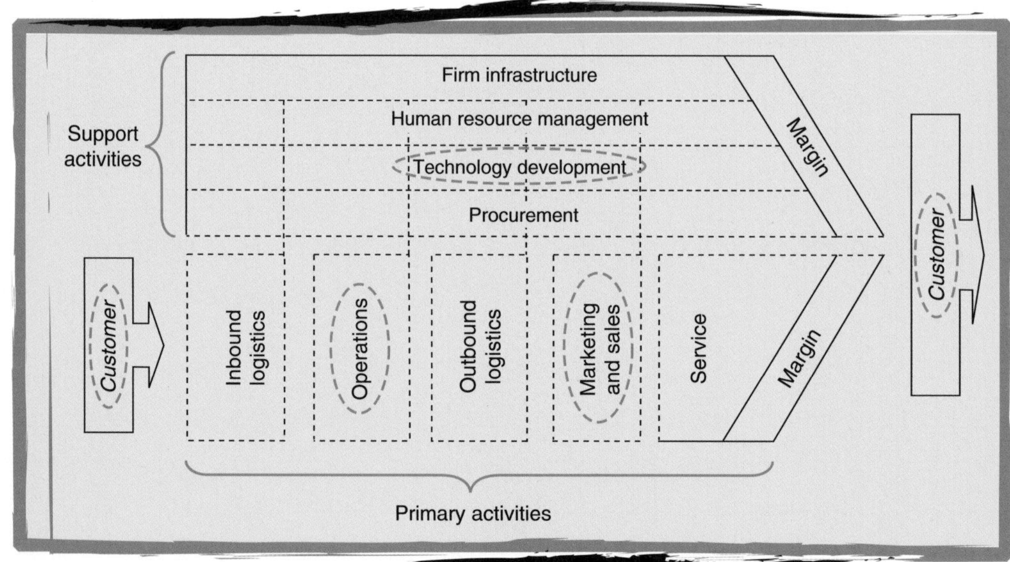

Figure 43 The value chain breaking up into little bits

relationships between suppliers and buyers. It allows suppliers to acquire up-to-date knowledge about production schedules and the market forecast. Suppliers can anticipate customers' needs and deliver what is required without the need for ordering. Internet technology enables this through intranets, where suppliers can link in to customers' networks and vice versa.

Transforming demand chains means creating new ways of dealing with customers, new ways of competing, new internal structures, and new systems to link and network the processes of companies in the chain. In order to be successful it involves re-engineering business processes and spaces – Internet technology and the World Wide Web have created a new market space, a moving space. It is in this space that NMS operates (www.nmsglobal.com).

About NMS – a catalyst of change

One of the world's leading new media firms – Newmedia Marketing Solutions (NMS) – is global, fast growing, profitable and offers customers a wide range of leading Internet marketing services. So what has built this firm's success?

NMS was created in 1999. The firm has built its strategy, business structure, processes and culture based on the digital age and moving space, and has used IT to create value for the business through efficient processes, specialist knowledge and innovative services.

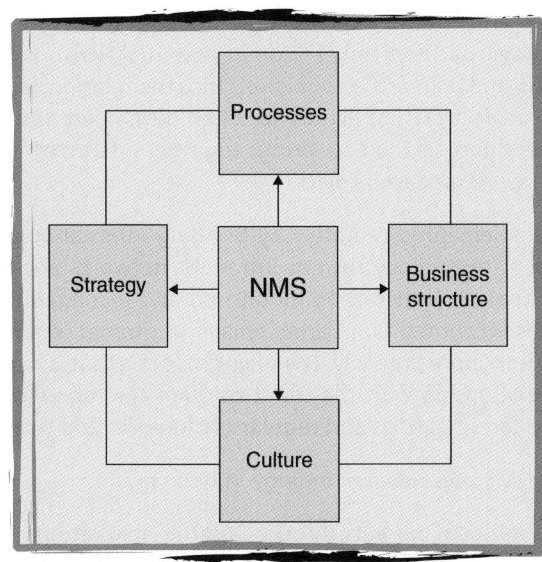

Figure 44 NMS – a catalyst of change

Many companies were investing in websites and IT systems that were not adding value to their business. They had no e-business strategies and those that did have them were not tailored to the business or to what the customers wanted. The most important stage – 'the human stage' – was being left out of most projects. Businesses expected technical teams to do the marketing and customer service as well as developing websites.
Alexea Grech, co-founder of NMS

NMS was established as a reaction to the numerous web development companies that had a 'factory approach' to creating websites for customers where 'the more, the better'.

The aim of NMS was to ensure that brick and mortar companies were advised how to use new technology appropriately in order to increase returns and business benefit. 'Companies can only expect returns from the use of technology, not from technology itself.'

The firm offers traditional businesses advice on e-business and Internet marketing, as well as implementation services. This meant that NMS could advise companies how to use technology to achieve maximum business benefit and then implement the project in order to ensure that successful results were achieved.

The story of NMS is an ideal example of how a clear vision of the future is necessary to take advantage of the technological revolution, both in its internal structure as well as the services it offers. This case study will address two main aspects:

1 The novel structure of the company.
2 The role of Internet marketing in a company's marketing strategy.

An international firm in moving space

NMS is an international firm in moving space. It has used technology to develop its global vision and target clients worldwide rather than just focusing on one local market. The firm has worked on projects with clients in Europe and North America in industries ranging from telecommunications and recruitment to financial services and Internet technology. It doesn't operate only in virtual space, however. NMS partners travel to meet potential clients around the world, where they advise and plan projects on-site. Once the relationship with the client is built, and the project plan of action has been developed, the operation then moves into virtual space as the firm brings together a team of the world's leading specialists to work on each project.

Each project is implemented remotely by bringing international skills together through the use of technology such as intranets, networks and email. Working this way means that projects can be monitored and managed more efficiently, since everything is accounted for in print, emails or intranet communications, and timelines are kept to more precisely. The major caveat is that it is nevertheless crucial to build a relationship with the client through traditional communications, including face-to-face meetings and regular conferences and conversations.

This shows how NMS uses new technology in two ways:

1 To target international markets through Internet marketing.
2 To communicate effectively with the selected team of specialists working on each project.

Differentiation through specialist teams

Through their use of remote operations and communications, NMS has developed a unique business model that utilizes its network of specialists all over the world. This means that a dedicated team is created for each project, where leading specialists in their field are able to deliver worldwide solutions.

Rather than being limited to a local team to choose from, this model makes it possible for NMS to select the top specialists in the world. The company has professional specialists working in the areas of e-business strategy, Internet marketing, intranets, usability testing, web development, multimedia and branding.

Utilizing a worldwide network reduces their reliance on a limited number of skills, where web developers are given design or database projects to do even though they are not experts in that area. All projects are more efficient because there is the incentive to perform well because NMS chooses its specialists based on suitability for the task and past project performances. And every project team is unique – sometimes all team members are working together from North America, other times there is a team including specialists from Sydney, San Francisco, the east and west coasts of America, and London. As the specialists on one side of the hemisphere are closing their laptops, the specialists on the other side of the world are waking up to start their working day. This allows NMS to work on projects 24 hours a day!

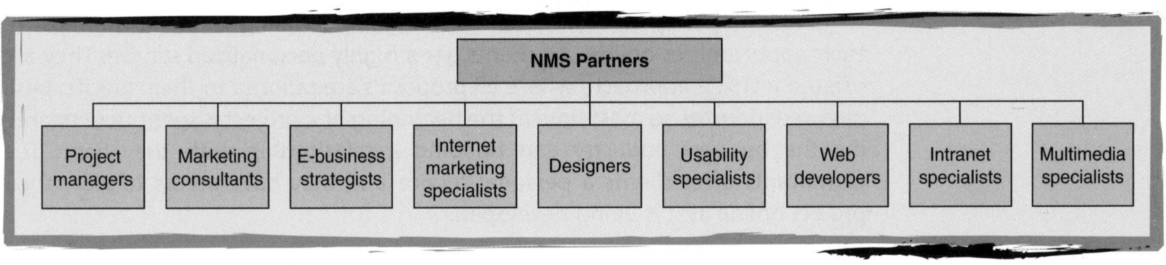

Figure 45 NMS structure

A business structure driven by technology

The NMS partners select all team specialists for their tasks, giving each of them a detailed project and creative brief outlining the project objectives, stages of development and activities they are each responsible for. Within these parameters they have flexibility and freedom to work in their own way. The specialists are paid a fixed fee for each project; therefore, they manage their own time cost-effectively and independently. The project managers brief their team on the project and together they develop the best solutions.

Table 15 'Win–win' benefits to all parties

Client benefits	NMS benefits	Specialist team benefits
• Specialist teams	• Successful projects	• Flexibility
• Added business value	• Satisfied customers	• Full creative control
• Industry specialists	• Specialist focus	• Focus on specialist skills
• High skills	• Wide-ranging skills	• Manage their own time
• Efficiency	• International team	• No commuting
• Leading solutions	• Cost-effective	• No bureaucracies
• Return on investments	• 24-hour efficiency	
• Accountable results	• Instant growth	
	• Instant downsizing	

A typical client project

NMS is not market specific and likes to deal with clients all over the world. However, it is company policy that the clients it works with must have the right mindset; therefore, it is highly selective. It does not matter whether clients are large or small, they must be open to change and willing to make the most of their opportunities online. All clients get a highly personalized service. They are offered a '1:2:1' approach, where all proposals are tailored to their specific business and industry, so most time at the beginning of a project is spent understanding the business, industry and building a relationship with the client. The consultants offer clients a personal service and they have access to view their project online as it is being developed.

NMS recently worked with a company whose business survived purely on 'existing customer relationships'. The company had invested in a website and internal technology; however, the internal procedures had not become more efficient and staff still dealt with customers over the phone and fax, much as before. The manager had given up hope of achieving online success.

An independent evaluation of the company's e-business potential was carried out. As part of this evaluation, the NMS team examined how the business worked internally, the processes, the target market and the potential market internationally, how to simplify the service for customers and communicating the essential information clearly. The industry, competitors and customers were all analysed as part of developing their e-business strategy.

Within a year the business has doubled and the majority of their business comes from the web. It took six months to implement the strategy, but how did they succeed? What are the secrets of achieving online success?

The client's website was recreated from scratch so that it was customer focused rather than based on industry technical specifications that the consumers did not understand or need. Instead, it offered simple and clear overviews which guided the customer through the process to a user-friendly order form enabling customers to conclude their business.

A database was developed to give customers immediate personalized advice based on their needs. The company developed a culture internally to ensure that web orders were serviced quickly and efficiently. A policy of dealing with emails within 15 minutes was implemented. The site was redeveloped using a distinctive design that was attractive and easy to navigate. This catapulted them ahead of all competitors in the industry.

By offering clear, concise information and online advice, as well as targeting international customers, the business also started using its website as a strategic tool to acquire and service customers. Marketing the site was a success because it was developed from a customer perspective – it was distinctive, simple, easy to use and customer focused, and as a result the orders and business enquiries quickly gathered pace.

The company's business doubled because NMS worked with them so that technology was used to design the online interaction from the client's customers' point of view. The system architecture had to permit easy navigation through the website and assist the employees in responding to orders and enquiries more quickly and easily than using conventional phone and fax technologies.

Developing an e-business strategy

This subsection covers the key issues companies need to address when developing their e-business strategy, as well as their Internet marketing tactics.

Traditional local marketplaces have opened up to a single worldwide marketspace; networks are global, teams are international and logistics have been completely redefined. There are opportunities for every business online, whether it is targeting

new international markets, looking for business partners or offering customers added value services online. The first step towards achieving success through online technology is defining and implementing an e-business strategy.

NMS develops e-business strategies that help clients focus on restructuring their business, processes and relationships so that they are more effective through technology. An e-business strategy addresses how the business should be developing methods of dealing with customers, partners and employees, as well as using technology to enhance the business and make its processes more efficient.

Key questions for developing an e-business strategy

- *What is the vision for your company online?*
- *How are other players in the industry utilizing their sites?*
- *What are competitors offering customers?*
- *What added value services are you offering customers?*
- *Why should customers come back to your site for repeat business?*
- *Have you communicated to the different user groups you want to attract?*
- *Have you undertaken usability testing?*
- *Are you attracting the right traffic to your site?*

Defining a successful e-business strategy is a task that must be undertaken by business development and marketing professionals. Many businesses hand it over to their IT department or expect their programmers to define their e-business strategy as well as implementing it – these companies will find it difficult to achieve business benefit online.

Internet marketing tactics

Once the e-business strategy has been developed and implemented, it is important to market the business online. To distinguish your company from the competition requires innovation, originality and creativity, and all marketing strategies should include Internet marketing. NMS partner, Alistair Jack, claims that today Internet marketing is the key differentiator to the success businesses have online.

The fundamentals of Internet marketing are exactly the same as the fundamentals in traditional marketing; however, Internet marketing is immediate, more flexible, more targeted, accountable and cost-effective. Internet marketing has revolutionized traditional marketing. Apart from being accountable and cost-effective, it is about:

- More revenue potential and generating results
- Attracting a targeted audience
- The possibility of entering new markets
- Global awareness and sales leads companies could not previously achieve.

There are a number of tactics that make up Internet marketing – the challenge is choosing the most effective techniques. NMS creates a short-, medium- and long-term Internet marketing plan with its clients to suit the business objectives, budgets and market.

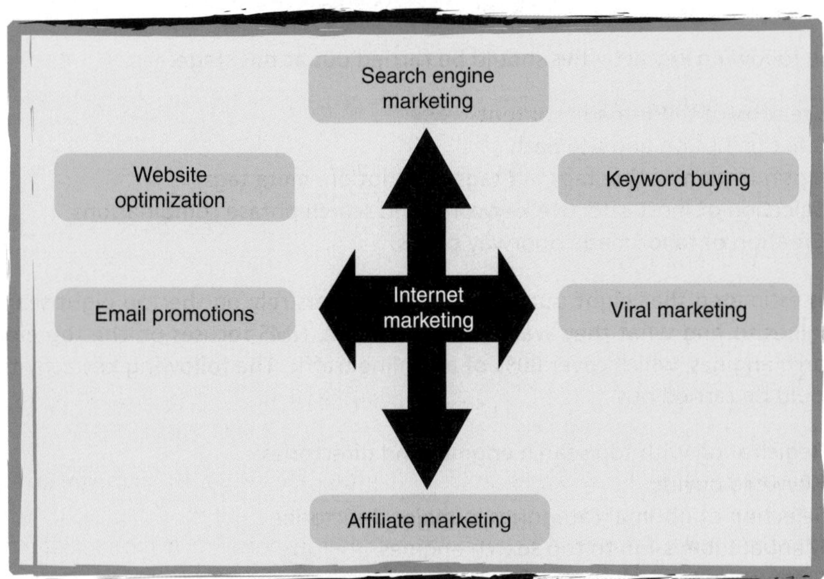

Figure 46 Internet marketing

The fundamentals of every Internet marketing strategy should include website optimization, search engine marketing and keyword buying.

The majority of company websites, even for *Fortune* 100 firms, are difficult to be found by search engines and many of them do not even use meta tags, which are the most basic form of optimization. It appears from this observation that most companies are doing an astonishingly bad job at the fundamental website optimization

activities. Internet marketing is generally far cheaper than any other offline marketing campaign companies conduct; therefore, it is important that businesses makes that effort to get it right.

By optimizing a website it makes it easier for search engines to spider it. As a result of successful website optimization, websites have a good chance of getting a high ranking once they are registered with the search engines. This means that businesses can target the customers who are actively looking for similar products or services. Good search engine rankings means that the website will attract potential customers who may not have known the company existed previously.

When optimizing a website it is important to create a team of specialists that includes search engine experts as well as industry experts. Search engine experts have hands-on experience, which means they know the complicated algorithms and keep up with their regular changes. Industry experts understand the business and can therefore guide the search engine specialists about the target audience, terminology they are likely to use when searching for similar products and services.

The following key activities should be carried out at this stage:

- Creation of tailor-made content
- Site description and site path
- Optimization of title tags, alt tags, description, meta tags
- Selection of most effective keywords and search phrase combinations
- Creation of tailor-made doorway pages.

It is estimated that eight out of ten Internet users rely on the top eight search engines to find what they want. For this reason, NMS focuses on the top eight search engines, which cover 80% of all online traffic. The following key activities should be carried out:

- Registration with top search engines and directories
- Keyword buying
- Selection of optimal categories in major directories
- Manual submission to top search engines
- Submission to market-specific search engines and directories
- Pay-per-click campaigns.

Once a website has been optimized and registered on the top search engines, it is important that companies give the responsibility of the Internet marketing to an individual or team. Ongoing activities should also include analysis and marketing, search engine ranking reports, website traffic analysis and regular site resubmissions, which help maintain and improve rankings.

Apart from website optimization, search engine registration and keyword buying, Internet marketing campaigns should also include innovative activities such as interactive added value features, email promotions, newsletters and viral promotions. This is what enables business success online.

Businesses must be imaginative and innovative in their approach to Internet marketing. They should:

- create interactive features that offer customers added value services
- develop innovative promotions that will help businesses stand out from competition
- promote the brand online through creative viral marketing tools
- create intriguing campaigns to excite people and arouse their curiosity
- lead customers to action rather than forcing them to click away.

Summary

With all clients, NMS makes a point of creating innovative solutions which give customers a reason to want to come back (see Creating Solutions). It has built its strategy, business structure, processes and culture based on the digital age and moving space. As a virtual firm it has used IT to create solutions through adaptive organization, efficient processes, specialist knowledge and innovative services.

References

Arefi, M. (1999) Non-place and placelessness as narratives of loss: rethinking the notion of place. *Journal of Urban Design*, **4** (2), 179–193.

Baudrillard, J. (1983) *Simulations*. Semiotext(e): New York.

Benjamin, W. (1955/2004) *The Arcades Project* (H. Eiland & K. McLaughlin, trans.). Belknap Press: Cambridge, MA, pp. 174–175.

Boisot, M. (1995) *Information Space*. Routledge: London.

Brady, M., Saren, M. & Tzokas, N. (2002) Integrating information technology into marketing practice – the IT reality of contemporary marketing practice. *Journal of Marketing Management*, **18** (5/6, July), 555–578.

Chung, C. J., Inaba, J. & Koolhass, R. (2001) *Harvard Design School Guide to Shopping*. Taschen: New York.

Clarke, D. & Purvis, M. (1994) Dialectics, difference and the geographies of consumption. *Environment and Planning A*, **26**, 1091–1109.

Coviello, N., Milley, R. & Marcolin, B. (2001) Understanding IT-enabled interactivity in contemporary marketing. *Journal of Interactive Marketing*, **15** (4), 18–33.

Davenport, T. (1994) Saving its soul: human-centred information management. *Harvard Business Review*, March/April, 119–131.

De Certeau, M. (1984) *The Practice of Everyday Life*. University of California Press: Berkeley, CA.

Dempsey, M. (2000) Customer-focus: embracing the CRM trend. *Financial Times*, 14 December.

Desai, C., Fletcher, K. & Wright, G. (1998) Barriers to successful implementation of database marketing. *International Journal of Database Management*, **18** (4), 265–278.

Dibb, S. (1998) Market segmentation: strategies for success. *Market Intelligence and Planning*, **16** (7), 394–406.

Domegan, C. & Doyle, D. (2000) Contemporary marketing practice and new technologies in Ireland. In conference proceedings of the American Marketing Association Conference, Argentina, June.

Fisher, M., Raman, A. & McClelland, A. (2000) Rocket science retailing is almost here – are you ready? *Harvard Business Review*, July/August, 115–124.

Giddens, A. (1990) *The Consequences of Modernity*. Polity: Cambridge.

Glazer, R. (1991) Marketing in an information intensive environment: strategic implications of knowledge as an asset. *Journal of Marketing*, **55**, 1–19.

Henry, P. (2000) Evaluating the implication for new media and information technology. *Journal of Consumer Marketing*, **18** (2), 121–133 (ABI Inform).

Ingram, J. (2005) *Theatre of the Mind*. Harper Collins: Canada.

Johnson, R. (1991) A strategy for service – Disney style. *Journal of Business Strategy*, September/October, 38–43.

Kardon, B. (1992) Consumer schizophrenia: extremism in the marketplace. *Planning Review*, 18–22.

Kotler, P. (2001) *Principles of Marketing*, 3rd edition. FT/Prentice-Hall Europe: Harlow.

Lefebre, H. (1991) *The Production of Space* (D. Nicholson-Smith, trans.). Verso: London.

Li, E., McLeod, R. & Rogers, J. (1993) Marketing information systems in the Fortune 500 companies: past, present and future. *Journal of Management Information Systems*, **10** (1), 165–192.

Mafessoli, M. (1996) *The Time of the Tribes. The Decline of Individualism in Mass Society* (D. Smith, trans.). Sage: London.

Malhotra, N. (1996) *Marketing Research: An Applied Orientation*. Prentice-Hall: London.

Massumi, B. (1992) *A User's Guide to Capitalism and Schizophrenia: Deviations from Deleauze & Guattari*. Swerve: London.

Mattsen, L.-G. (2000) Relationships and networks. In: *Marketing Theory* (M. Baker, ed.). Thomson Learning: London, pp. 150–160.

Minkel, J. (2002) Hollow universe. *New Scientist*, 27 April, p. 23.

Morley, D. & Robbins, K. (1995) *Spaces of Identity: Global Media, Electronic Landscapes and Cultural Boundaries*. Routledge: London.

Peppers, D. & Rogers, M. (2000) *The one-to-one future – building business relationships one customer at a time*, 3rd edition. Piatkus: London.

Reichheld, F. & Schefter, P. (2000) E-Loyalty – your secret weapon on the web. *Harvard Business Review*, **78** (4), 105–113.

Shields, R. (1992) *Lifestyle Shopping: The Subject of Consumption*. Routledge: London.

Van Raaj, W. F. (1993) Postmodern consumption. *Journal of Economic Psychology*, **14** (3), 541–563.

Varun Grover, V. & Davenport, T. (2001) Perspectives on knowledge management: fostering a research agenda. *Journal of Management Information Systems*, **18** (1, Summer), 5–21.

Wedel & Kamura (2002) *Market Segmentation: Conceptual and Methodological Foundations*. Kluwer Academic: Boston.

Zuboff, S. (1988) *In the Age of the Smart Machine*. Heinemann: Oxford.

[illegible], J. (2003) *Theft of the Nation*, HarperCollins, Canada.

Johnson, R. (1989) A strategy for service – Disney style. *Journal of Business Strategy*, September/October, 38–43.

Kahn, B. (1995) Consumer variety-seeking behaviour in the marketplace. *Planning Review*, 15–42.

Lancaster, G. (2001) *Essentials of Marketing*, 3rd edition, FT/Prentice Hall, Europe, Harlow.

Lefebvre, H. (1974) *The Production of Space* (D. Nicholson-Smith, trans.), Verso, London.

Li, E., McLeod, R. & Rogers, J. (2001) Marketing information systems in the Fortune 500 companies: past, present and future. *Journal of Management Information Systems*, 18(1), 151–172.

Maffesoli, M. (1996) *The Time of the Tribes: The Decline of Individualism in Mass Society* (D. Smith, trans.), Sage, London.

Malhotra, N. (1996) *Marketing Research: An Applied Orientation*, Prentice Hall, London.

[illegible] (1993) *A Manager's Guide to Marketing Research* [illegible], London.

Mattsson, L.-G. (1998) Relationships and networks. In *Marketing Theory* (M. Baker, ed.), Thomson Learning, London, pp. [illegible].

Mayer, J. (2002) *Newsweek*, New York, 27 April, p. 23.

[illegible] (2001) *[illegible]*, [illegible], London.

Peppers, D. & Rogers, M. (1993) *The One-to-One Future – Building Business Relationships One Customer at a Time*, 2nd edition, Piatkus, London.

Reichheld, F. & Schefter, P. (2000) E-loyalty – your secret weapon on the web. *Harvard Business Review*, 78 (4), 105–113.

Shields, R. (1992) *Lifestyle Shopping: The Subject of Consumption*, Routledge, London.

Van Raaij, W.F. (1993) Postmodern consumption. *Journal of Economic Psychology*, 14 (3), 541–563.

[illegible], V. & Davenport, T. (2001) Perspectives on knowledge management systems. *Journal of Management Information Systems*, 18 (1), Summer, 5–21.

Wedel, M. & Kamakura, W. (2000) *Market Segmentation: Conceptual and Methodological Foundations*, Kluwer Academic, Boston.

Zuboff, S. (1988) *In the Age of the Smart Machine*, Heinemann, Oxford.

Index

Above-the-line agencies, 63–5
Actor-network theory, 119
Ad literate consumers, 61–2
Advertising, 63
  ambient advertising, 65, 66
  frequency, 67
  industry players, 63–4
  noise, 67
  post-campaign research, 67
  pre-campaign research, 67
  provocative/offensive advertising as stimulation, 108–9
  timing, 65–7
  see also Communications
Agencies, 63–5
Amazon.com, 83, 182–3, 258
Ambient advertising, 65, 66
Analytical capabilities, 185–6
Ann Summers parties, 68
Armani, 234–5
Automated teller machines (ATMs), 141, 155

Barclays Bank, 177, 183
Bear Factory, 71
Below-the-line agencies, 65
Benetton, 109, 211
Biological business metaphor, 30–1
Blue Screen Technology, 160
Blueprint programme, 55
Body Shop, 213
Boots, 212
BP, 183
Brand communities, 123, 215
Brand diffusion, 234–5
Branding, 197–8
  film and television, 200–1
  Internet, 201–2
Brands, 61, 102, 198–200
  brand identity, 74
  brand image, 75
  brand stretching, 199–200
  brand values, 70
  celebrity brands, 200, 202–4, 226
  corporate brand, 210, 211–13
  fashion brands, 220–2, 224–8
    creation of fashion brand experience, 228–33
  high street brands, 198
  household brands, 198
  lifestyle brand extension, 233–5
  luxury brands, 199
  own-label brands, 200
  reinvention of, 76–7
  sub-brands, 199
British Airways, 214
BT, 75
Bundling, 263–4

Camper, 232
Carnegie Corporation, 16
Cash flow enhancement, 181–3
Celebrity brands, 200, 202–4, 226
Chanel, 108
Chinese culture, 6, 24
Choice, 25
Clothing, versus fashion, 223–4
Coca-Cola, 73–4, 84–5, 101, 216
Cold War, 16
Collaboration, 6–7
  types of, 6
Comme des Garcons, 229–30
Commercial knowledge, 164
Commitment, 43–4
Communications, 59–78
  communication process, 67–8
  creativity, 62
  cultural differences, 60
  initiation, 63–5
  integration, 69
  internal marketing communication, 70
  post-purchase communications, 69–70

Communications (*contd*)
reach, 66
semiotics, 60–1
switching behaviour and, 73–6
thinking outside the box, 65–6
timing, 65–7
with new customers, 68–9
see also Advertising
Competition, 4–5
between buyers, 5
between buyers and sellers, 5
between sellers, 4–5
Competitive advantage, 5
corporate identity and, 216
elements of, 6
Concept testing, 163–4
Consumerism, 95
Consumers, 116
ad-literate, 61–2
consumer identity, 118
creation, 119–21
displaying, 118–19
corporate identity influence on, 211–16
basic functions, 211–13
knowing the company behind products/brands, 213
loyalty, 214
trends, 214–16
culture and subcultures, 121–4
ethnographic studies, 121–2
disadvantaged consumers, 128–9
IT awareness, 156
model of, 166–7
prosumer role, 116–21
satisfaction, 126–8
see also Customers
Consumption, 180
as performance, 124–6
implications of, 126
culture, 99–101
genealogy of, 117–18
labour, 96–8
materials and energy, 95–6
meanings and signs, 101–2
stimulation, 104
use or utility, 98–9
Contemporary marketing practice (CMP), 47–50
Contracting out, 21–2
Corporate brand, 210, 211–13
Corporate identity (CI), 206–10, 211
graphic design approach, 208
influence on consumers, 211–16
basic functions, 211–13
knowing the company behind products/brands, 213
loyalty, 214
trends, 214–16
interdisciplinary approach, 208
marketing approach, 208
organizational studies approach, 208
perspectives on, 208–9
responses to environment, 216–18
Corporate image, 210–11
Corporate strategy, 175, 186
Couriers, 267–9
Cultural values, 25
communications and, 60
Culture:
consumer culture and subcultures, 121–4
ethnographic studies, 121–2, 165
consumption of, 99–101
of poverty, 129
organizational, 171
Customer behaviour, 16, 166
switching behaviour, 73–6
tracking, scanning and surveillance, 254–6
see also Consumers
Customer databases, 72–3, 250–1
see also Information
Customer information, 248
collection of, 249
see also Market research
Customer intimacy, 20
Customer loyalty, 50–2
corporate identity influence, 214
encouragement of, 71–2
loyalty cards, 8, 71
loyalty ladder, 51
switching behaviour, 73–6

Customer relationship management (CRM), 26, 172–3
capabilities, 183–6
analytical capabilities, 185–6
directional capabilities, 186
integration capabilities, 185
learning and market orientation capabilities, 183–5
operational capabilities, 186
process of, 173–83, 187
customer value process, 179–80
information processes, 177–8
performance measurement process, 181–3
strategic planning process, 174–7
software, 252–4
Customer relationships, 41
de-selection, 76
end of, 74–5
see also Customer relationship management (CRM); Relationship marketing
Customer satisfaction, 126–8
Customer strategy, 175–7, 186
phase-driven strategies, 175–6
segmentation strategies, 176–7
Customer value, 44
delivery, 175, 180
judgements of, 181
process, 179–80
relationship marketing and, 43–4
See also Value proposition
Customers:
customer as king, 25–6
retention of, 41–2
see also Consumers
Customization, 159

Data mining, 251–2
Data warehouse, 251
Database management, 72–3, 250–1
Database marketing (DM), 48
Debenhams, 183
Dell, 80–4, 159
Demand chain, 272–3
Diesel, 232
Diffusion brands, 234–5
Direct marketing, 72, 76
Direction capabilities, 186
Disney World, 249–50

E-business strategy development, 277–8
E-suds technology, 158
EatMyHandbagBitch, 221
Ecological values, 30
Enacted environment, 14
Enchanted illusions, 113
Enis–Paul index, 51
Environmental context, 11–14
corporate identity and, 216–18
environmental scanning, 13–14
materials and, 262–4
Ethics, 27–8
marketing ethics research, 28
Ethnographic studies, 121–2, 165
Event sponsorship, 225
Exchange theory, 4
Exchanges, 243–4
relational, 82–3, 84–5, 143–4
External marketing context, 11–14
external scanning, 13–14

Fantasy and fiction, as consumer stimulation, 111–13
enchanted illusions, 113
hopeful fantasies, 112–13
hopeless fantasies, 113
Fashion, 220–36
fashion brands, 220–2, 224–8
creation of fashion brand experience, 228–33
fast fashion, 222
versus clothing, 223–4
Films, branding in, 200–1
Five senses, 106–7
Ford Foundation, 16
Forecasting software, 258
Freight companies, 267–9
French Connection, 109

General Motors, 159
Geographical information system (GIS), 258
Grey market, 227

Guanxi, 6, 25
Gucci, 234

Harley Davidson, 215–16
Henrion, Ludlow, Schmidt, 210
High street brands, 198
Home Depot, 264
Home improvement programmes, 105–6
Household brands, 198
HSBC, 60, 181

IBM, 20
Identity, 207
  brands, 74
  consumers, 118
    creating, 119–21
    displaying, 118–19
  corporate, *See* Corporate identity (CI)
Ikea, 106, 116
Image:
  brands, 75
  corporate, 210–11
IMP (Industrial Marketing Group), 7, 41
Information, 7–8, 162, 247
  customer databases, 72–3, 250–1
  geographical information system (GIS), 258
  marketing information system (MIS), 257
  processes, 177–8
    acquisition, 162–4, 177, 249
    dissemination, 177
    use, 177, 247–8
  see also Market research
Information technology (IT), 152–3, 247, 256
  challenges, 259
  consumer awareness of ITs, 156
  consumer perceptions of innovations, 157
  consumer wants, 157–9
  forecasting software, 258
  market research and, 250–6
    customer relationship marketing software, 252–4
    data mining, 251–2
    data warehouse, 251
    database management, 250–1
    tracking, scanning and surveillance, 256
  marketing and, 153–6
    orientations, 153–5
  marketing decision models, 258
  road ahead, 161
  solutions through, 159–60
    customization, 159
    interactive products, 159–60
    remote delivery, 160
Innovation, 148–9
  consumer perceptions of, 157
  diffusion of, 156–7
  from insights, 169
  see also New product development
Insights, 168–9
  innovation from, 169
Institutions, 82
  roles in marketing relationships, 82–3
Integration capabilities, 185
Intel, 21
Interaction approach, 41–2
Interaction marketing (IM), 48
Interactive products, 159–60
Internal marketing, 10–11
  communication, 70
Internationalization, 216–17
Internet:
  branding, 201–2
  demand chain and, 272–3
  shopping, 244
Interpretation, 107–8

Japanese business methods, 6
J.Lo, 202–3

Kellogg, 212
Kinder Surprise, 201
Kodak, 217
Koolhass, Rem, 220, 244
Krantz, Judith, 113

La Chaussee d'Antin, 265–6
Labour view of consumption, 96–8
Latent loyalty, 50
Lauren, Ralph, 221–2, 233–4
Learning capabilities, 183–5

Lego, 215
Levi Strauss, 181–2
Lifestyle brand extension, 233–5
Logistics, 265–9
  definition, 265
  key activities, 265
  role in marketing, 269–70
  technology role, 269
Logos, 61
Lopez, Jennifer, 202–3
Love Kylie, 203
Loyalty building, 50–2, 71–2
Loyalty cards, 71
  information collection, 8
Loyalty ladder, 51
Luxury brands, 199

McDonald's, 61, 209
Macro-environment, 12
Manolo Blahnik, 201
Mappoint2000, 258
Market orientation capabilities, 183–5
Market research, 162–5, 250
  client perspective, 167–9
  in new product development, 163
  information technology and, 250–6
    database management, 250–1
  professional perspective, 165–7
Market value, 18
Marketing communications, *see* Communications
Marketing contexts, 10–14
  environmental/external context, 11–14
    external scanning, 13–14
  organizational/internal context, 10–11
Marketing history, 14–17
Marketing information system (MIS), 257
Marketing oriented organizations, 10
Marketing strategy continuum, 42–3
Marketing values, 24–31
  biological business metaphor, 30–1
  ethics, 27–8
    marketing ethics research, 28
  social values, 28–30
  sustainable and ecological values, 30

Markets:
  as competitive arenas, 4–5
  as exchange, 3–4
    roles of institutions, 82–3
  as information systems, 7–8
  as networks, 6–7, 41
  researching, 164–5
  types of, 7
Marks & Spencer, 74
Materials:
  availability, 264
  bundling, 263–4
  consumption of, 95–6
  definition, 261–2
  environmental influences on buying, 262–4
  moving, *see* Logistics
Max Mara, 230
Media management, 225
Memory, 110–11
  nostalgia, 111
Micro-environment, 11–12
Minogue, Kylie, 203
Miss Sixty, 231–2
Motivation, 104–5
  needs and wants, 105–6
  see also Stimulation
Movies, branding in, 200–1
Myth, 125–6

NE Choices programme, 53–5
Needs, 105–6, 117–18, 141
Neo-tribe concept, 122–3
Network:
  meaning of, 80–2
  network thinking, 84–5
Network marketing (NM), 6–7, 48
New intellectuals, 121
New product development (NPD) process, 147–8
  market research, 163
  role of technology, 148–51
New York, London, Paris syndrome, 226
Newman, Paul, 203–4
Next, 228
Nike, 21, 101, 207

NMS (Newmedia Marketing Solutions), 273–81
  as international firm in moving space, 274
  business structure driven by technology, 275
  differentiation through specialist teams, 275
  e-business strategy development, 277–8
  Internet marketing tactics, 278–81
  typical client project, 276–7
Noise, 67
Nostalgia, 111

Offensive advertising, 109–10
Operational capabilities, 186
Operational excellence, 20
Opinion leaders, 68
Opodo.com, 201–2
Organizational capabilities, 171
Organizational context, 10–11
Organizational culture, 171
Organizational processes, 171
Own-label brands, 200

Parallel distribution, 227
Pepsi Cola, 216
Perception, 106–9
  five senses, 106–7
  interpretation, 107–8
  memory, 110–11
  subliminal perception, 107
Performance:
  consumption as, 124–6
    implications of, 126
  measurement process, 181–3
Portugal Telecom, 218
Positioning, 175, 176
Post-campaign research, 67
Post-purchase communications, 69–70
Prada, 220–1
Pre-campaign research, 67
Product leadership, 20
Product life cycle (PLC), 144–5, 223
Products, 95–6, 142
  as solutions, 141–8
  customization, 159
  interactive products, 159–60
  levels of, 142–3
  new products, 145–6
    development (NPD) process, 147–8
  placement, 200–1
    technology, 160
  signified nature of, 144
  utility concept, 98–9
Prosumers, 116–21

Qualitative data, 255
Qualitative research, 164–70
Quality, satisfaction and, 127–8
Quantitative data, 255

Ralph Lauren, 221–2, 233–4
Reality television, 116–17
Relational exchanges, 82–3, 84–5, 143–4
Relationship marketing, 6–7, 41–52, 143, 214, 253
  abusive marketing relationships, 55–7
  contemporary marketing practice (CMP), 47–50
  customer value and, 43–4
  definition, 43
  future developments, 44–6
  implementation of, 46–7
  loyalty building, 50–2
  relationship management chain, 46, 47
  see also Customer relationship management; Social marketing
Relationships, 83, 84–6
  choice of, 83–4
  roles of institutions, 82–3
  see also Customer relationships; Relationship marketing
Remote delivery, 160
Rolex, 199

Sainsbury's, 84–5, 183
Sales oriented organizations, 10
Sales promotion, 71
Satisfaction, 126–8
Sears Catalogue, 160
Self-service technologies, 157
Semiotic analysis, 166
Semiotics, 60–1, 101–2

Service quality, 127
Services, 117
SERVQUAL rating scale, 127
Sex and the City, 105
Shareholder value (SHV), 181–2
Situational scripts, 125
Skoda, 77
Smoking, promotion of, 55–7, 108
Social groups, 100
Social marketing, 29–30, 53–7
  abusive marketing relationships, 55–7
  NE Choices programme, 53–5
Social values, 28–30
Solutions, 141
  products as, 141–8
  technology role, 148–51
  through IT, 159–60
    customization, 159
    interactive products, 159–60
    remote delivery, 160
Sony Playstation, 62
Spurious loyalty, 50
Stimulation:
  by provocative/offensive advertising, 108–9
  fantasy and fiction, 111–13
  nostalgia, 111
  of consumption, 104
Strand cigarettes, 108
Strategic planning process, 174–7
Sub-brands, 199
Subcultures, 122–4
Subliminal perception, 107
Sustainable loyalty, 50
Sustainable marketing, 30–1
Switching behaviour, 73–6
Symbolism, 60–1, 101–2

Target audience, 59
  communication with, *See* Communications
Target markets, 248
Tattoos, 120
Technology, 148–51, 256–7, 272–3
  application areas, 150
  role in logistics, 269
  self-service technologies, 157
  see also Information technology
Television:
  branding, 200–1
  reality TV, 116–17
Text messaging, 155
Theatre of the mind, 249
Through-the-line agencies, 65
TiVo, 160
Tobacco promotion, 55–7, 108
Top Shop, 222
Total market offering, 96
Toyota, 246
Transactional marketing (TM), 42, 48
Travel agents, 266–7
Trust, 43–4

USC, 230
Utility concept, 98–9

Value:
  creation, 18, 20, 23–4
    co-creation, 117
    relationship marketing and, 43–4
  customer's voice in, 23–4
  defining, 24
  definitions of, 18–20
  delivering, 24
  developing, 24
  shareholder value (SHV), 181–2
  see also Customer value
Value chain, 20, 21–4
  extended, 22
Value proposition, 18, 20–1, 175, 176
  definition, 179
  delivery, 180
  development, 179–80
  see also Customer value
Values, 25
  brand values, 70
  see also Marketing values
Virgin, 199
Virgin Mobile, 73
Virgin Vie parties, 68
Virtual brands, 201–2

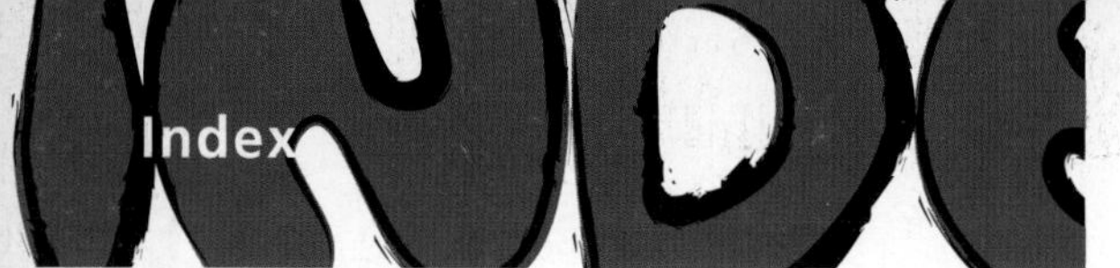

Vision, 175, 176
Volvo, 70

Wal-Mart, 251
Wants, 105–6
  from technology, 157–9
Websites, 270

Wolff Olins, 209–10
Wonderbra advertising campaign, 66

Yves Saint Laurent advertising campaign, 66–7, 108

Zara, 222